Voiceless Victims

What truly hurts is our conscience that aches when we oppose it, and dies when we betray it – Kahlil Gibran

Voiceless Victims

Rebecca Hall

Foreword by Brigitte Bardot

Wildwood House Limited

First published in Great Britain in 1984
by Wildwood House Ltd
Jubilee House, Chapel Road
Hounslow, Middlesex, TW3 1TX

Hall, Rebecca
    Voiceless victims.
    1. Zoology, Economic
    I. Title
    591.6   SF84.3

ISBN: 0 85117 0500 2

*The publishers wish to thank the League Against Cruel Sports and British Union for the Abolition of
Vivisection for generously providing the photographs used on the cover of this book.*

Typeset in 11 on 12pt Baskerville by Tellgate Ltd, London WC2
Printed in Great Britain by The Camelot Press, Southampton

Contents

The author wishes to thank Graham Wilson who made an initial suggestion as to how the idea of this book might be developed; Oliver Caldecott who commissioned that idea; Kim Stallwood who supplied encouragement at its inception; all of those people who have given so freely of their time, information and goodwill; those who gave introductions and those people and organizations whose writings have been quoted in these pages; my editors for their help; my sons, Matthew and Cassian Hall, who put up with and understood the many difficulties; and Brigitte Bardot who so readily and generously provided a Foreword in the true, courageous spirit of the idealist battling amidst the ageless struggle against species discrimination.

This book is dedicated to all those who with perseverance and courage continue to carry the light of compassion among the dense clouds of cruelty which darken our planet, if only each one of us can be sure that, in the words of Kahlil Gibran:

I shall follow the path to wherever my destiny and my mission for Truth shall take me

and to Animalkind, forced into slavery by the human nation, to serve not only with their presence, their work, their suffering, but with their lives.

Foreword

Who has given Man (a word which has tragically lost all its humanity) the right to exterminate, to dismember, to cut up, to slaughter, to hunt, to chase, to trap, to lock up, to martyr, to enslave and to torture the animals? Who has given legal sanction for his power, backed by every modern means, to be used against their helpless innocence? Who authorizes the genocides, the atrocities, which lead to the extinction of whole species? Why is there so much carnage, so much suffering, so much inhumanity, on this earth where men rule?

We must be reminded that every second of every day an animal dies in an experimental laboratory; a slow death and, for the most part, a useless death, a hellish death, a death endured in terror at the hand of sadistic evil (for our survival. . .).

We must be reminded that each morning as dawn breaks, millions upon millions of animals are slaughtered for food in town and village the world over: death on production lines, death en masse, industrial death; they see it, they smell it, they know it is coming. Neither their sight nor their instincts deceive them. They *know*. More horrible still is death by ritual slaughter, drawn out to last as long as the prayers said over them! What God could want that (for our survival. . .)?

We must be reminded what transportation means for them – by sea, by road or by train. Destined for the slaughterhouse, crammed together without food or water, they trample each other in the pounding vehicles or heaving seas. Hooves broken, eyes blinded, they die for lack of air, freeze to death or expire from the heat. What does it matter? . . . they are to die in any case (for our survival. . .)!

We must be reminded of the shameful traffic in exotic animals; for each one which survives, a hundred others are left dead. Animals traumatized, uprooted, often smuggled in crates with false compartments, left in customs so long that they die and no one knows (for our survival. . .).

We must be reminded about the hunters, stalkers and beaters who turn our forests, our countryside, into battlefields. These men, dressed for combat, armed to the teeth with the latest weapons, slaughter everything that moves, kill anything that lives. For these people, the death of one small animal is a victory.

We must be reminded about the persistence of those who live by killing animals for their fur; those who set traps and snares for the smaller animals, lay poisoned meat, use helicopters and machine-guns to kill wolves, smoke foxes from their earths – the females emerge unable to breathe, their little ones still clinging to their teats, to be killed at point-blank range by these greedy men.

And then the mass murder of the baby seals, the only babies in the world to have the privilege of being killed for their beautiful white fur (and all for our vanity).

We must be reminded of the battery animals whose universe is a concentration camp, forced to live an intolerable, mechanized existence. The unbearable lives of those who, like machines, eat, lay, give birth, excrete and sleep to order; worn out, fattened in spaces so small that they cannot move. They know neither the sweetness of straw, nor the colour of the sun, nor the fragrance of the meadowland. They live to die an economically quick death (for our survival. . .).

We must be reminded of the distress of the animals condemned for ever in zoos, in menageries, behind bars, for us to take pleasure in their pain.

And, finally, we must be reminded of the massacre of the whales for oil which goes into beauty products, the wholesale killing of the elephants for ivory, the kangaroos for tinned meat.

We know what has caused all this extermination, incarceration and injustice, but we do not know where it will end. Because there is no end. Who justifies, who permits, who allows, who suggests, who promotes that collective indifference, which will lead sooner or later to the complete destruction of the animal kingdom?

Greed, cruelty, violence, sadism: these qualities, alas, are all too typical of present-day *human* behaviour. It is time to act, high time – if we want to regain the dignity the animals have never lost. If we really wish that the world might become once more what it was at the beginning of time: a shared Paradise.

Parts of this book make painful reading. I truly hope that even those who have lacked compassion and generosity of spirit on this issue will be deeply moved and inspired to action.

Brigitte Bardot

Introduction

'One stupendous Whole whose body nature is'
Pope

And how we have abused that body of which we are a part, but it *is* possible for each of us to contribute to changes.

The idea for this book grew partly out of an awareness that the animal rights movement was sadly fragmented and therefore losing a huge proportion of its potential power for good.

In these pages many of the issues of animal abuse and exploitation are explored, along with suggestions as to what may be done and details of the main organizations campaigning for animals.

Every care has been taken to maintain factual accuracy throughout this book, and all chapters have been read by experts or people who have worked closely on the specific issues covered. Information on organizations is as up-to-date as possible at the time of going to press.

The object has been to be as *positive* as possible – it is always easier to be critical than to be usefully constructive. This is in the hope that, if 'moderates' cannot say a good word for the courage and energy of 'militants', or the much-needed publicity which they attract to the dire suffering of animals – with which none of the sane among us can live in any kind of peace – they will at least remain silent. In the hope too, that where 'moderates' appear to be letting down the 'militants' but are not actively damaging the cause, they will not be openly attacked but valued for what they are able to give. In this way all factions could move together in greater numbers, with greater force, forgetting human egos which only hamper the struggle against the iniquity of animal exploitation.

Unfortunately, there are omissions, but this is inevitable as the field is so huge and one book so limited in what it can cover.

Sea creatures – the whales, seals, dolphins, the turtles left to die on their backs, roasting in the sun, for turtle soup – and others, the reptiles and snakes who die for shoes and handbags, the birds, massacred in their thousands, and animals used for so-called 'luxury foods' – Indian frogs dismembered while fully conscious, their frozen legs sent to fill the restaurants of the West, leaving an ecological gap for insects upon which those frogs once fed, so expensive toxic pesticides have to be sent *from* the West as the 'solution' for its gourmet greed; the force-fed geese of France, the Balkans and Israel, their agony ingested by the ignorant who call their lack of sensitivity sophistication, the camels of the desert literally felled to the ground so that their throats may be reached for the cutting, the dogs and cocks bred to fight on behalf of man's lower nature.

Some larger issues have not been covered as they might have been – factory farming, for instance, as not only have there been three good books published on this shame of our time[1], but for the person who truly believes in reverence for life, vegetarianism is the only answer. For this reason, slaughter has been covered at length, both to dispell the myth that in Britain food animals are killed humanely and because the subject has not been written about as other issues have. Hunting and fishing have been covered, but not shooting – a 'prestigious' sport which attracts many trigger-happy foreigners to our shores to massacre alongside the jolly British natives and which employs thousands of gamekeepers who take it upon themselves to decimate wildlife in order to 'preserve' millions of gamebirds, intensively reared – and sometimes debeaked to prevent cannibalism under these conditions – to enjoy a 'sporting death'. I recommend Charles Causley's poem 'I Saw A Jolly Hunter'[2] which says all one can say on the matter in its last verse: 'Bang went the jolly gun/Hunter jolly dead/Jolly hare got clean away/Jolly good I said.'

The enormous issue of the use of live animals for experimentation is discussed, but it is a large and complex one on which several good books have been written. Cancer research, next to psychological and behavioural experiments, seems to have created the most devastating waste of animal life.

[1] Ruth Harrison, *Animal Machines* (Stuart, 1964); Jim Mason and Peter Singer, *Animal Factories* (Crown, NY, USA, 1980); Mark Gold, *Assault and Battery* (Pluto Press, 1983).
[2] Charles Causley, *Collected Poems, 1951-75* (Papermac, 1975).

The multi-million cancer con research industry continues to use emotional blackmail on a gullible, fear-ridden public in order to keep its steamroller wheels well oiled as it trundles its destructive way, mowing down lives, but offering nothing in return. This subject will hopefully be covered in the way it deserves in another book now in its planning stages

I make no apologies for the unrestrained, campaigning style of the book. The word 'campaign' originated with its military meaning and we are indeed in the midst of a battle between those who, insofar as possible, wish to live by a philosophy of respect for all that lives, which would in turn lead us into harmony with Nature and Natural Law, and those who wish selfishly to pursue their own ends, no matter what the cost to other life forms, which in turn would lead us to destruction and devastation.

Hippocrates talked of 'One common flow/One common breathing/All things in sympathy,' which is the natural order of things; an order, a communion, we have forgotten, which we ignore to the detriment of ourselves and all that lives. R.D. Laing has talked of 'the disarray of personal worlds of experience, whose repression, denial, splitting, projection and general desecration and profanation our civilization is based upon'. One of the problems is that, for most people, inner and outer worlds are at best out of touch with each other and at worst in total opposition. The disease which so plagues mankind but has not touched the animals is alienation. Unfortunately, this alienation plagues those working within the Animal Rights Movement as it does those who are not, albeit to a lesser extent, so that in order for constructive progress to be made, it is up to every individual to look for blocks within him- or herself and become realigned with the common flow of the Universe.

This particular point was articulated by 'Cal', a member of the Porton Women's Camp for Peace and Animal Liberation: 'We are making a conscious effort towards co-operation and harmony within and among ourselves – none of us should just point to the "baddies out there" and ignore the violence within ourselves.'

Whether or not you agree with the ideas and ideals of a peace camp – though surely everyone must recoil at the horrors perpetrated behind the prison walls of Porton Down, where chemical and biological weapons to kill man are tested on thousands of animals – the concept of this particular camp was revolutionary in that its instigators were attempting to lift the common despair about the violent mess we are in; to invite people to *question* and to break down the individual's sense of unimportance: 'The State with its oppressive mechanism is very glad that people don't make connections. Our educational system militates against it.' We are all victims of conditioning, but only the ignorant man or woman is helpless. By seeking self-knowledge, individuation, integration, we can begin to replace this clamouring dischord of pain and suffering with love, or at least compassion and harmony.

For those who still say, 'but what can I do?' *some* of the answers to that question lie in these pages. It is a book meant to provoke thought, pity, anger, compassion and action, to provide a few pointers once the conscience is stirred. To all those who know or have begun to know the supreme importance of Animal Liberation, the words of C.G. Jung must provide a spur: 'The progress of the race is always in the hands of the *individual*, for the masses are blind. . .'

He was not necessarily talking of the poor, the uneducated, but the masses who live in spiritual ignorance, and that will include the hunting vicar, the coursing country landowner, the wealthy turkey farmer, the vivisecting scientist with a string of acclamations from academe trailing after his name, the government minister who from his high estate sanctions the export of live animals or the quick-witted businessman who breeds primates for research. They are all a part of the masses living in the darkness of ignorance, without the circle of compassion. There must be a thousand ways of drawing them in, most of all by compassion which radiates and gives strength from within each individual.

Animal Liberation is a quest; the wretched ones who 'stand and wait' behind locked laboratory doors, in the dark, overcrowded cells of factory farms, in the holds of overloaded ships – where 'natural wastage' is counted in the financial calculations – those from the sea whose blood is yearly spilt on the beaches of Canada and South Africa because humans want to tear their skins from their living bodies to bedeck their own, those whose bodies are torn apart in the name of pleasure, or whose home is the bars of a cage, cannot wait.

The Time is Now! For another million animals and more, They will come in the morning. Martin Luther King declared that to passively condone an evil is as bad as to perpetrate it. How many of us can carry such a burden?

1 Cruel Sports

Hunting

> *Hunt saboteur*: 'Oh my God, I can't see, I can't see . . .' as hunt supporters smashed the windscreen of his car, sending slivers of glass into his eyes.

> *Master of the Essex Union Hunt*: 'Horse-whipping a hunt saboteur is rather like beating a wife. They are both private matters.'

Hunting animals for pleasure is a pastime which stretches back into history and is often associated with daring and courage. It has been linked with training for war, yet the enlightened of all ages have spoken out against it. It is the indulgence of a primitive instinct refined to a curious degree – primitive man does not kill simply for the fun of it, though man soon learns to enjoy the perverse 'thrill' of killing.

Philip Windeatt, in his excellent little book *The Hunt and Anti-Hunt*[1] provides a potted history of hunting, revealing the merciless savagery through the centuries towards people who got in their way as well as towards their quarry. He tells us that Xenophon (who chronicled the Persian Wars) proclaimed hunting to be the 'best training for war', a tenet so dear to the military that until 1977 Sandhurst Military College had its own pack of foxhounds – for which English taxpayers had to pay.

Foxes

Perhaps the fox, most of all, has suffered from 'futile arguments'. Many myths have grown around it, all raised to

[1] Pluto Press, 1982.

support the hunters' cause. Man, who decimates wild and domestic life, accuses the fox of plundering creatures which he is rearing to kill for himself, yet careful studies have shown the case for the prosecution to be very shaky.

Fox myths

The killing of lambs and chickens Despite the fact that for part of the year the fox's diet may be up to 40 per cent vegetarian, it stands accused of stealing countless healthy lambs and chickens. But in the *Sunday Times* (21 May 1978) John Barrington, a Scottish shepherd, claimed that it is largely untrue that foxes kill young lambs. He said that the fox is a friend rather than an enemy to the shepherd, because voles, one of which can eat 50lb of grass a year, form a major part of its diet. Barrington also stated that on the rare occasion when a fox does kill lambs, (as distinct from carrying off the bodies of lambs which are already dead) it is as a result of human interference – such as the killing of its mate. He also said in the *Scottish Farmer* that the Ánimal Breeding Research Organisation has estimated that 17 per cent of all lambs born on Scottish hills are either still-born or die within twenty-four hours. The fox is usually blamed because remains are found in their earths, but it is now known that the main cause of early death is poor nutrition of the ewes in winter.

Brian Hamilton, himself a farmer, reported his findings in the *Farmer and Stockbreeder*,[1] after studying the carcasses for over twenty years with post-mortems on two hundred lambs. All had died before mauling. Seventy per cent of missing lambs had died within forty-eight hours and were born of ewes who had insufficient milk. The remaining 30 per cent were unaccounted for but many of these would have succumbed to disease and general weakness. He wrote: 'During our investigations we found a strong link between bad shepherding and "lamb losses due to foxes. . ." When I found four foxes prowling round my flock one night, I felt no concern; they were waiting for the afterbirth or dead lambs.' In addition, of his 10,000 free-range poultry only sixty were lost to predators and most, he claimed, were his fault.

Foxes, as confirmed by countrymen I've talked with, will also eat carrion. Even the Duke of Beaufort, a notorious hunter,

---

[1] Reproduced in *Cruel Sports*, vol.9, no.2, new series II 68.

admitted in the *Sunday Times* (13 March 1955) that although he had ewes lambing next to fox coverts, he had not lost a single lamb. This was confirmed by Monica Hutchings in *A Farmer's Wife Looks at Hunting*:[1] 'We have always had foxes on our farm and have never shot, poisoned or trapped them, neither have we ever lost a lamb or had poultry taken. In the main our foxes keep down small rodents, slugs and beetles and do more good than harm.'

Even the British Field Sports Society which has a vested interest in vilifying the fox says: 'It is probably true to say that about 5% of all foxes in Christendom . . . taste domestic poultry.' (Nowadays 95 per cent of poultry are in batteries and deep litter houses and not wandering around freely.)

John Bryant,[2] who ran the Ferne Animal Sanctuary in Somerset, has received two letters from the Ministry of Agriculture in reply to his enquiries, stating that loss of either lambs or chickens to foxes is thought to be 'insignificant' and 'small' respectively.

Foxes have small stomachs and usually feed on rodents, beetles, rabbits and berries. (It is interesting to compare this fact with the discoveries of naturalist Farley Mowatt[3] who studied Canadian wolves. They, too, ate mainly rodents and, contrary to popular myth, were not at all vicious, but were pleasant, organized, friendly, family-loving creatures, who made no attempt to attack him even though he had set up camp on their trail, and never killed needlessly.)

A lady I talked to in Reading had formerly run a poultry farm and had banned the hunt from her land. As a result, foxes would go to seek refuge there and even dug an earth under a hen house. *But she lost not a single chicken to them.*

The killing of cats It is also commonly thought that foxes kill cats – but they hardly ever do. They might in utter desperation, in the depths of winter, but many people will have watched the television documentary in which foxes were filmed encountering cats near city dustbins at night. It was usually the fox who turned away first. John Bryant states that at the Ferne Animal Sactuary he witnessed eight-week-old kittens drive an

---

[1] Booklet published by the National Society Against Cruel Sports.
[2] Information quoted from his article in 'The Beast'.
[3] Farley Mowatt, *Never Cry Wolf*, Dell, 1963.

adult fox away from food and eat it themselves!

What is more, foxes venture into towns not because there are too many of them, but because they see an easy food supply – humans throw away an awful lot of food.

Population control The continual defence put up by huntsmen and women is that foxes 'must be kept down'. David McDonald, an authority on foxes (known for his film *Night of the Fox*), and Eric Ashby (who made *The Private Life of the Fox*) both agree that if there were no fox control the population would not expand to problem proportions. Food supply and territorial factors would limit it, but there would always be some who would not be happy with the population statistics.

'Rogue' foxes who occasionally raid and plunder would in any case not be dealt with by a hunt, because a farmer with a gun usually tackles such a problem immediately. However, foxes who do steal easy food in this way usually do so because a mate has been killed – by humans – and there is a family to be fed by one parent. Fox hunting has been abolished in Germany and such problems do not appear to be worrying the Germans.

The League Against Cruel Sports sponsored an independent survey carried out by a market research company in which it took no part, the results of which it published in a leaflet entitled: 'Facts about Foxes and Farming':

> Only 27% of farmers consider the fox to be harmful, the majority consider it not to be so. Almost ½ (49%) who do not consider it harmful think it of value in controlling rabbits, mice, rats, etc. Of the farmers who thought it harmful, 27% said 'by assumption', 59%, 'eye witness account' and 15%, 'other means'. 2% said 'impossible to know' and 4% 'didn't know'. Most farms suffering damage from foxes put it at no higher than £25 for a whole year – this applies to all regions.

Foxes are preserved and reared especially for hunting which leads to an artificially high fox population and thus the apparent need for fox control to keep down the numbers.

The Hunt

I sought wild animals only to hunt and kill. The blood of
thousands is on my hands. And I am deeply ashamed. I want
to wash away the blood I have spilled. Not just by making
friends with wild creatures, but by setting down for everyone
to read my confession as a hunter, especially of foxes.
(Captain Robert Churchward, ex-Master-of-Foxhounds.)

Some unpleasant facts

* The Earl of Yarborough is known to have weaned young
cubs with the intention of hunting them when fully grown.[1]
* Vera Sheppard, veteran anti-hunt campaigner, had plenty
of evidence of artificial fox earths being made for hunts.[2]
* Foxes are moved round the country from places where there
are many to where there are none. Suddenly finding themselves
in a strange place the foxes may, according to Captain
Churchward, an ex-Hunt-Master, take easy food such as
poultry and as a result may be poisoned or inexpertly shot and
may die slowly of painful wounds.
* Gamekeepers who kill foxes are in the employ of people
making a lot of money out of rearing gamebirds for massacre,
often by incompetent people who treat a weekend of killing, for
which they may be paying £200 or more as they would a
weekend of golf. But no special skill is required. Mrs A. Collett
who worked in an hotel to which businessmen flocked for a
weekend's shooting in the country, overheard one enthusiast
ask, 'Is there anything at which we're not supposed to shoot?'

The truth about hunting

Hunting, it can be categorically stated, is:
Damaging to farmland To crops, livestock, fences and hedges;
to gardens and pets – many of which have been 'accidentally'
killed – and it is a possible potential carrier of foot and mouth
disease and other diseases. It is rare for adequate compensation
to be given, especially to tenant farmers of hunting landlords,
some of whom make sure that leases do not allow the exclusion

[1] LACS.
[2] *My Head Against the Wall*, 19.

of the hunt. Those who protest run the risk of non-renewal of leases.

To horses: they may like a good gallop, but they could sustain injuries on jumps or barbed wire, etc. Severe injuries mean they will be shot – in which case they are often fed to hounds.

To terriers who are sent in to chase out foxes from their refuge for further hunting and who may get badly injured by the terrified victim. A government report – the Scott Henderson Committee – in 1951 called this practice, termed 'bolting', needlessly cruel. Terriers may also be sent into holes to occupy the fox while the hunters dig down to it.

To the hounds who are trained to be unnaturally vicious, and in effect, cannibalistic. Hunters encourage children to pat the 'nice doggies' on hound parades at Agricultural Shows to show how friendly the hounds are, but it is unnatural to train them to chase and kill their wild brothers. The hounds are shot by the hunt at an average age of five or six, earlier if they show any indiscipline in the pack.

Morally degrading   Violence and aggression are encouraged in both adults and children. All want to be 'in at the kill': 'Although I had found the reek of stiffening blood upon my face almost unendurably revolting, I had done my best to conceal my disgust for fear of ridicule,' said Captain Churchward about his 'blooding' as a young child. (Blood from a severed tail is sometimes smeared on the child's face and he is told not to wash it off, though this happens less today than formerly, thanks to bad publicity.)

Dishonest   Foxes are moved about the country to artificial earths and breeding areas, they are sent from the grouse moors to the shires, for instance.

Huntspeople do not want to 'keep foxes down' – they want to clock up their number of kills each season.

Too big a number of foxes in one spot, however, may be a distraction for the hounds who may split up, which will annoy the hunt.

An exhausting (for the fox) chase is artificially set up by the stopping of its earth while it is out on the night previous to the hunt. If it is clever or fortunate enough to be able to take refuge in another hole a few miles away, it will be dug up and shot, or bolted with terriers and hunted again.

The fox will be chased as far as possible so the marauding

horde won't be disappointed, sometimes for an hour and a half, sometimes for much longer.

Cubs are hunted in August. 'Cubbing' is 'necessary' for the training of the hounds. Many are dug up and torn apart before the vixen, given no chance to escape.

Cubs are sometimes left to starve if the vixen is killed. The hunting season runs from November until April inclusive, and fox cubs are born in late March or early April.

A fox's natural lifespan could be ten years, but not many are allowed to live beyond two years.

A strange status symbol 'Hunting is turning into a hard commercial advertising business, cashing in more and more on its status symbolism in order to keep going.'[1] It is attracting the new rich ever seeking ways of getting in with the 'right' people. This kind of attitude is comparable to that of the empty-headed tourists who keep Spanish bullfighting alive – a sport which otherwise might have died a natural death – simply because they think they are doing the 'authentic' thing, while many Spaniards are ashamed of the 'sport'.

It is often said by huntspeople that the fox enjoys being chased and that quite a few 'get away' anyway. John Bryant maintains that fox hunting is particularly cruel because the fox has physically evolved to be fit for short sprints, not for a long chase, as the deer, for example. He has found exhausted foxes on his sanctuary land which have 'escaped' the hunt, but which inevitably die from exhaustion. That kind of exhaustion can be agonizing and must involve suffering for the fox, not to mention those which are caught by or thrown to the hounds and torn limb from limb.

Other perils

Foxes are also suffering from the demands of the fur trade – fox fur seems to be enjoying a new popularity. To obtain the skins, the fox will be killed by trapping or poisoning, both of which are extremely inhumane. It can take ten skins to make one coat.

There is hope, however, for the fox. In spite of the tenacious desperation of the old guard and the simpering determination

[1] Captain Churchward.

of the new, disapproval of fox hunting among the general public grows by the day. Successful anti-hunting campaigns and a new wave of pity and anger are threatening their security. The editorial columns of *Horse and Hound* now contain a note of hysterical defensiveness which would be amusing were it not for the fact that their victims will suffer until fox hunting is abolished by law, relegated once and for all to the annals of a shameful past. Up to 30,000 foxes are killed every year by the hunt.

A sensible alternative

Drag hunting could easily replace the hunting of a live quarry. A sack or bundle of cloth containing liquid simulating live-quarry scent is pulled across the ground by a runner for the hounds to follow.
* It involves no cruelty.
* It is safer for all humans and animals concerned.
* As the trail is *chosen*, no damage need be done.
* Hounds will not go out of control. (They sometimes endanger their own lives and those of others, causing accidents on railways and motorways, for example.)
* There will be no artificial fox population.
* The same riding pleasure can be obtained.
Source material: The National Society Against Cruel Sports. *The Beast*. League Against Cruel Sports, with special help from John Bryant.

Hares

Each outcry of the hunted hare
A fibre of the brain doth tear
                    William Blake, 'Auguries of Innocence'

It seems from evidence to be found from Ancient Egypt, Assyria and Greece that the hare has been hunted since pre-history: in Britain the hare was the preferred victim before the deer and fox and was praised for giving a chase as long as four miles.

Hares are pursued in three different ways; by coursing, hunting on foot (beagling), or by mounted riders (harriers) as in fox hunting.

Coursing

Hare coursing, described by a former president of the British Small Animals Veterinary Association, Noel Ormrod, as 'senseless and wanton cruelty' is purely a form of entertainment, kept alive by betting, which can run into thousands of pounds at the Waterloo Cup.

Coursing, which takes place from September until March, differs from hunting in that only two dogs are used. The aim of this 'sport' is for two dogs, usually greyhounds, to compete against each other in pursuit of the hare.

In 'static' coursing, the competition takes place in an enclosed field into which the hare is driven. The idea of coursing is not to kill the hare, but to give competing greyhounds a chance to demonstrate their agility as they go after the hare, which turns sharply as it tries to escape them. Points are given according to the dogs' skill and ability in turning after the hare. Spectators remain outside the coursing field and are expected to remain silent.

Hares may be driven half a mile or so into the field by thirty or more beaters. The two dogs are then released by the 'slipper' who gives the hare a recommended start of about eighty yards, or sometimes less. Having been already chased, the hare must then run for its life.

The judge, mounted on horseback, waves coloured handkerchieves in the air to indicate results. The hare may, or may not, escape. When both dogs catch the hare at once, there may be a horrendous tug-of-war as the victim is torn to pieces.

Hare-coursing supporters say the hare is always killed instantly, but this is not so. A large proportion are caught. They scream a human-sounding scream during those long minutes approaching death.

Death itself depends on how quickly the handlers or pickers-up reach the dogs. When they do reach them, the hare may still be alive, in which case it will be taken from the dogs and killed, usually by having its neck broken.

Hares are often coursed in the open. This is called 'walk-up' coursing. A line of beaters, or beaters, spectators, and owners, walk over the fields, driving hares out in front of them. They stop when a hare is moving and the dogs are released to chase it. It is possible for the dogs to catch the hare and run off with it so that the pickers-up may not be able to reach it to kill it quickly.

Many clubs throughout England and Wales organize these kinds of meets, the biggest being the notorious Waterloo Cup, held at Altcar in Liverpool in February each year. This is the course to which all coursing greyhound owners aspire.

Hunt saboteurs are effective against hare coursing; they clear the ground of hares by beating against the beaters, making a great deal of noise or using smoke screens.

A good deal of unorganized coursing also takes place outside the auspices of the National Coursing Club. People go out with dogs, generally three – two greyhounds and a terrier. The terrier bolts the hare out into the open (hares do not live in holes like rabbits) and then the greyhounds go after it. This is mostly done for sport, casually and for the hell of it, and so it is irrelevant to these people whether the hare is killed or not. Sometimes hares are killed for eating, in which case one dog is used, not two, so it cannot be called coursing.

Beagling

The hare is hunted by humans on foot, using either beagles or bassets. Some English public schools have beagle packs. These hunts have the usual officials – a master, huntsmen and whippers-in. The pack is sent out searching for hares and, when one is located, it is chased down and killed. Hares can sprint fast over short distances but, because the hounds are bred for stamina, they will always move in on the exhausted hare and kill it. The absolute cruelty of this is graphically described by the old Norfolk farmer, Arthur Harmer, who – while he shot hares to control them – was very much against bloodsports:

> I once shot one running away from the hounds . . . and carved it up so the hounds didn't find it. . . . When I opened that hare I was never so much surprised. There wasn't a mite of blood in it . . . (it) was all pink bubbles. She'd been chased then for over a quarter of an hour . . . had run the life out of herself.[1]

Hares are getting scarce in some parts of the country, a fact admitted by hunting reporters. The Ilminster Beaglers have frequently said they have trouble in finding hares. And so the

[1] George Ewart Evans and David Thomson, *The Leaping Hare*, Faber, 1972.

usual hunter's argument, that hunting conserves the hunted species, crumbles.

Harriers

Harriers, named after the hounds they use, which are rather like foxhounds, hunt hares on horseback. These are the same kind of people who go fox-hunting and it has been said of them by one who has watched their activities that they 'will kill anything they come across'. Like the beaglers, they hunt from October to March, officially, but will go from September until the end of April, and so pregnant does may be caught and killed. A hare may have been chased for miles – perhaps four – and the kill is not always controlled. It may happen out of sight of the huntsmen. If a hare finds shelter, it is officially supposed to be either left or killed immediately, but these 'sportsmen' – 14 stone men on 15cwt horses – give no 'sporting rights' to their harmless 8lb quarry; the hares are often flushed out and rehunted.

All huntspeople show little concern for the dogs they train to do their dirty work. Any hounds which are either not very good at their work or show signs of slowing up are killed and fed back to the other hounds in the pack. At the end of each hunting season the hounds which look as though they are lagging behind are chosen to be destroyed so that new ones can be introduced. From a pack of thirty, five or six will be selected to be killed, so that over a five- or six-year period there will be a completely new pack of hounds. Occasionally a particularly good hunter may be allowed to live longer, perhaps till he's nine or so, but that is not very common.

People come from many countries – from as far away as the USA – to watch the killing of English hares, especially at Altcar in February, and even the righteous are prone to the rape of the fair; many vicars are officials of hunts.

Stags and Deer

> . . . the spot is curst . . .
> Some say that here a murder has been done,
> And blood cries out for blood: but, for my part

I've guessed, when I've been sitting in the sun,
That it was all for that unhappy Hart.
                    William Wordsworth, 'Hartleap Well'

In fact, Grace was blooded twice. Once into fox-hunting and
for a second time into deer stalking. Her second blooding was
when she was the mother of four children . . . the stalker
came towards her with a piece of the stag's body and
smeared the blood not only upon her cheeks, but on her
forehead, nose and chin . . . (she) went into dinner at a smart
hotel with her face set hard in a mask of blood. There she
received the congratulations of the distinguished guests.

So wrote Captain Robert Churchward. Deer stalking is not stag
hunting, but the blood ritual is the same, and the hunting even
more cruel.

Deer hunting, not instituted in its present form until the
eighteenth century, is probably the most barbaric of all field
sports. The RSPCA published a leaflet affirming the terrific
cruelty of the hunt, to which it has been opposed ever since,
even though there seems to have been a notable lack of
campaigning activity. In an attempt to lessen the cruelty
involved, the RSPCA presented the stag hunts with humane
killers and these, or guns, are now sometimes used for the final
killing. However, the shooting may not be carried out by the
most skilful, and the man with the gun or humane killer may
not arrive in time and deer are still sometimes killed by having
their throats cut. But shooting is the only legal method of killing
deer under the Deer Act of 1963.

There are now four deer hunts in England and two in
Ireland. The New Forest Buck Hounds hunt fallow deer and
say they kill only five or six deer a year, while the Quantock,
Devon and Somerset, and the Tiverton hunts kill 150-200
animals a year between them. These three hunt only red deer.
The season begins on 1 August when they hunt what they call
spring stags, until 1 November. A few years ago the hunt would
stop on 9 October to allow the stags some peace through the
rutting season, but now it continues right through it – which is
upsetting to a good many people. A strong stag fights to gather
his harem of hinds, but the strong stag will be selected to be
chased and killed, which in turn means that weaker ones mate

with the hinds, thus weakening the deer population. This is entirely the responsibility of the huntsmasters who are oblivious to complaints on the issue.

Nora Harding of the Devon and Somerset Hunt stated: 'We hunters really love the deer. We love to see them and look after them,' and admitted to her interviewer that deer exist *solely* for sport, but went on to say that huntsmen are a deer's best friend.[1]

These inhumans hunt stags until 1 November, take a week's break to get their dogs used to the changeover, and begin at once to hunt hinds, which they continue to do until 1 March.

By March many of the deer they are hunting are heavily pregnant, and the ones which aren't generally have young at foot. One of the most sickening aspects of deer hunting is the chasing of a hind with its calf. The calf is unable to keep up with its mother and the mother, wanting to escape but distressed about her young one, keeps turning back, trying to chase off the hounds, desperately trying to lead her calf away, not knowing that for all her brave attempts they will be shown no mercy. John Hicks, who is employed by the League Against Cruel Sports as their sanctuaries manager recounted,

> I have seen the hinds when they have calves at foot hunted down very quickly. This spoils their fun and so the hounds are whipped off and a rider is sent to chase the hind and calf on. In ten or fifteen minutes they will chase after her again.

Arthur Harmer, a Norfolk farmer, told how his grandmother had seen hounds catch a deer on the far side of a river so that the hunters could not get to it.[2] 'The hounds pulled that deer to pieces, joint from joint. And when that was killed, it was like a copper of boiling water . . . and there were two little ones inside the animal while it was being hunted.'

From 1 March until the end of April, or 1 May, stags are hunted once again. The deer are left alone only during May, June and July.

When a stag comes to bay, the hounds will attempt to attack him. This happens when the hunt goes over rough terrain where it is difficult for the huntsmen to keep up with the

[1] Mark Rossell of the *Sunday Independent*, 27 February 1983.
[2] See George Ewart Evans and David Thomson, *The Leaping Hare*, Faber, 1972.

hounds. Huntspeople claim that deer are always humanely despatched with a shotgun, but this is a gross distortion of the truth.

Hinds, particularly those with young at foot, have no protection at all and it is certainly not unheard of for them to be ripped to pieces before the hunt turns up. When they do arrive, the hounds are whipped off, and the deer shot through the chest.

Mike Huskisson of the League Against Cruel Sports has witnessed many kills. In his experience, the autumn stags are nearly always shot, either with a shotgun or with a pistol at close range. The hounds seldom actually kill a stag because he can fight so well with his strong antlers, but they do sometimes manage to bite at his hind quarters, especially if he is caught in thick brush or is swimming out to sea. Other witnesses have stated that for hinds, dying can be very different. They have seen a hind disappear into a thick wood, and by the time they have reached it, all that remained was the head and feet. One got herself caught on barbed wire and was suspended upside down, the hounds biting at her while she hung there helpless, before the huntsman got near enough to shoot her. The spring stags have antlers and usually manage to keep the hounds back. Hunters declare that their hounds never get near the quarry, but the League have plenty of photographs and film which prove that they lie. It is true, however, that hounds do not usually attack deer long enough to kill them.

The hunters also claim that one shot kills a stag. Mike Huskisson has seen stags killed only after three shots have been fired.

It is generally felt that deer do now need to be controlled because we have eliminated their natural predators (wolves). On Exmoor, wild land adjoins farmland so that deer wander towards the farmland to feed. If the population were not controlled, they would eat the crops or suffer as they do in Scotland, where large numbers die of starvation for lack of food. Many consider that the more humane way would be selective killing with a high-powered rifle by a skilled man employed to do the job. This would eliminate the idea of 'sport'. (The Forestry Commission keep a ranger on Exmoor who culls about as many deer as the stag hunt kills, working over the same area. He costs them £11,000 a year in total. At a conservative estimate the Devon and Somerset stag hounds cost £¼ million a year. Only twice in six years[1] has the ranger failed to kill instantly with the first shot.) More and more people are campaigning for what they feel to be the more humane approach.

After the kill, a standard ritual takes place in which the animal is gutted, its feet cut off, and the stomach and innards taken out and fed to the hounds. These, a larger type of foxhound, are trained by 'education' from the older members of the pack. A handful of new hounds are introduced each year. They are bred by the huntspeople who have their own kennels.

Stag and deer hunting is a far more expensive pastime than fox hunting. The fees are larger and the status greater. The distances are long and the terrain rough, so that many horses are killed each year. Many more are injured or killed than in fox hunting, but the figures are closely guarded.

Hind hunting begins at about 11am and goes on until dark, while stag hunting starts at about 3pm in August, because of the midday heat, and goes on until 9 or 9.30 in the evening. This is timed so that visitors to Exmoor are less likely to see a kill. The aim is to kill the hunted animal just as dusk is falling. To the huntspeople, that is a perfect day's hunting. One animal may be chased for eight hours; from the first hour the creature is experiencing 'absolute, sheer terror'.

While huntspeople claim that 'they [the deer] don't feel anything', John Hicks said, 'I have seen stags and hinds after being hunted for just an hour, absolutely petrified. You can see the white of their eyes and they're gasping. They don't know which way to turn. Then will follow seven hours of pure hell for them.'

There is a difference between stag and deer hunting. For stag hunting a harbourer goes out to select a 'warrantable' stag two days before the hunt takes place. He will go back to check on its whereabouts very early on the morning of the hunt. A stag will settle in one place for the day, and would remain there undisturbed were it not for the tufters (the best hounds – the best scenters and the most reliable) which are taken in by the huntsman to flush him out. When the whole pack is laid on, the hunt begins.

[1] *Sunday Independent*, 10 July 1983.

In the hunting of hinds, no deer is selected, but tufters are still used to chase them out of their cover. Once the deer is out, they select a hind, or hind and calf, but they do not preselect.

The majority of local people in hunting country are against the stag and deer hunts – in a small Quantock village referendum the vote was three to one for a ban.

Besides the huntspeople, lesser mortals like to be in on the act. These include mounted followers, car followers, supporters and a vast array of riders on motorbikes. Said John Hicks, 'I have seen them at a kill – they all jump out of their cars and off their bikes and shout "hooray, we got it, we've killed it, hooray".'

Motorbike boys will drive the deer in, chase them in the desired direction. On an average hunt about a hundred motorbikes are out. At an opening meet there might be two hundred riders, between fifty and a hundred on motorbikes, and 100–200 cars.

Followers tend to be tough types. John Hicks has first hand experience:

I was dragged out of my van – which has League Against Cruel Sports written on the side of it – and my head was smashed against it. I was punched in the stomach, kicked, dragged across the road by four or five men and had my head beaten against the landrover. I was then pushed back into the van and told not to show my face again. I think they only stopped then because there were some more sensible huntspeople around who tried to restrain them and there were also television cameras about that day. The motorbike and car supporters are much worse than the riders.

Official complaints were made to the police, with photos and the registration numbers of their vehicles, but the police said that no one could identify them and that the number plates must have been false. . . .

The huntspeople themselves are prone to hooliganism and absolute disdain for the law and other people's wishes and feelings. On one occasion the hunt approached Holford, a Quantock village, and a stag ran to hide on land belonging to a person who happened to be anti-hunt. The owner refused to let anyone disturb it but after three-quarters of an hour he couldn't hold them back any longer and a group of supporters ran in and chased the creature out. It then ran into a field of a neighbour who was also anti-hunt. The stag was so worn out that, as it jumped the fence, seven or eight supporters physically jumped on it and sat on it for over twenty-five minutes, until all of the hunt had gathered around to see it killed.

The owner of the first piece of land had informed the hunt that his neighbour was anti-hunt, but they ignored him and after twenty-five minutes they shot the stag.

The League Against Cruel Sports was asked to prosecute for armed trespass and poaching. There were photos of the event and the hunt even admitted to what they had done, yet the magistrate ruled that they were not poaching. There was no appeal and there was no point of law on which to appeal. The League is now taking out a High Court Injunction to protect its own sanctuary land – the Devon and Somerset Hunt was caught trespassing on eight or nine occasions in the 1982/83 season by the sanctuary manager.

LACS owns 2,000 acres with thirty-three sites in the West Country. These sanctuaries are difficult to patrol, but most are visited each day and night as there are many voluntary helpers. Near hunt time, there is always someone checking the ground. (Deer belong to the ground they are on.) John Hicks, sanctuaries manager, knows what he is up against:

> I would never patrol at night without a shotgun because I know, sooner or later, I'll be assaulted. There are so many people who hate me so much. Last time I received only minor injuries, but I consider mine to be a very dangerous job. To be without a shotgun would be very stupid.

Many farmers are forced to allow the hunt over their land. Either they are tenant farmers who daren't or can't stop the hunt or else the sporting rights of their farms are owned by the Badgeworthy Land Company, a firm set up to buy land and preserve the hunting rights.

This was financially backed by the huntspeople until it became self-supporting. The company buys land, reserves the hunting rights, keeps it for a short time, and resells at a profit, then buys more. This is an escalating procedure so that more and more hunting rights are gained.

In addition, farmers are still afraid of their livelihood being affected. If it is found that a farmer has banned the hunt, he might find it difficult to sell his hay or animals at the market because hunting farmers put the word around and people in the area will then refuse to bid for these farmers' goods. Thus farmers can be bullied into accepting the hunt.

Source material: John Hicks; League Against Cruel Sports; Mike Huskisson.

Otters and Mink

Otters are now very scarce in England and the hunting of them has been illegal since 1978. However, the same people hunt mink and coypu and may still even be killing otters.

The same rivers are now inhabited by mink which, having been imported and farmed for making fur coats, have escaped and bred. They are hunted in the same way as otters were, with otterhounds and foxhounds, the season running from April to October. These same men and women, dressed in a strange uniform, carrying their poles on which to notch their kills, have just told their dogs they mustn't kill otters now – *if* they manage to find any.

Even supposing that human and canine hunters abide by the law, they are still harming the otter. The otter needs to be left alone in order to re-establish itself; if disturbed while with cubs, a mother will either abort or eat her young. They are extremely susceptible to any disturbance.

The hunters are desperately trying to maintain that mink are a major disaster for the English countryside, but scientific evidence shows this not to be so. Mink have simply found a natural niche and do very little damage, and in many ways are beneficial in that they keep down the rat population.

The case given against mink is that they take many fish, including trout, that they take poultry and have even been accused of attacking newly born lambs.

Research has shown the mink to be a poor swimmer – it cannot catch healthy fish and so only takes the sick and injured. Most poultry are living in battery houses, where even daylight cannot reach them, let alone other animals. The last allegation has been shown to be absurd. Mink may raid poultry, as many other carnivores, but their impact is nothing compared to that of rabbits and rats on agriculture. Dr John Birks, a zoologist from Durham University wrote: 'In most situations the level of predation upon native prey populations by feral mink cannot objectively be regarded as excessive; if it were one would expect to find evidence of serious and continuing declines in prey numbers where mink are well established. Such evidence has yet to present itself. In this respect the mink is an unfortunate victim of "scaremongering" ' and furthermore: 'scientific investigation suggests that there is a niche available in Britain for a generalist waterside predator such as the mink.'[1]

The remaining concern is that they take ducks. They do, but waterfowl have always had natural predators to cope with, many of which have been hunted or trapped into extinction – the polecat, for example, which has been trapped out of existence by gamekeepers who are also killing a great number of stoats and weasels. There is not sufficient evidence to suggest that the mink is such an efficient hunter that it is seriously affecting the waterbird population, but their human predators, hunting for 'fun' are certainly disturbing much river wildlife, including swans.

Maureen Duffy has graphically theorized on the psychology of fox and otter hunting:

> The fox and the otter both have prized tails and no great insight is needed to divine what they represent. Even the folklore characters of these animals are phallic. . . . Their body shape too isn't hard to see as a phallus and both are traditionally sexy beasts and dwell in holes. From their own angles both men and women can find pleasure in hunting and conquering them, a pleasure that isn't accessible to reason since it's based on these strange psychological needs.[2]

'If this seems far-fetched,' she writes, 'there are dozens of examples in popular literature of hunting as sexual pursuit and the reader is referred to any unbowdlerised collection of broadsides.' She goes on to say that it would be 'a simple desire

[1] *RSPCA Today*, summer 1982.
[2] Maureen Duffy in *Animals, Men and Morals*, R. and S. Godlovitch and R.J. Harris (eds.), Gollancz, 1971.

not to face facts to pretend that it wasn't so' as such songs were sung in the taverns by the very participants.

Here is one ballad on hunting in which the word 'coney' is purposely misspelt and in which the 'joyful rise in the air' refers to male erection:

'Some in the Town go betimes to the Downs,
To pursue the fearful Hare;
Some in the Dark love to hunt in a park
For to chase all the Deer that are there:
Some love to see the Falcon to flee
With a joyful rise in the Air
But all my delight is a Cunny in the Night
When she turns up her silver Hair.'

Referring to shooting and fishing and the obvious phallic connotations of the rod and the gun, she states: 'Those who are familiar with dream symbolism will know at once that the thing hunted behind these two animals is the same as that behind fox and otter.'

Hunters and shooters to whom I have pointed out the hidden psychological reasons for their activities have turned long faced and run away at such taunts from a woman. Albeit beyond their comprehension, some chord was struck.

Massacre in the Waters: The Plight of Fish and Wildfowl

Roy Plomley: Could you catch your own food – would you be able to fish?
Tom Keating: No, I wouldn't do that. I don't like killing.
Desert Island Discs, Radio 4, 1983.

Fish have for far too long been excluded from the Animal Rights Movement. Only vegetarians and vegans have given them consideration. But even they have not publicized their plight; they have merely refrained from eating them.

During the Vedanta conference on Animal Liberation held in Bath in August 1980, Swami Avyaktananda, a dedicated devotee of 'Ahimsa' or non-violence, brought attention to the suffering of fish:

Our conscience has been suppressed completely as far as fishes are concerned. They are mercilessly taken from their natural environment, heaped up and subjected to slow death by the pressure of the heaps, gasping for breath. Live and half-live fishes are cut up for sale in many countries; live and half-live fishes are fried and boiled without scruple. In Eastern countries fish are to be found struggling out of water for many hours after they are caught.

Millions are caught every day and are more ruthlessly treated than animals in experimentation, whose numbers are fewer. But fish, too, are used in experiments. Cruelty, torture and killing perpetrated throughout the world on fish is completely overlooked.

Angling is unworthy of man. An innocent creature with a similar love of life to ours, is tempted onto a hook and compelled to bear the pain. When it is removed by force from the water, it is brought to a foreign environment where it cannot breathe, and suffers a slow death.

People have been so thoughtless, callous and heartless about fishes; they have no conscience about torturing and killing them. If we resort to cruelty and killing for food, we forsake morality. We face a tremendous ethical problem when we consider both blood sports (angling) and the regular slaughter of creatures for food.

A walk through a port like Lisbon where fish restaurants crowd the streets reveals live crabs and lobsters struggling in shop windows – hundreds destined to meet death by being boiled alive. We cannot imagine that they do not suffer.

Given the fact that we are not going to see a vegetarian world in the near future, and that a tiny minority of the world's population probably needs fish for its survival, we should at least deplore the catching of fish for pleasure.

As a result of pressure by concerned people, the RSPCA commissioned an independent, expert Panel of Enquiry in 1976 to report on cruelty in angling and shooting,[1] and to formulate definitive policies.

The panel was to be uninfluenced by the RSPCA, free to seek

[1] Report of the Panel of Enquiry into Shooting and Angling (1976–9), available from Mrs A.V. Delany, c/o School of Environmental Sciences, University of Bradford BD7 1DP (£1).

evidence from any appropriate source and to be composed of outside experts – 'sportsmen', conservationists and scientists. Chaired by the Earl of Cranbrook, a country landowner, farmer and a zoologist of some repute, the panel deliberated for more than three years.

By far the most important information to come out of this enquiry was the evidence indicating that vertebrate fish feel pain as much as other mammals. The mouths of fish are 'well endowed with sensory organs and free nerve endings'. Pain research has revealed the presence of something known as 'substance P' which is associated with the transmission of pain in the nervous system of mammals. This has now been found to be present in the bodies of fish. 'The presence or absence of substance P . . . provides another pharmacological test for pain-transmitting elements in a nervous system. It is known to occur in all mammals so far investigated, as well as in birds and frogs.'[1] Dr Kelly of the Medical Research Centre in Cambridge tested for its presence in fish.

The panel concluded:

> there may still be some people who will argue that we cannot prove beyond question that any vertebrate other than man, feels pain. We, however, conclude that if any do, then the evidence suggests that all vertebrates (including fish), through the mediation of similar neuro-pharmacological processes, experience similar sensations to a greater or lesser degree in response to noxious stimuli.[2]

Strangely enough, fish have been included in Britain's legislation concerning cruelty to animals ever since the 1876 Act (which prohibits painful experiments on all animals other than vertebrates), the 1911 Protection of Animals Act, which includes fish, the Protection of Animals (Scotland) Act 1912 – which is the same as the 1911 Act which covers only England and Wales – the Welfare of Animals Act (N. Ireland) 1972 (in which 'animal' is meant to include fish) and the 1973 Transit of Animals (General) Order.

It is a pity, therefore, that most of this legislation *remains flagrantly unenforced.*

[1] Para 44 of Cranbrook Report.
[2] Para 57.

The panel stated that 'in relation to the 1876 Cruelty to Animals Act . . . this basic practice by which angling is defined (taking fish by rod, line and hook), if performed in a laboratory on unanaesthetised fish, without licence, would very probably be in contravention of the Act.'[1] Yet there are over 3¼ million anglers in Great Britain. It also stated: 'Any hook causes tissue damage when it catches and thus, in medical terms, inflicts an injury.'

Anglers realize not what they do:

The degree of trauma experienced by fish handled out of water may not be fully appreciated by anglers. The tissues of a fish, when it is removed from water, are subject in air to pressures greatly reduced and differing in nature from those they are subject to in water. . . . Bleeding tends to occur from the gills and, instead of dispersing, the blood coagulates and reduces the effective respiratory surface.[2]

Even more serious is the effect on the epidermis which in fact covers the scales and which provides a delicate waterproofing and a barrier to diseases caused by micro-organisms found in water. Handling, either by hand, or in a net, damages this delicate layer. The epidermis can heal very quickly, but if severely damaged, circulatory failure or extensive infection can result. Both mean ultimate death.[3]

Prolonged 'playing' of fish can completely exhaust them and if those fish are later returned to the water, they will be almost unable to move for several hours, which will put their lives at risk.

Coarse fishing is particularly to be deplored. This is angling for inedible fish in competition. Well over 1½ million people participate in this highly organized spectator sport with large cash prizes and wide publicity for those who catch most. After being hooked and landed, fish are kept up to five hours in crowded 'keep nets' (often contaminated by carbon-dioxide and chemicals) and then examined, weighed and photographed before the survivors are returned to the water at the end of the match.

[1] Para 252.
[2] Para 262.
[3] Paras 263 and 264.

Specimen-hunter anglers join clubs which specialize in the capture of a single species and usually return their victims to the water. Any dead fish are usually rejected at weighing-in time. On the other hand, match fishermen see fish as expendable. These people aim to catch as many fish as possible in the shortest time possible.

Fish hardly enjoy their period of imprisonment in the keep nets. Cruelty is obviously involved because the Report states that 'Inconsiderate treatment of fish by match or other coarse fishermen is periodically anathematised in the angling press.'[1]

The list of suffering inflicted on fish seems endless: rough handling, or any handling; rough nets, nets sited so as to create poor conditions for the fish, overcrowded nets; fish which escape with hooks in their mouths, the use of barbed hooks; the use of live bait – the live fish used may succumb to stress or injuries inflicted by the predatory fish or tear free from the tackle, thus increasing the severity of its impalement injuries; the use of a gag to hold open the jaws of such fish as large pike; the injuries caused to eels which are often accidentally caught by anglers and which often swallow baits so deeply that uninjurious disgorgement is impossible; the deliberate catching of eels for sport; the use of dangerous (to the fish which escape) lures for game fish; and the landing by use of a gaff (a stout hook on a staff which is impaled through jaw or body).

In addition, game fishing – the catching of fish for the table – involves a good deal of interference by man. Fisheries may be restocked from special hatcheries and 'some degree of vermin control may also be practised, including destruction of predatory fish and fish-eating birds such as the goosander in Scotland.'[2]

After a game fish has been landed – dragged from the water – by net, gaff or tailer (when it will be dragged by the tail), it will be killed by a blow on the head. How then, can fishermen say that fishing is not violent? In sea angling, fish are traditionally returned to the water alive but 'Many in any case, are likely to be too severely damaged in catching and landing to permit their recovery'[3] and it is not usual for the fish to be accorded a coup de grace unless the angler's safety demands it (for example, if he

[1] Para 151.
[2] Para 167.
[3] Para 174.

has caught a shark or conger). Sharks are also known to be very badly treated. The Cranbrook report states: 'we have seen a private report (in correspondence) of callous ill-treatment accorded to a captured shark on board a boat in waters off south western England.'[1] I have also personally heard an account from a merchant seaman of gross cruelty towards a captured shark.

Fish farming too involves some suffering. Cruelty is likely to be involved in the water provision, handling and grading and transportation to the release point. When the water provision is not adequate, the problems become equivalent to those in an intensive poultry farm. Shortage of water can mean a shortage of oxygen and pollution when the degree of excretory products becomes too high. When temperatures rise in summer the water can carry less dissolved oxygen, so the fish suffocate.

Although fish are now farmed on a large scale, they are not covered by welfare legislation comparable to that which seeks to protect conventional farm livestock, nor are they covered by the provision of the Veterinary Surgeons Acts (1948 and 1966).[2]

Angling litter is also a huge problem:[3] discarded fishing tackle causes much misery to wildlife. The angling litter lout is likely to be in breach of at least three Acts of Parliament: The Litter Acts of 1968 and 1971 and the Control of Pollution Act of 1974. Nylon which does not rot and in which animals and birds become entangled is a particular nuisance. Added to this, the ingestion of lead by swans has caused many deaths. Swans may pick up lead shot and ledger weights and use it as stone to grind the vegetation which they eat. The pieces are retained in a swan's gizzard and gradually poison the bird. 'Clinical symptoms include progressive paralysis of the neck, offensive greenish diarrhoea and acute weight loss. The treatment of affected birds is rarely successful.'[4]

In December 1977 the British Trust for Ornithology published an article by Alan Hunt of the Ministry of Agriculture Fisheries and Food Agricultural Development Advisory Service, who works at the Veterinary Investigation Centre at Loughborough. He stated that of 206 dead swans

---

[1] Para 178.
[2] Para 196.
[3] The Keep Britain Tidy Group is also involved in a campaign against careless fishermen.
[4] Para 196.

collected from the Midlands, 107 had died as a result of lead poisoning. The lead pieces found in swans' guts appeared to be 'split shot' used by anglers to weight their lines. On 16 June 1978, at the start of the coarse fishing season, the Young Ornithologists Club launched an enquiry to draw attention to these problems. They received fifty-one full reports covering an average of 30·4 miles of freshwater margin, and the results are remarkable: they found along the banks searched an average of 808 feet of line per mile of bank, 86 pieces of split lead shot per mile, and 7 hooks per mile. Because of the difficulty in finding split lead shot in vegetated areas, the average of *86 pieces per mile is probably only a fraction of the total actually present.* In addition, 4 lead weights, 5 floats, 1 disgorger, 1 swivel, 1 spinner and 7 flies were found.

The following birds were reported to the YOC as being found dead or injured as a result of becoming entangled in fishing line: 1 cormorant, 1 heron, 5 mute swans, 11 mallards, 4 moorhens, 3 coots, 1 black-headed gull, 2 herring gulls, 1 gull, 1 swift, 1 sedge warbler, 1 robin, 1 fieldfare, 3 blackbirds, 2 song thrushes, 1 mistle thrush, 1 great tit, 1 magpie, 1 species unknown. One hedgehog was also found entangled in line.

One more problem, admitted by serious fishermen, is that of inexperience and lack of skill in young people. There are angling instructors, but often children, especially young boys, who do not know what they are doing, go fishing, and by their inexpertise involve fish in suffering.

Many who already feel fishing is cruel and or unnecessary, will also be surprised to learn that public funds go towards the upkeep of this 'sport'. Regional Water Authorities in England and the Welsh National Water Development Authority have a duty to provide for the maintenance of fisheries and may allocate large sums of money for the purpose. Your water rates may be going towards the supporting of this sport. The National Anglers Council (NAC) *receives an allocation of public funds* and concerns itself with all matters relating to the welfare and promotion of the sport.

There are now over two hundred qualified instructors in coarse fishing and their fees are paid for by local education committees responsible for the adult education institution in which they teach. This money will come from your rates. While, if there are to be fishermen, it is better that they should be experts – because that means *less* gratuitous cruelty – it is objectionable that those of us who do not agree with them should be forced to pay for them.

Many supporters of the sport will argue that, but for them, many stretches of river which are now clean would be horribly polluted. They are almost certainly correct. We all want clean rivers which support life and growth, but not so that we can kill and maim the inhabitants for our own selfish reasons.

Few people are aware that 'the apparently harmless digging of rag or lug worms for anglers' bait is likely to have serious effects on a fragile eco-system.'[1]

It took me longer to stop eating fish flesh completely than it did to stop eating animal flesh. But gradually I grew to be revolted by it. These were living, moving, breathing creatures, just as much as the ones which lived on land. Their bodies lying on plates were corpses. They had surely felt a joy in being alive and had clung at the last to each dying gasp.

Man is ingesting increasingly high levels of harmful chemicals such as mercury via the fish that he eats. Ronald Lockley, a naturalist living in New Zealand, who left his home in Wales because of growing pollution, wrote:

> Mercury levels are rising everywhere, even in the bodies of penguins – absorbed through their fish and krill food. . . . In Tasmania I was told that Hobart's broad river Derwent was so horribly impregnated with mercury waste from factories upstream, that it was dangerous for humans to eat fish taken in the estuary; this river spewed forth its waters upon the Tasman Sea, where the prevailing currents carried the pollution to New Zealand shores. . . .[2]

Then there are oil-fired power stations which send sulphur into the sky, ships which spill their oil and chemical cargoes, sewage waste poured into rivers and seas, and radioactive waste dumped into the oceans.

Man could learn from the ordered, integrated life of underwater creatures. Instead, he chooses to plunder and kill.

[1] *Sunday Times*, 20 March 1977.
[2] Ronald M. Lockley, *Whales, Dolphins and Porpoises*, David and Charles, 1979.

Arrogance versus Terror: The Bullfight

It may be a national custom, but it is a custom which degrades us. (Nineteenth-century poet, Zorilla, in a maiden speech to the Royal Spanish Academy)

To unload all the blame onto Spaniards would be wrong, for in Europe, at least, it is tourists who are keeping the spectacle alive. The Spanish press has stated that only 7 per cent of the Spanish population support the bullfight.

A. Invernon, a Spanish journalist who specializes in bullfighting, wrote: 'Man created this entertainment called the bullfight to entertain the nobility and the people . . . manly, but not cruel . . . it represents the whole of Spain, not the Spain of the tambourines, but that of deep popular roots.'

That violence runs deep in the alienated soul of mankind is not to be denied, but if this 'sport' is 'manly', then man can only be an object for derision. The gruesome cruelty of the decadent Roman circus is living history which survives like a rotting mould eating at the heart of our civilization.

The bullfight originated in Spain, but it was exported to South America, especially Mexico – the world's largest bullring is in Mexico City. Bullfights also take place in Venezuela, Guatemala and Peru on a minor scale.

The bullfight is important to the British in that many British tourists, in their ignorance, are helping to keep alive a pastime in which many Spaniards are losing interest and which many others would like to see abolished.

The bullfight, or *corrida*, as the facts will show, is not a display of manly prowess, but one of cowardice in which men, brutalized by bloodlust, torture to death an innocent and noble creature. In fact, being a bullfighter is a fairly safe occupation: certainly safer than working on an oil rig or even driving a car. The Spanish Tourist Office published statistics which showed that in the 215 years over which figures were available, 51 matadors were killed, plus 5 mounted bullfighters – or one every four years out of all who were taking part in both Spain and South America. In contrast, every year 6,000 bulls are slowly killed in Spanish bullrings alone. Two hundred horses are crushed to death against the barrier or are disembowelled. Injured horses are patched up and used again until they die.

A *corrida* normally consists of the killing of six bulls by three matadors and each individual bullfight is divided into three 'phases' or *tercios*.

The bull, contrary to myth and propaganda, does not normally want to fight. The unwilling bull, before entering the ring, is often handicapped. He may be driven into a small box and either beaten with sandbags or electric cattle prods. Vaseline may be put into his eyes so that he cannot see his opponent too clearly. Sometimes the bulls' horns are ground or blunted and the nerve exposed, so that they will not easily penetrate the bullfighters' flesh and the animal will be less likely to attack than he otherwise might because of his discomfort. Bulls are injected with sedatives if too excitable or with stimulants if they are not animated enough.

Banderillos de castigo – darts with fuses which frighten the weakened bull – are now supposed to be against the law, but the law is not always adhered to.

One nostril may be plugged with cotton wool, which interferes with breathing so that the bull tires quickly; laudanum may be poured into his ears or a darning needle stuck through his testicles which both gives intense pain and helps subdue any bull, however wild.

The bull which enters the ring is usually a bewildered young creature, merely seeking a way back to his herd from which he has been forcibly taken.

Bill Jordan, a veterinary surgeon, investigated bullfights in Madrid in 1975 when he was employed by the RSPCA and gave a full report on what he saw:[1]

During phase one of the fight, the picador, mounted on a horse, thrusts his pics or lances into the bull's neck muscles – which causes the animal to lose the power to throw his tormentors. This process happens three times 'so that there is ample opportunity to do a great deal of damage to the bull's strong neck muscles and ligaments, weakening the bull and causing a fair amount of haemorrage, and generally slowing the bull down.'

Phase two is for the planting of the *banderillos* in the shoulder muscles, which not only causes the bull intense pain but so disables him that he cannot turn swiftly. 'This makes the work of the matador much safer and easier, for by now the bull is not

[1] Report for the International Council Against Bullfighting.

only weaker, but to a significant extent is maimed and distracted.'

The next phase is the infamous 'dance of death' (*faenas*) when a totally disabled and exhausted animal is slowly slaughtered. This torture lasts about twenty minutes. The report states:

> If the bull has been correctly maimed by the picadors and the banderillos and winded by dashing about a ring, the matador is in very little danger. . . . The matador appears to get the bull to stand quite still in front of him and he will then turn and walk away. Any stockman or veterinary surgeon who knows anything about bulls will tell you that this is a very easy procedure, for bulls will generally stand and take stock. . . .

These matadors will almost certainly have practised in slaughterhouses where they are allowed to kill with the *descabello* (a special sword). The captive cattle are forced to endure repeated sword thrusts until at last death frees them from their agony. According to Madame Marsans Comas, a prominent Spanish animal-welfare worker, 'practise in abattoirs is an important part of any matador's training.'

In every *corrida*, six consecutive bulls are baited and slaughtered. In Spain, where seven impresarios arrange all the bullfights which take place, the season lasts from Easter until the middle of September.

Santiago Esteras Gil wrote:

> Have you ever seen a bull die in the ring? His shoulders are drenched in blood still oozing from wounds in which are stuck half a dozen banderillos. A sword is thrust deeply between the shoulder blades, cutting at his vitals as he moves.
>
> He goes slowly towards the barrier. Instinct warns him to leave the centre where only harm befell him. He tries to avoid the torment of the capes waved at him on both sides; he bellows in pain, but it is only a hoarse sound which issues from a throat burning with thirst. I implore you to think earnestly on the shamefully cruel death of a bull in the bullring.[1]

[1] *La Fiesta de los Toros y sus Tristes Verdades*, Ochoa Logroño, Spain 1962.

At least six horses are used in most *corridas* – all are injured and some killed; survivors will be forced to fight another day. These are usually old horses that have already given a lifetime's service. Some are jettisoned racehorses. They are shown not an ounce of humanity or consideration. Before the fight their vocal chords are cut and sometimes they are made blind.

The founder of the Asociacion Contra La Crueldad En Los Espectaculos (ACCE), the late Conde de Bailen, wrote:

> The public do not realise what the horses have to suffer from the moment they arrive at the Plaza de Toros. . . . Because of the 'peto' (covering) often they do not know when a horse has been injured and, if it is able to stand, it is patched up, doped and sent back to face the bull again, or to be used in another corrida.

One eyewitness who had been to a bullfight in Mallorca wrote to the International Council Against Bullfighting about the atrocious treatment of horses in the ring:

> I had studied at length this particular horse prior to the corrida in the outside yard. His stitches from previous gashes were abominable, and he was painfully thin. . . . We watched one boy spend 15 minutes . . . trying to make him trot, but it was impossible to get the beast to do more than walk for a few feet at a time. He was almost totally lame on his nearside foreleg and could only, obviously with pain, shuffle along. . . . Instead of going near the 'white circle' the picador propped himself and his steed against the wall. . . . The bull was drawn across to this equine wreck by the cape, and thus he charged the horse . . . he toppled and was ripped underneath on the second rush . . . finally the horse lay shattered and exhausted on the ground, and the bull was drawn off him. Five assistants dragged the horse onto his weak, twisted legs and pushed and pulled him the twenty feet out of the ring.

Many tourists attend one bullfight and are so shocked by what they see that they never want to return. Some write to express their horror, as did Mr D.F. Barry from the Cambridge School of English: 'I am one of those tourists who attended a bullfight in Barcelona recently . . . we went out of curiosity. . . . The horror of watching six bulls systematically tortured to death cannot have been remotely what I had been led to expect.' He goes on to suggest that the tourist propaganda relating to bullfights is totally misleading, that if the description of the bullfight given to tourists was 'sober and detached' then he for one – and probably many more – would have left curiosity unassuaged.

The aficionado (supporter) of the *corrida* is almost certainly the same kind of person as the stag-hunt supporter: cowardly, well out of harm's way, they pay others to do the 'dangerous' act.

Their own level of behaviour was tragically demonstrated when the terraces of Sincelejo bullring in Columbia, South America, collapsed in 1980. The *Liverpool Daily Post* reported: 'It was terrible. Women and children who fell during the stampede were trampled without anyone bothering to help them. . . . None of the drivers would lend their cars to take the injured to hospital . . . some scrambled frantically, trampling children and adults in their path.'

However, bullfighting in Spain is becoming less and less profitable and in order to promote it the impresarios have attempted to export it – without success – to Yugoslavia, Cyprus, Brazil and Japan.

In addition, they have made strenuous attempts to win the interest of children. This, in Spain and Mexico, has included mini-bullfighting with calves in schools – in Mexico schoolchildren are allowed, indeed encouraged, to kill calves for the fun of it.

The biggest Spanish impresario, Manuel Chopera, attempted to take female calves to schools so that pupils could practice killing them with swords. One religious school agreed to this, but it was stopped due to the efforts of Madame Marsans Comas and the International Council Against Bullfighting. In Madrid, Chopera also offered free *corrida* tickets to children under fourteen, in order to attract their interest. Chopera, who has met with much public disapproval, thinks that children should be encouraged to 'love bullfighting as they do football'; he even asked the government to establish a special department for the *corrida*, so that a bullfight lottery might be formed and all his problems thus be solved! Albert

Schweitzer asked 'When will the time come when public opinion will tolerate no longer any popular amusements which depend on the ill-treatment of animals?'[1]

What You Can Do

Hunting

Some self-help directives   Get your local council to ban the hunt. Vince Smith, well-known anti-hunt protestor, reported how a concentrated effort, with representatives from eighteen animal welfare organizations, including the Hunt Saboteurs, the RSPCA and the National Society Against Cruel Sports, brought about a ban by Brighton County Council. From now on the anti-hunt clause will be written into the leases of tenant farms in that area as a new tenant takes over.

Vince Smith gave step-by-step advice to those who want to attempt the same in their own area: make one person responsible overall for the campaign to avoid duplication of work. Finance should come from all those groups who join in the lobby but in case of difficulty contact one of the main anti-hunting organizations. Proceed as follows:

1   Find out from the town hall how much land the council owns and *whether it is used by hunts*.
2   Try and find a councillor who will introduce the motion – if you find this difficult, consult an established animal welfare organization. They may know of someone. (If your council has banned the circus, the Captive Animals Protection Society of 17 Raphael Road, Hove, Sussex will tell you which councillor helped with the ban.)
3   If possible, get someone from each political party represented on the council to sign the Notice of Motion which will help avoid partisanship when it comes to voting on the issue.
4   When the date of the debate is known, it is time to start lobbying. There will probably be about one month in which to work on them.
5   Ask the town hall for lots of copies of their list of councillors

[1] Albert Schweitzer, *Out of My Life and Thoughts*, trans. C.T. Campion. NEL (NY) 1957.

which gives names and addresses of them all.

6   Send a copy to as many animal-welfare organizations as possible and include a letter asking for their help. Ask local groups to write a letter to each political party or if possible to each individual councillor.

7   Print leaflets asking local residents to write to councillors to support the ban.

8   Circulate the leaflets to all animal-welfare groups in your area and to other community organizations such as the WI, residents associations etc., which will be more effective than street leafleting.

9   Ask the local churches if they will carry an article against hunting in the parish magazines.

10   If you think the local press will be sympathetic, use them in any way you can. If they are pro-hunt don't inform them at all because they may push out propaganda.

11   Use local radio as much as possible.

12   During the actual debate, remain quiet, do not heckle as this could upset councillors wavering on the brink. After the debate, relay the result to all groups and organizations who have helped.

You, the hunt and prosecution   If you are involved in a hunt incident:

1   Obtain names and addresses of witnesses if possible.

2   Do not accept any apology, offer of money, or any gift from the hunt before referring the matter to the League (LACS). By doing so you could affect your legal right to adequate compensation.

3   Ascertain the name of the hunt and if possible the person in charge. It is common belief that the hunt may go where it likes. This is not so – it may only enter private property with the owner's permission. Trespass by hounds *alone* is actionable and usually results in the hunt having to pay damages to the land owners.

The League Against Cruel Sports will help any member of the public who has been involved in a fracas with the hunt *free of charge*. If hounds have come onto your land or into your garden against your wishes, or have killed a pet, a telephone call to the LACS twenty-four-hour answering service will bring help. The number is 01-407 0979.

Protest If you can protest in any way, full listings of all hunts are published each year in *The Horse and Hound* as the season starts.

Stag and Deer Hunting

Hunts can be hindered by hunt saboteurs. So far, they have not been as effective as they could be, for lack of organization in that area. First, they must know the ground intimately, and they must know the hunt, and the movements of the deer and which woods they would run through. They have to know where the hunt is meeting, where the deer are harboured, or the hind hiding. Then these woods can be cleared and the creatures dispersed. If the run is known, the runs can be followed up with antimate spray. Once the hunt is underway, it is very effective to use holloas. In the case of fox hunting, it is possible to turn up at a strange hunt and be effective because you know that they are not going to move out of that area, but stag hunting covers such vast distances and moves so fast that a strategy must be worked out beforehand.

* Join the hunt saboteurs, especially if you live in the West Country.
* Write to your MP.
* Keep writing to your local newspapers and radio stations, especially in the West Country.
* Support the League Against Cruel Sports (see pp. 36-42) and help their sanctuaries to thrive and grow; support their campaigns.

Bullfighting

* Boycott the bullfight. Do not even go once out of curiosity. This helps to keep it alive.
* Support the International Council Against Bullfighting.
* Write, giving your opinions to the Director of the Spanish Tourist Board in London, especially pointing out the misleading nature of their propaganda.
* Write to your Euro MP on the matter as soon as Spain gets into the Common Market.
* Try to place free ICAB literature with travel agents.
* Complain whenever bullfighting is given publicity or in any

way promoted on radio, television or in newspapers or
magazines.
* Write to the Spanish Embassy expressing your views.
* When in Spain, do not buy souvenirs connected with the
bullfight as these are directly concerned with arousing the
tourist's interest in the *corrida*.

Angling

* If you want to extend your knowledge of this subject, read the
Cranbrook Report.
* Look out for litter louts.
* Find out what proportion of your rates or water rates is going
towards supporting angling.
* Do any youth groups, activities involved with your children's
schools involve fishing? If so, object.
* You now have the evidence that fish suffer and feel pain.
Spread the knowledge.
* Support the work of the Council for the Prevention of Cruelty
by Angling.

Organizations to Join

The League Against Cruel Sports[1]

The League Against Cruel Sports (LACS) campaigns in as
many ways as possible for the abolition of all cruel sports. The
League has developed into a well-known and influential
organization working in the mainstream of the anti-hunt
protest. It was founded in 1924 and at that time its concept was
very radical, even revolutionary: 'It was in effect a challenge to
the upper classes.'

The League has undergone some changes in the last ten years
or so. It used to have a more conservative image. Its supporters
shunned active political involvement or the kind of radicalism
we are now seeing. The executive committee of the League has
gradually changed; now it is

perhaps   the   best   committee   of   any   animal   welfare

This section is based on a talk with LACS director, Dick Course.

organisation in the world – the 12 members are capable, dedicated and intelligent. They are ordinary people who work in completely different fields. They all have a proven track record in animal welfare campaigning and an ability to make sound judgements.[1]

The League claims to represent 'the views of the ordinary man and woman in the street' and endeavours to present itself in that way. Its prime aim is to bring about legislation to prohibit hunting with hounds and shooting – the killing of wildlife for pleasure. It specializes in bloodsports but it also tries to assist other animal-welfare organizations wherever possible in order to maintain consistency of approach to all animal abuse. The League finds that its accumulated knowledge and ability to react with speed is all the greater for being specialized.

The main focus of its work to gain legislation is, of course, Parliament. Dick Course feels that Private Members Bills have proved to be

a dead loss, because they can either be talked out or thrown out by the other chamber. We've had about 20 and they've all either been talked out or lost in various ways. When the last Private Members Bill was adopted by the government – the Bill to abolish hare coursing in 1976 – it got through the House of Commons with a majority of 117, but was thrown out when it reached the House of Lords. We were not particularly au fait with Parliamentary procedure at that time, but Michael Foot who was then leader of the House and Merlyn Rees – then Home Secretary – explained that although there is no written constitution, the Constitutional situation is that if a political party puts an issue in its manifesto, then it is quite all right for the Commons to over-rule the Lords, but if it is not a manifesto issue, then the House of Lords can claim that the lower house was not elected to enact certain legislation and therefore, they have every right to oppose it.

The League then decided to seek a manifesto commitment to achieve its aims so that those kind of obstacles would not be

---

[1] Dick Course.

encountered again. This decision was taken quite independently of any other animal-welfare organization. It was evident at the time that the Labour party was almost certainly the most likely to make such an inclusion in its manifesto – although the Liberal party were also expected to make this move.

Close contacts were needed with the political parties and this caused a troublesome internal row in the League as many of its members felt that there should be no involvement with politics, but Dick Course feels that most of the dissenters were ardent Conservatives who did not want to compromise their allegiance over the bloodsports issue. He states that as 'an organisation whose members specifically commit us to seek the abolition of bloodsports, not to do so would be a breach of the articles of association'. The 1979 row led to the expulsion of many of the old executive committee by the members who were then replaced by a more radical group. There were some misgivings among the membership over this but soon the new committee was functioning well, behaving responsibly and constructively. Contacts with politicians from all parties were made and they lobbied at party conferences. Other animal welfare societies became interested in what they were doing.

Lord Houghton and Clive Hollands approached the League when they set up GEECAP (General Election Campaign for Animal Protection). The next general election loomed and it was decided that rather than just campaign for the abolition of bloodsports – because should the Labour party take it up, it could look like a class issue rather than a welfare one – it should be made clear that all the major animal issues were of importance. Whereas fox hunting is a sport for wealthier people, all classes participate in hare coursing, for it involves little expense. Shooting falls into different categories – members of syndicates pay £1,000 a year or more to shoot pheasants, but working people shoot pigeons. 'It doesn't matter who does it, it's totally wrong, so the Labour party should get that message across,' says Dick Course, 'but to take up animal welfare as a broad issue was beneficial so that any accusations of class warfare could be refuted.'

The Conservative party were not interested in doing anything about bloodsports, but because of the momentum created by party-political involvement, they were inundated with letters from genuine Conservatives who wanted their party to take up animal-welfare issues. When the manifestos were finally published, the Conservative party included an animal-welfare commitment for the first time, albeit a lukewarm one: to reform the 1876 Experimentation Act, to make some changes in the export of live animals and to look at intensive farming.

The Liberal party made encouraging reference to animal welfare in their manifesto.

The Labour party declared that they would look at several different issues but that it would definitely abolish hare coursing and stag hunting – not fox hunting or shooting, which was rather incongruous. But the Conservatives won that election and did nothing for animals.

Because of upheavals in the Labour party, certain changes are occurring which will make the parliamentary Labour party more accountable to conference. This has given the League a new impetus for campaigning. Dick Course feels that if they work hard with Labour party activists and so get a motion for animals through conference, then

> we will see that conference motion implemented by the parliamentary Labour party, so of course we have a lot of sympathy for the 'working faction' of the Labour Party which wants more control over what goes into the manifesto. This is where we concentrate the bulk of our efforts.

The League also works in other practical ways, searching out and talking with as many landowners as possible, asking them to prohibit bloodsports on their own land. As there are so many, in order to save time and energy, only those most likely to sympathize are approached. Labour-controlled county councils are more likely to respond but surprisingly, when the campaign for local authority hunt bans was begun, it was Tory-controlled Brighton which first banned the hunt. This was followed by Derbyshire County Council and Nottingham, Mid-Glamorgan, two Scottish county councils and others followed suit. These councils have banned the use of county-council controlled or owned land for the use of bloodsports – mostly hunting with hounds, but also some shooting (but not fishing, which will be the last cruel sport to be abolished as the anti-angling campaign is the most recent and most difficult to pursue).

The League also buys land. As little as 60 acres can, if it is strategically placed, affect thousands of acres as far as the hunt is concerned. If the hunt approaches the League's borders it is leapt upon without hesitation. The sanctuaries have wardens, but it is a difficult task to police hundreds of acres effectively. When anyone is caught abusing wildlife in any way, they are not warned or told off but sent straight to court. *The League also provides a free legal service for anyone who wants to prosecute a hunt for trespass or damages.*

The League prosecutes for hound trespass (when hounds run out of control) as well as damage, and achieves about fifty prosecutions a year. Trespass and damage is a civil action, so there are no fines as such, but the League usually manages to prove its case, using expensive solicitors so the defendants have heavy costs to pay – their own as well as the League's. Hunts have to pay an extra amount if a pet animal is killed, but those costs are set extremely low – around £20 or £30 for a pet cat. One hunt even managed to kill a donkey in Hertfordshire a few years ago.

When a hunt damages a garden the costs can run to between £500–£600. LACS is pressing ahead with as many prosecutions as possible – once a prosecution for trespass is secured, a hunt will not return to that particular area.

> Even though it may be only 10 or 20 acres [says Dick Course] it may give an area of up to 100,000 acres which will effectively be a wildlife sanctuary. This way we are easing the pressure on wildlife, creating huge no-go areas all over the country.
>
> If you read the hunt journals, *The Field, Hare and Hound, Shooting Times*, and so on, you'll notice that we are really making our presence felt. We don't give them a chance, we are hitting them wherever we can – in Parliament, in the council chambers, in prosecutions, in our own sanctuaries and in blatant propaganda. The hunting fraternity are now desperately trying to find ways of improving their flawed arguments. But it does require tremendous effort on the part of our organization; it's a lot of hard work, but we aren't going to ease up – we are going to increase the pressure.

The League offers rewards for information leading to the

conviction of people involved in such activities as cat, dog or cock fighting or badger baiting. Its area of concern is anything which can be termed a cruel sport.

It tries to promote drag hunting, an extremely acceptable alternative (see p.8). The League would also like to see the Grand National abolished and has so far campaigned effectively – some of the fences are now considerably lower than they were, for example.

The League does have some liaison with the Hunt Saboteurs Association, but acts independently. Many people who join are also HSA members or become HSA members. But LACS cannot condone illegal activities in any way as it needs parliamentary support. What is more, should a huntsperson fall from a horse and blame a hunt saboteur, the hunt would attempt to sue the League rather than the HSA if there *were* close links, as the HSA has no money, whereas LACS is a much more likely target with its land holdings and healthy bank balance. As a matter of expedience LACS takes care of its own income. The HSA never sets out to break the law, but in heated situations, odd incidents do crop up. 'People cannot credibly oppose violence by the infliction of violence,' says Dick Course.

Opinion polls reveal that about 5 per cent of the population are actively opposed to legislation to abolish bloodsports and, due possibly to the concerted efforts of all concerned in this particular battle, the percentage of people who oppose cruel sports has gone up steadily year by year. Despite enormous hunt propaganda, backed by the BBC who have tended to report one-sidedly on this issue, awareness is growing.[1]

LACS now has about 15,000 members. Some remain fairly passive, but occasionally contribute constructively, supplying information, writing letters and so on:

> Our members don't go out disrupting hunts, that really is a young people's game, but they do draw up petitions, go to their local councils, go to their MPs. Some have been doing these things for so long that they get a little jaded, but new members are always coming in to replace those who fade away. Our turnover of members is fantastic; we may lose three or four thousand every year and gain the same number, which can only be good. Anyone who has been a member has

[1] See Vera Sheppard, *My Head Against the Wall*, Moonraker Press, 1979.

read the journal and knows the arguments and will never support field sports again and so we've done our job. It is better that we don't have a stable membership which never changes because in the end, we shall have reached a good many more people.

It is the older section of the membership which tends to donate most of the money and give solid support. Younger people are impatient for immediate change, and don't understand that Parliament is designed for slow change, not quick and easy victories, but all kinds of enthusiasm are vital to the cause.

The basic advice from the League to those who wish to see cruel sports abolished is that we should each examine the political party we would like to see running this country and campaign within our chosen party to secure a positive commitment to a policy which encompasses all aspects of conservation and cruelty to animals, including bloodsports. We should use our democratic rights to work for the protection of our environment.

Dick Course urges people to take more personal responsibility:

People should involve themselves politically, whether it's banning the bomb or abolishing bloodsports. There is far too much political complacency in this country, especially among the young, and that is a very dangerous situation. We are getting general election turnouts of 70 per cent. That is disgusting. It means 30 per cent – around twenty million people – don't care who is going to be in control of the legislation of our nation. I want to see more and more people not just voting in the polling stations, but formulating the policies of the political parties. It's time for action.

The League Against Cruel Sports, 83-7 Union Street, London SE1 1SG.

The Hunt Saboteurs Association

The HSA was formed in 1964, in Brixham, Devon, by a journalist named John Prestidge. There was an apparent need for more active opposition to hunts than could be provided by the League Against Cruel Sports.

By 1965, there were HSA groups in Brixham, Street in Somerset, Bristol, Hampshire, Northampton, Birmingham and Weybridge, Surrey. The initial financing came from publicity - there were two donations of £500; the rest came from subscriptions and donations. An office was set up in Brixham, but this lasted only for a short while as the central organization in that town collapsed within two years, following court appearances and a mass binding over to keep the peace. Magistrates had imposed this after an incident in which thirty otter hunters had attacked a carful of saboteurs, breaking the driver's jaw. One hunter was fined £10 for this.

But by 1966–7, the HSA was based in London, run by members of the Weybridge group. Following advertisements in animal-welfare journals and in *Private Eye*, new contacts were gradually made throughout the country. The HSA carried on quietly working; by 1972 it had a membership of 200–300.

The turning point came in 1972 when the journalist, Jill Tweedie, accompanied protestors on a Dorset otter hunt. Her half-page article appeared in the *Guardian* bringing a flood of finance, and more than doubling HSA membership. By 1975, there were groups scattered throughout the country.

In November 1975, the HSA were given an Open Door programme by the BBC. Despite protests from the bloodsportsmen, it was repeated the following week. From this came 3,000 letters of support, and 30 of abuse. By mid-1976 there were 1,500 paid up members and the four-monthly magazine *HOWL* (Hounds Off Our Wildlife) was published. Membership has since grown to 5,500. When joining, subscribers are asked to state whether they wish to be active in the field. But although 90 per cent answer positively, only about 10–20 per cent actually manage to carry out that intention. However groups are scattered throughout the whole of the UK with links in Eire and N. Ireland; the USA, Canada, France and Scandinavia. The organization, steered by a twelve-person committee, is self-financing with no paid workers, the greatest outgoings being for postage and printing.

It is interesting to note that the proportion of members living in rural and urban areas and their political beliefs are in the same ratio as those of the adult population. Most but not all of the active saboteurs are in the 18–35 age group.

The HSA considers itself solely an 'animal rights'

organization, dedicated to direct action against any sport involving the hunting to death with hounds of wild animals such as foxes, deer, hares, otters, mink and coypu. They are also officially opposed to hare coursing, seal culling and whaling. Many members are vegetarian or vegan; some are also actively engaged in fighting other forms of animal abuse.

Their rules are strict and include absolute non-violence and adherence to the country code – any violence comes from the hunters, not the life-saving saboteurs. As successful hunting depends upon close harmony between the huntsman and his hounds, their methods are designed to disrupt it and create confusion to allow the hunted animal to escape.

Fake hunting cries (holloas) are given to draw the huntsman to a non-existent quarry, and hounds are drawn to strong false scents which cover those of the hunted animal while hunting horns are used to vie with the huntsman for control of the pack. Many noises are used to distract the hounds, and to move the hunted animal away from danger, but if the gap between the two is dangerously narrowed, smoke bombs are sometimes used. Saboteurs are, however, very careful not to do anything which could possibly harm hounds, horses or riders in any way.

Hunting now has many factors not in its favour – increasing costs, urbanization, motorway construction, the demands of agriculture and so on. Parliament must eventually legislate against it, but there are still many huntspeople in the Lords and the Commons. Apart from saving the lives of individual animals, saboteurs help to keep the issue alive as their activities are often covered by the media.

Anyone can help the hunt saboteurs by becoming a member. Members are sent a copy of *HOWL*, a list of area contacts, sheets covering recommended tactics to employ against hunts and hunt maps. Members may operate alone or join a group. Even non-active members can help by liaising with the press, letter-writing, fund-raising and so on.

This small association has been the life-blood of the new militant activist movement for animal rights and liberation as its history shows. It was, in effect, the first organized militant animal rights organization of the current era.

In the middle and late 1960s and for most of the 1970s, the HSA was a primary introduction to the concept of animal rights for many young militants. Hunting, by its blatant nature, has always been one of the main targets for those concerned about cruelty to animals. The HSA provided an opportunity for people to show their colours exactly where the action was taking place. Hunting was open to this, whereas other forms of cruelty – vivisection/experimentation, factory farming and so on – are hidden away and so less likely to be the target of 'local' active opposition.

Apart from the obvious achievement of having saved countless wild animals from the jaws of death, one of the HSA's other big achievements has been to keep the public's awareness of bloodsports to the fore. The hunters have always wanted to keep their activities in the field well away from public gaze, but the press coverage resulting from such activity has ruined that secrecy. This has been particularly true of hare coursing. Mass demonstrations at major coursing events like the Waterloo Cup have brought the horrors of the sport into sitting rooms – on TV newsreels and in the national press. This has brought the necessary support for petitions and letters sent in to relevant people at crucial times when the subject has come before Parliament. The same has also been true for fox, otter, hare and deer hunting. Media coverage helps to polarize the public's views on the subject and makes hunting a topic of public and parliamentary interest.

The HSA, by attracting young idealists, also helped to dispel the belief that it was only 'old ladies with cats' who felt that hunting was wrong. The hunters did not understand the old ladies, but were never too worried about them. Neither did they understand the young militants and mistakenly believed that they would go away before too long. They never did.

Instead, these militants managed democratically to take control of the League Against Cruel Sports. The *Hare and Hound* actually expressed sadness at the departure of Raymond Rowley, previous chairman of LACS!

The LACS, while not officially working with HSA, now have three committee members who were formerly HSA committee members and at least half of the LACS committee have at some time sabotaged hunts, and so awareness of the enemy is far greater than it had been previously.

The parliamentary activities of the LACS together with the in-the-field activities of the HSA, have formed a formidable threat to the existence of bloodsports.

In addition, that leading members of the HSA support the ideology of vegetarianism has been a major factor in spreading the 'rights' gospel among activists.

The HSA also spawned the Band of Mercy (well-known animal rightists, Ronnie Lee, Cliff Goodman and Robin Howard who were fined or imprisoned for BOM activities in 1975, were all, at one time or another HSA committee members). Later followed its more famous descendant, the Animal Liberation Front.

The HSA also helped to provide ammunition and tactics for the militant takeover of the BUAV, which has proved enormously successful, in that public awareness of the horrors of experimentation has grown by leaps and bounds since that takeover.

The Hunt Saboteurs Association began life in the afterglow of the first CND/Committee of 100 Campaigns. Militancy had proved its value in attracting media and parliamentary notice. From there it has grown and continues to make its sincere and important presence felt.

Hunt Saboteurs Association (HSA), PO Box 19, Towbridge, Kent TN9 1AA.

National Society for the Abolition of Cruel Sports

The NSACS (a company limited by guarantee and not having share capital) is a small organization which stresses the educational, humane and moral principles of the case against cruelties inflicted in the name of sport. It advocates all peaceable, non-aggressive and non-violent methods to achieve its ends and does not favour practises which can disrupt or confuse animals connected with hunts.

Founded in 1932, the NSACS almost had to restart from scratch in 1966 when the incumbent secretary died slowly at his post, losing society records in the process. The society was subsequently dominated by the well-known spiritualist editor Maurice Barbanell until his death early in 1981. There was an attempt to begin revitalizing the society later in that year, but little seems to have happened in the interim.

The aims are to obtain for wild animals the legal protection at present afforded domestic animals and many birds; to educate public opinion to demand, by every lawful means, the prohibition of the hunting and coursing of Britain's native wild creatures; to obtain the interest and cooperation of naturalists and nature lovers in the preservation – unconnected with conservation for sporting interests – of the countryside's wild life and, where necessary, its humane control under proper and authorized conditions; to secure the total abolition of killing for sport, whether by the above-named practices or by shooting or falconry.

The society is opposed to militant action, but has, in the past, published some useful material on hunting. It could now play a useful part as a conservative lobbying faction in the anti-hunt movement, but very little is happening within the society, which is a pity as all resources and existing channels for diverse shades of public opinion with a common goal are needed and could potentially play a useful part in the abolition of all cruel 'sports'.

Details are available from John D. Doherty, 33 Forest Rise, Crowborough, East Sussex TN6 2EP.

The Council for the Prevention of Cruelty by Angling

The CPCA was set up by William Maxwell Brodie – with the patronage of Brigid Brophy and Lord Houghton – in 1980 after the publication of the Medway/Cranbrook Report into Shooting and Angling.

The council was set up because the established societies were not prepared to take on angling as an issue. Societies opposed to blood sports believe that the public will not donate money to combat angling and are concerned that their battle may be much longer and harder if they include this 'sport' in their campaign. The society has a difficult task – until recently most people have never considered angling to be cruel and the opposition is very highly organized and well-funded. Millions take part in fishing for sport.

The council is composed of an executive committee, four officers and four members. The council is still feeling its way, but has received both sympathetic and serious media attention. Its primary aim is to publicize its purpose. Its more specific immediate aims are:

1   To obtain the abolition of live-bait angling, a recommendation made in the Cranbrook report.
2   To obtain prosecution of anglers under the relevant parliamentary acts (Litter Acts 1968 & 1971 and Control of Pollution Act, 1974).
3   To demonstrate at angling matches.

Since the Cranbrook report, the RSPCA has taken no action whatsoever and is shying away from the angling issue. CPCA produces a newsletter distributed to members: *HOOKUP*. The first issue contains the typescript of an excellent speech given by Brigid Brophy.

Council for the Prevention of Cruelty by Angling, PO Box 14, Romsey SO5 9NN.

The International Council Against Bullfighting

The ICAB was formed by the late Mrs Speedwell-Massingham in 1958 to campaign for the abolition of bullfighting. A small society, with a thousand members in twenty-six different countries, it works together with other societies, including the World Federation for the Protection of Animals, in a co-operative effort to stop the promotion of this form of 'entertainment'.

While its aim is abolition, it seeks to inform potential visitors to the *corrida* of the true horrors and suffering involved and to thwart publicity and propaganda for the 'fiesta of blood and sun'.

International Council Against Bullfighting, 13 Greystone Road, Tankerton, Nr. Whitstable, Kent CT5 2J4.

2 Badgers

Till kicked and torn and beaten out he lies
And leaves his hold and cackles, groans and dies.
                                        Badger, John Clare

The badger and its close relative the otter (now almost hunted
to extinction) are ancient members of Britain's wildlife. They
have probably been with us for some 500,000 years. Badgers
live throughout Britain and Ireland, except for most of the
islands off the Scottish coast. Their population is particularly
dense in the South West of England and they become scarcer
towards the north. Their estimated number is 75–90,000
(according to the Gwent Badger Group) though Tim Clarke of
Friends of the Earth gives an estimated figure of 50,000.

One of our best-loved wild animals, the badger is, under the
Badgers Act of 1973, a protected animal but it is still persecuted
– for sport, illegally, and by the Ministry of Agriculture, who
obtained the necessary legal loophole in an Act of 1975.[1]
Digging and baiting – traditional country pastimes – though
now strictly illegal still go on. The gassing of badgers was
conducted by the Ministry of Agriculture.

Digging means the removal of the badger from its sett where it
lives with its family group. This is usually done when the sow
has small cubs because she will then be more aggressive in
defence of her young. Terriers are sent in to locate her; once
located, the men dig into the tunnels and haul her out. She will
fight easily, but when a dog is injured, a new one is sent to tackle
her. The dogs may suffer extreme injury – a face can be bitten
off – or may even be killed, but the badger cannot win. Her

[1] Conservation of Wild Creatures and Wild Plants Act, 1975.

death is lingering. Pulled out with badger tongs, she may have her jaw broken by these 'sportsmen', her skull fractured, she may be blinded or have her claws removed, so that her fighting ability is hampered. The Gwent Badger Group has a photograph of a badger with a chain attached to her leg and seven dogs attacking her. Whenever she got the better of the dogs, the chain was pulled to expose her vulnerable underside.

From their booklet comes the story of a courageous sow who broke away from the fight and, running back down to save her single cub, ran a quarter of a mile with it to a sett which was too rocky to dig. Despite being savaged by nine dogs, she refused to leave her cub and managed to escape to rear it.

Badger baiting was made illegal 150 years ago. It often meant staking a badger to the ground by its tail and putting dog after dog to it, until it died of wounds and exhaustion. Sometimes a badger was put into a barrel and dogs sent to pull it out. Baiting still goes on today. The *Sunderland Echo* made its own investigation in 1981 and found it to be all too common. Men were engaged in the sport simply because it was a family tradition. The Leicester RSPCA reported three badger setts dug up in 1980 and the Nottinghamshire Trust for Nature Conservation warned that organized gangs were digging out badgers for baiting. Prosecutions were also brought against badger diggers and baiters in Surrey, but unfortunately fines were low and magistrates often too lenient.

Gassing/trapping The greatest threat to these creatures lies in the Ministry of Agriculture's fanatical extermination policy. In 1975 the Ministry of Agriculture first announced that the gassing of badgers in certain areas – the South West and Dorset – could be justified because, they claimed, badgers were giving bovine tuberculosis to cattle. Many found this bureaucratic edict hard to swallow, especially since only two years previously the Ministry had announced that the badger was not responsible for passing this disease to cattle and had substantiated their claim with figures. It was felt that it had given in to pressure from the National Farmers Union.

In 1971, a badger was found in Gloucestershire heavily infected with bovine TB. Lord Zuckerman in his Report to the Minister for Agriculture Peter Walker[1] says it was found by 'an

[1] HMSO, 1980, £5.20.

observant farmer', omitting to inform us that he was also a Ministry vet, Mr Roger Muirhead, who admitted to the *Western Daily Press* eight years later that evidence linking badgers, cattle and bovine TB 'is still totally circumstantial'.

Following this, the NFU and farming press mounted a kill-the-badger campaign. Later in the same year, eighteen more infected badgers were found, two in areas where there was no trouble with cattle. Trouble with TB also occurred in Cornwall and in 1973, the MAFF published a report assuring farmers that badgers 'were nothing to worry about', virtually stating that badgers were not the cause.

But in 1974, the Ministry changed its mind, and began to demonstrate badger snares. Mrs Ruth Murray, a noted badger expert, sued the then Minister and one of his officials for cruelty, but was unsuccessful. Under the Badgers Act 1973, it is an offence 'if any person wilfully kills, injures or takes, or attempts to kill, injure or take any badger.' The badger was made a protected animal, but in 1975, at the whim of the MAFF, an amendment was made to the Act enabling badgers to be killed under license in those areas where both cattle and badgers are infected with TB. All badgers within 3 sq km of any incident involving badgers and cattle were killed with cyanide gas by MAFF officials. Gassing was begun in 1975 and continued until public opinion called for suspension of gassing *new* setts and led to Lord Zuckerman's enquiry. By then more than 10,000 badgers had been killed in 3,589 setts. The report came out on 30 October 1980 and gassing, at his recommendation, was resumed.

Ruth Murray said that Zuckerman visited her in April 1980 and told her what he would report – which she claimed, showed him to be already prejudiced. She feels that the badger is a victim of politics.

Between 1975 and 1978, MAFF personnel and other 'authorized' individuals gassed over 3,500 setts, causing approximately 10,000 to die a horrible death. These are the *official figures*, but an unknown number of unofficial killings sparked off by Ministry propaganda may be added to them.

Reassurances were given in 1975 that investigations had proven badgers to be the only possible source of TB infection and it was stressed that the utmost discrimination was to be exercised to ensure that badgers were not gassed outside 'problem areas'. Here is an extract from the first Ministry report on Bovine Tuberculosis in Badgers, November 1976:

> Early in 1976 the Ministry undertook to collect and examine post-mortem all badger carcasses found by members of the public . . . the results of the examination of the carcasses received up to 31st August 1976 . . . show no evidence of tuberculosis in badgers outside the south west region except in a part of Surrey, where further investigations are being made. . . .

Peter Roberts of Compassion in World Farming and himself a dairy farmer who also examined this data could see no evidence of TB inside the South West either. Out of 118 carcasses tested, only one was found to be infected. 176 corpses were tested and only 3 carried TB – one in Cornwall and 2 in Surrey.

Later figures showed that out of 412 badger carcasses received throughout the country, only 7 carried signs of TB, 4 in areas where there was no significant problem with TB in cattle.

The Ministry claims that examination of casually collected corpses is not an effective method of detection. Why then did it ask for these to be collected?

Further Ministry research in problem areas showed the badger to be the most likely cause of TB in cattle – not surprisingly, because they focussed their research almost entirely on one animal. Nonetheless, out of 2,270 badgers, only 410 were seen to be carrying infection – 18·6 per cent. This was enough to warrant the wholesale gassing of the badger anywhere where there were TB infected cattle and no other obvious cause existed. Such animals as rats, feral cats and farm dogs were hardly examined at all – unfortunately for the badger, but perhaps fortunately for the other animals because mass destruction seems to be the usual Ministry solution.

In addition, an experimental centre was set up at the Central Veterinary Laboratory in Weybridge, Surrey to test the feasibility of transmission from badgers to cattle. This was described in an RSPCA report:

> The transmission experiment between badgers and cattle was done by housing together in a concrete yard 3 calves, each separately with experimentally infected badgers, and all fed off the floor. This was repeated with 9 infected badgers

housed the same way with 3 calves. In this second experiment, after a year in captivity, 2 badgers died and a third was killed in poor condition. One calf reacted to the tuberculin test after 6 months, one after 8 months, and the third after 10 months.

The RSPCA pointed out that these experiments merely show the *feasibility* of transmission and not that the disease is transmitted after ten months. John Bryant, ex RSPCA Vice Chairman said,

> This concrete environment (covered, thus excluding even the disinfectant properties of sunlight) in which 9 wild animals and 3 growing calves were forced to co-exist, measured about one sixth the size of a football penalty area. Despite these appalling conditions it was 6 months before the first calf reacted to a tuberculin test – demonstrating quite clearly just how unlikely it is that badgers transmit TB to cattle in fields.

David Coffey, a working, ex-Ministry vet stated that it is even more significant that this experimental work has never been published: 'Any scientific work to be meaningful, must be published so that the results can be reproduced. In effect, unpublished experiments cannot honestly be put forward as evidence.'

The facts about badgers and bovine TB raise disturbing questions:

1   There are cases where TB has occurred in cattle, but no nearby badgers are infected.
2   There are persistent cases where one farm has infected cattle and a neighbouring farm has none, yet both are on the same badger run.
3   In other areas badgers have TB yet there is no evidence of the disease in cattle.
4   Cattle are said to pick up infection from badgers' sputum on pasture grass, but how this happens nobody has satisfactorily explained. It is quite possible that badgers get TB from cattle and not the other way round because they may root under cow pats for worms and beetles and so on. Lord Zuckerman admits

this himself ('No one knows the answer,' he says), even though he chooses to disregard it: 'on the assumption, which I am ready to accept that cattle give the disease to the badger, and not the other way round'[1]. Comparing the British situation to the one in New Zealand where the possum – the badger's equivalent – is suffering from TB on a large scale, he writes: 'No one; of course, has actually seen possums in the actual process of passing tubercle bacilli to a cow, any more than the transfer has been watched in the case of the badger. But the fact that this does happen is nonetheless incontrovertible.' The last statement is made, on the admission of a scientist himself, with *no tangible proof whatsoever*!

5   Why are badgers infected in some areas and not in others?
6   If badgers are such a potent cause of TB in cattle, why has it been possible to reduce the national incidence of disease in cattle herds so dramatically over the past twenty years? If badgers catch bovine TB how did they escape its ravages before 1960 when up to 30 per cent of the national herd was infected?
7   Why are there no tests of corpses in gassed badger setts – or at least no published figures?
8   Why are the Ministry so inconsistent in their vigilance? A veterinary strike in Ireland during 1975 and 1976 meant that no herds were screened for TB and yet no restrictions were placed on the importation of cattle into this country. Until the strike Irish cattle were tested every other year, but in November 1974 the vets responsible stopped work until June 1976. Southern Irish cattle have much more TB than British cattle. In 1977, 14,540 Irish herds reacted to the TB test, compared with 90 herds in England. *In spite of this known risk there was no attempt to suspend importation, or even to test them on arrival.*

During the first nine months of 1977 there were four reports a month of TB in cattle that had come from Ireland. These were not shown up in tests, but in the discovery of open lesions in the cattle during slaughter. This was permitted at the same time as badgers were being subjected to wholesale slaughter. (Zuckerman attributes reduction in TB in herds in the South West in 1976–8 to badger gassing, but using his statistics, Peter Roberts has shown that an exactly similar reduction took place outside the gassing area. The peak in TB reaction coincides with the importing of untested Irish cattle. The Ministry said

[1] Para 34.

that the Irish cattle did not go to the West Country, where most herd breakdowns occurred, but checks with importers showed this to be untrue. Peter Roberts states that at that time there were regular sales of Irish cattle at Banbury and staff at the Auctioneers there told him that 'buyers would come from different parts of the West country for heifers, rather than store stock'.)

9   Why have badgers been singled out as culprits when other animals have been ignored?

10   Why has there been so little research into alternative methods of TB control? A vaccine, for instance?

11   Why is the incidence of TB in human populations lower in the SW (10 per 1,000) than virtually all other parts of Britain (average for England and Wales is 20 per 1,000) (figures from Tim Clarke, Friends of the Earth)?

Although statistics indicate that the incidence of disease has dropped in Dorset since gassing was introduced, this could be co-incidental. In October 1975, when gassing was begun, TB was detected in 19 herds, whereas by August 1977, there were no reported cases. But in August 1974 there were 73 TB infected herds in the area, reduced to one, by May 1975, *before* there was an anti-badger campaign. Figures also show that in the South West extermination has made no significant difference to the amount of TB in cattle.

Gassing was called 'humane' by the Ministry, but the RSPCA believed that sub-lethal doses of hydrogen cyanide may have caused unnecessarily prolonged suffering. The Cornwall Badgers Protection League is also worried about the way in which badgers are being snared. It says that the snares the Ministry is using are considered by some authorities to be the least humane design and liable to cause extreme suffering.

Although only authorized Ministry personnel are supposed to kill badgers, some farmers have taken the law into their own hands. There has been a good deal of *illegal gassing*, trapping and digging, often in areas where there is no problem with TB infection. Although the Ministry condemns this, it is in fact responsible for it happening. In any case, badger expert Eunice D. Overend, says that it is very unlikely that all infected badgers would be killed by the gassing of a sett, and survivors could join other groups and spread the disease. She also says that TB is known to be 'precipitated by stress'. Previously healthy animals may become diseased by the stress of losing their social group. Cleared setts are often repopulated.

We could not believe the Ministry when it said that badger-gassing operations 'should prove of benefit to the long-term future of the species'. It is not concerned about the health of the badger. We are their only natural enemy. Badgers are also affected by illegal sports involving them, droughts, increasing road traffic – hundreds are killed on the roads – and increasing destruction of habitat. Lord Zuckerman claims that there are 38,110 setts in existence in this country. Dr Ernest Neal, badger expert, puts the figure at 9,381. Paul Patchett, Badger Recorder for the Mammal Society in West Yorks said that Lord Zuckerman's figures came from the Mammal Society who admitted in a letter in his possession that the figures were an inspired guess. He said that neither he nor any of the other 53 county badger recorders were asked for figures. Lord Zuckerman estimates 250 setts for West Yorks. Patchett says there are only 35. Zuckerman says 1,400 setts in Cornwall, Dr Neal says there are 256. Eric Ashby, badger expert and maker of the BBC's *At Home with Badgers* says that these animals are very susceptible to stress and Ministry monitoring in some areas could make them vulnerable to disease.

Farmers and huntsmen are also badger enemies. Huntsmen will stop setts and sometimes thereby suffocate the occupants. Badgers may be the innocent victims of poison put down by gamekeepers to kill foxes or birds of prey illegally. Gin traps are also far too commonly found at sett entrances, despite their having been illegal for years. Badgers may also dig up and eat worms treated with strychnine to kill moles.

The anti-badger campaign has kept a larger number of civil servants in costly employment – people have drawn up expensive reports, teams have investigated badger health, laboratory experiments on the transmission of infection have been set up, experimental work on badger faeces and urine has been carried out, research on badger behaviour and ecology in Gloucestershire has been done and the misnamed 'fire brigade' – the exterminators who go out killing – are kept employed. Obviously this kind of expense has got to be justified and Lord Zuckerman appeared to do just that.

In August 1980, his report to Peter Walker was complete.

The NFU was very happy about it – a spokesman for its Animal Health Committee said, 'We are delighted that the Zuckerman report has vindicated MAFF policy.' Criticism of it was effectively squashed.

Evidence available from Professor D. Chant, head of the Department of Biological Control, University of California, was omitted from the report. Of 40 per cent of cattle infected in 1932, only 2 per cent were infected in 1961 after a campaign to eradicate the disease. Professor Chant stated that this is an extremely low level, but that it is not possible to eliminate such disease entirely as freedom from disease means loss of immunity and therefore a very much heightened susceptibility to infection should a source of re-infection occur – this source could be imported cattle, local pigs, humans, rats or dogs and cats. Other animals have also been mentioned – rabbits, voles, foxes, hedgehogs.[1] Could they all come under the same crude extermination policy?

But the report plays on fears over public health when Zuckerman states: 'If the incidence of bovine TB in cattle were allowed to rise unchecked, not only would more human beings be at risk, but those affected would then become carriers'. However, Dr Norman Littler, a retired consultant who specialised in TB criticised this 'biased report' saying that 'Bovine TB as a cause of human disease in Britain today is almost non-existent' and called Lord Zuckerman's references to public health 'scaremongering'. 'Humans,' he says, 'are mostly affected by the human, not the bovine strain, those affected by the latter are usually *stockmen working in close contact with cattle breath/sputum.*'

The Ministry told Compassion in World Farming that in any herd breakdown all stockmen, cowmen, farmers etc. in contact were screened. But in fact no tests are done, only 'discreet enquiries made as to their health.' Black's *Veterinary Dictionary* states: 'The prevalence of tuberculosis in animals bears a direct ratio to the intensity of the methods of agriculture in an area. Cattle closely confined and housed to a great extent in buildings, are much more often affected.' It also states: 'Cattle are susceptible to humans suffering from bovine TB and serious breakdowns in attested herds have been traced to cowmen

[1] Robert Howard, *Badgers Without Bias*, Abson Books with Avon Wildlife Trust, 1981.

suffering from the disease.' Cattle can also contract it through wounds after dehorning.

Lord Zuckerman ignores the fact that infected Irish cattle came into this country for almost two years. (Disease had predictably shown occasional flare-ups, particularly in the South West where a quarter of the National Herd is concentrated. The Gwent Badger Group, in its informative booklet *Briefly on Badgers* forgets to mention this when it states that a high density of badgers in the South West – according to the MAFF – may have been the cause of continuing infection in that area. Infection can also be carried in streams and there are apparently more streams than water troughs in parts of the West country. Writing in *The Field*, Phil Drabble reported that one farmer believed that most of the infection in holiday areas comes from people stopping on roadsides to urinate. Farmers in Widdecombe Valley had suffered with bovine TB only in fields adjacent to picnic and camping sites.)

There have been some important criticisms made of Zuckerman's report. Some examples follow:

The World Wildlife Fund put out a press release saying, 'It is simply a review of the inconclusive evidence that was already available when the original gassing operations were suspended.'

David Coffey, a vet who has experience of testing cattle, worked in TB hospital wards and in the Central Veterinary Laboratory when the Ministry's tests for badger-cattle transmission were being carried out, says that the report is 'statistically inadequate'. Zuckerman more or less admits this when he states:

> It would help to meet the criticism that this animal has been made a scapegoat in the story of TB in cattle were surveys to be made systematically of all wild mammals that can be found on farms where breakdowns occur. To discover how vulnerable they are relative to the badger would, however, necessitate the testing of a fairly large number.

David Coffey and Dr Littler, say that no reference is made to Russian research which shows that pastures may remain infected with bovine TB for up to twelve months and that guinea pigs fed on grass on infected soil contracted the disease.

No investigation of soil conditions in the South West has been carried out.

Coffey (who believes with others that the solution to bovine TB lies in vaccinating cattle) says that at one time the Ministry encouraged farmers to 'get rid of badgers' by pumping slurry down the setts (liquid manure from cattle) – a possible source of infection to badgers and a horrible way of drowning the occupants.

The Mammal Society was quoted in *Nature* as saying:

It is our belief that there is no unequivocal evidence that the present gassing policy is likely to produce a long-term solution to the problem. We suggested that the Zuckerman report is one-sided in its interpretation of the evidence and that the conclusion and recommendations in the report are too categorical and do not take sufficient account of the complexity of the problem.

Finally, Mr John Alexander-Sinclair who complains of gross anomalies in the report puts forward important information from Switzerland which Lord Zuckerman did not include:

The conclusive evidence is provided by an authoritative report (in German) dated 1964 by the 'Schweizer Archiv fur Tierheilkunde' provided by the Swiss Embassy in London in 1975, whose letter of transmittal says, in part (the whole is at the disposal of Lord Zuckerman or of the Minister for Agriculture on request from me or from the Swiss Embassy), as follows: 'No new cases of infected badgers have been found since 1960 and it is very interesting to note that the number of tuberculous infected deer (the principal object of the enquiry) and badgers has dropped almost to NIL since the eradication of bovine tuberculosis in Switzerland.'

Experience in FIVE major cattle breeding countries has proved that cattle infect badgers but that, with rare exceptions, a 'return' infection does not occur. The only way to solve the problem as has been done in five countries, is by eradicating bovine tuberculosis in cattle.

Lord Zuckerman had, in his report, recommended that the toxicity of hydrogen cyanide given to badgers be investigated.

Tests were later carried out by the Chemical Defence Establishment, Porton Down. One balks at contemplating what those tests may have meant to the animals involved in them – and it was concluded that badger gassing was inhumane and that there was doubt as to whether the badgers in the gassed sett died quickly. As a result, gassing was suspended as a means of control in the summer of 1982. (The Scott Henderson Report of 1951 (Cruelty to Wild Animals) had stated that 'gassing' is undoubtedly the most effective and humane method of killing badgers. Obviously the assessment was not thorough enough.)

Badgers are now trapped alive in cage traps and then shot – this system of killing to be 'supplemented only when necessary by other methods such as shooting by a marksman, netting and snaring.'

Although the Ministry is aware that the public object to snares, they defend their use by stating that under Section 11 of the Wildlife and Countryside Act 1981, snares are required to be inspected at least once a day while in position. A strong wire noose is set low on the badger's runway so that the creature will run into but not through it. The intention is to catch the badger around the abdomen, not the neck as happens with rabbits and foxes. It is stated that Ministry inspectors will endeavour to inspect snares every two hours and that lactating females up until the end of April will be released. It cannot be categorically stated here that they are as conscientious in practice as they have proposed to be in theory.

There have been several occasions on which distraught landowners have been physically restrained by Ministry men while they went about their slaughtering.

As I write, badger baiting is spreading, the Ministry badger-victim is still being killed. He remains a hounded victim.

Source material: John Alexander-Sinclair, Peter Roberts and 'AG' vols 54, 61 and 62; Tim Clarke and John May, *The Beast*, vols 4, 8, 9 and 10; Gwent Badger Group, *Briefly on Badgers* and Lord Zuckerman's Report: *Badgers, Cattle and Tuberculosis*, August 1980, HMSO PO Box 569, London SE1 (£5.20). Particular help from John Alexander-Sinclair and Peter Roberts.

Reports from MAFF. Animal Health Division 111 (Branch A) 10th Floor, Tolworth Tower, Surbiton, Surrey KT6 7DX.

What You Can Do

*   Protest against the massacre of the badgers. Write to the MAFF (address above) and the Minister of Agriculture.
*   Write to your MP giving the facts and asking him/her to protest to the Ministry of Agriculture.
*   Help to bring prosecutions against those illegally killing badgers. Report any possible cases to the RSPCA.

3 Slaughter and Farming

The British Public would react strongly if it were known that considerable suffering frequently results from present slaughtering methods. (Farm Animal Welfare Co-ordinating Executive paper to the Ministry of Agriculture)

In 1979 3,996,000 cattle, 11,634,000 sheep and lambs, 14,672,000 pigs, 450,000,000 birds,[1] were slaughtered, including broilers, spent hens (mainly from battery cages), turkeys and ducks, in this country. The industry kills 3,000 animals every minute of every working day.[2]

Most people believe that slaughtering in Britain is humane, that the interests of the animals from the farm to the dinner table – where they mostly cease to resemble in any way what they once were – are satisfactorily covered and guarded by law. There are laws which attempt to set down standards whereby the animal is not deliberately or unnecessarily ill-treated, but in practise the law is neither upheld, nor is it adequate.

Laws on Slaughter

The first law which makes reference to slaughtering is the 1911 Protection of Animals Act which prohibits deliberate cruelty and makes the causing of unnecessary suffering illegal both by the general public and by knackers.

The first private members bill concerning slaughterhouses appeared in 1927. This came about following concern about conditions in slaughter houses after World War I and

[1] The Ammerdown Group Report, Seminar, April 1980.
[2] From the Vegetarian Society of the UK Ltd.

eventually became law in 1928 after amendments which allowed exemptions for 'religious slaughter'. This was the Slaughter of Animals (Scotland) Act.

Efforts by private members to obtain a slaughter bill for England and Wales were under way from about 1930 in the face of much government apathy, but in 1933, the Slaughterhouse Act became law. It only covered cattle, calves and in some cases pigs. David Whiting says that this

> is not specifically a slaughter Act. So far no government has seen fit to introduce a bill to improve the welfare of animals for slaughter and it reflects shamefully on those who set themselves up to lead us, that the present legislation is the result of Private Members Bills. Our democratic dictatorship even now in this so-called enlightened age continues to oppose progress and attempts to reduce the suffering behind the meat trade.

The 1933 Act requires that the animals be rendered unconscious before being bled. This used to be done by hitting the animal over the head with a large sledgehammer, commonly known as a poleaxe. This is heavy work and the stunning blow is only as effective as the muscle power of the man wielding the hammer. So in smashing the head of hundreds of animals a day, the man will tire and become less efficient. A slaughterman, by the very nature of his job, will switch off mentally from the reality of his task and so will gradually become insensitive to the suffering he is causing.[1]

David Whiting, a vegetarian since 1951 and an animal-welfare field worker since leaving his career in aerospace science, has taken a slaughterman's licence in order to work in slaughterhouses to understand the problems and investigate ways of making the killing process more humane. His stepfather Lord Dowding worked hard to promote humane

[1] The following reports in particular indicate that pre-slaughter stunning by captive bolt pistol, electricity or CO_2 gas is not always effective:

(i) Review of pre-slaughter stunning in the EC (Commission of the European Communities, Information on Agriculture, No 30, March 1977).

(ii) Report on the Working Party on Slaughterhouse Hygiene (Environmental Health Officers Association, London, 1977).

(iii) Hearing on Pre-Slaughter Stunning (National Food Administration, Uppsala, Sweden, 1978).

slaughter from 1948 onwards. Finally, in 1953, the work he did became law as the 1953 Slaughterhouses Act, which has now been replaced by the Slaughterhouses Act of 1974. Part 2 of that Act says that an animal must be rendered instantaneously insensible to pain until death supervenes, by a mechanical instrument in a good state of repair. There are also other regulations from 1958 which, among other things, state that an animal must not be slaughtered in the sight of another animal.[1] The 1911 Protection of Animals Act states that

> If any person shall cruelly beat, kick, ill treat, over-ride, over-drive, over load, torture, infuriate or terrify, any animal or shall cause or procure or being the owner, permit any animal to so be used, or shall by wantonly or unreasonably doing or omitting to do any act, or causing or procuring the commission or omission or any act cause any unnecessary suffering, or, being the owner, permit any unnecessary suffering to be so caused to any animal

shall be committing an offence under the Act.

Furthermore, there is *no legislation* for the killing of rabbits. Rabbit meat is now big business.

Cattle

Stunning of cattle (and *sometimes* sheep) is normally done with a device known as a captive bolt pistol. Except for small animals – calves and sheep – the trigger-operated pistol can be, and is, frequently open to incorrect use, because the slaughterman from his difficult position in the slaughter pen is trying to stab the muzzle of the gun accurately on the small target area of the animal's moving head as it shies away with fear. The trigger is frequently pulled before the gun is in contact with the head and therefore the bolt often does not penetrate to the full depth necessary to produce total and instantaneous unconsciousness.

More modern developments in captive bolt equipment are of a cylindrical design; the bolt fires as a result of the muzzle striking the animal's head, instantaneously firing the cartridge and ensuring full penetration of the bolt. If the shot has been

[1] The Slaughter of Animals (Prevention of Cruelty) Regulation 1958 (no.2166).

accurately placed, the animal immediately collapses, oblivious of any further pain. This is fast but a lot of commotion precedes this act.

The placing of the head is vitally important, and the restraining pens into which the animals are put do not make this an easy task. David Whiting feels that this is especially so when the animal – as he has seen – is badly mistreated on the journey to the abattoir and does not want to go up the ramp of the stunning pen. He has seen animals 'urged on' with buckets of scalding hot water tipped over their back parts 'until the skin literally peels off'. In fact F.P. Lawton, DVSM, MRCVS, of the Health Dept Manchester Abattoir, stated that 'all movements on and around the slaughtering floor should be gradual and unhurried so as not to cause excitement to the animals and to assist in the prevention of accidents'.[1]

Meat eaters who find such facts horrifying, might remind themselves that the slaughterman is only doing their dirty work. He is on piecework, is encouraged to hurry when he should take his time, and isn't paid a great deal. He is handling sharp knives, moving on bloody, slippery floors, works amid bad smells and high humidity. In its demands for cheap meat, society hasn't given him the tools or conditions to do the job adequately, but demands that he do it.

The Association of Meat Inspectors[2] stated

common problems arise at lairage, overcrowding, lack of cleanliness and disinfection, occasionally *lack of feed and adequate water*. [my itals] The demand for speed and the general practice of piece-rate work for abattoir employees is not conducive to attendance on these matters, and it is known to result in maltreatment at stunning which is not always effected skilfully or sufficiently to cause unconsciousness.

If an animal is stubborn – a young bull, for instance – it might be frightened and want to go backwards down the ramp, but can't because there are others behind it; it can't go back down the line, it can't turn. The men will then beat it with sticks, or

[1] UFAW Symposium, 1971. Humane Killing and Slaughterhouse Techniques.
[2] National Seminar, AMI, 1979. Interim Report by the Association's Centralisation Sub-committee.

twist and break its tail. When the animal is thoroughly ill-treated, it becomes terrified and more adrenalin is released into the blood. The slaughtermen and lairage attendants fail to realize that they are then producing a lower quality meat. Highly stressed animals produce meat which will not keep so well, partly as a result of a high level of adrenalin released into the muscle fibre. The recording of accidents and injuries to the animals in slaughterhouses is not compulsory, whereas accident or injury to people is.

Slaughter could be carried out in a much more kindly manner than at present, though we must question the word 'humane', for it is almost impossible for slaughter to be humane.

Stunning boxes are, on the whole, badly designed. The pen usually has a vertically sliding door, which in the better abattoirs is operated by compressed air. In the more old-fashioned ones – the majority – it is operated by means of a heavy counterweight and rusted old pieces of greased cable. When the heavy iron door is pulled down it sometimes thumps the animal on the bony part of its back. If the animal is driven badly up the ramp it may try and jump out of the pen and can end up looking over into the so-called hygienic area – where carcasses are being cut into joints.

The slaughterman is standing above the animal and has to lean over it, which puts him off balance while the animal is throwing its head about – and if it has horns, it is of some danger to him – and then has to place the gun in a theoretical position across the animal's forehead, taking diagonals from each ear to the opposite eye, where the two lines cross the forehead. The gun should be pressed right up against the animal's forehead and, if trigger-operated, the bolt fires and is into the head by the time the slaughterman has finished pulling it; the animal is already on the ground. But if it flicks its head at the last minute and he misfires, and the thing goes into an ear for instance, then it will be in agony, will be enraged and will possibly fall to the bottom of the pen, half-stunned, almost out of reach. If the gun is held perhaps half an inch away, penetration may be only 2½ inches, which will leave a large animal still conscious to outside stimulus. The gun then has to be reloaded, which will take time. It should be mandatory to have a second gun to hand for this very reason. But, at present, no such thing is required. It is not known how often the captive bolt pistol fails, necessitating a second shot, in addition to which the correct strength of cartridge is not always used.

But even if a second gun is to hand, the manoeuvres are not easy. It has to be loaded, and the slaughterman has to lean over, perhaps hooking his feet on a rail – if there is one – and then lean upside down to get the gun into the animal's head, between it and the end of the pen, or alternatively, to put a shot in the back of the animal's neck, which requires a great deal more skill and a fairly powerful gun. After stunning with a captive bolt pistol, the slaughterman may, or may not, put a pithing cane down the hole in the head – a coil wire spring about two-thirds of a metre in length. This, pushed down through the hole, is riddled up and down so that it completely mashes the brain and severs the connections to the spinal cord. This stops any kicking reflex and is done as a safety measure. If the animal is not pithed and if the bleeding were to be delayed, it could regain consciousness, but it would have a hole in its skull and brain. EEC regulations discourage pithing as it introduces dirt into the carcass. When some of the more modern guns are used, pithing is not considered necessary.

Contact guns made by Accles and Shelvoke of Birmingham are in fact better than the trigger type because they go into action on contact rather than having a trigger. A light tap will fire the bolt, but the gun must be positioned correctly. There are basically two types of contact firing guns: the most common type relies on the bolt penetrating the skull. However, in order to reach an acceptable compromise in attempting to provide humane stunning prior to the act of ritual slaughter, experiments have been done with contact-fired guns modified to deliver a powerful blow with a blunt head which stuns by concussion without penetrating the forehead or damaging the brain. The difficulties with the latter are in obtaining the correct balance and strength of cartridge – too much will crack the skull, too little means the animal will regain consciousness. This demonstrates the kind of engineering problems involved in creating accurate equipment at economically viable prices.

The captive bolt industry is financed by the turnover in cartridges, not by the selling of guns. High volume cartridge sales are the only source of viable income from which finance can be diverted into research and the development of new equipment. Humane slaughter costs money.

In the report of the Ammerdown Groups Seminar[1] it is stated that 'Restraint of calves to ensure accurate and effective stunning is difficult, and this may lead to their being stuck (the neck arteries cut) while still conscious.'

The slaughterman and lairage hands have less than enough understanding of animal psychology – perhaps if they had, they would not be doing the job? – so unnecessary suffering results. Lairage hands may be lazy or on a tea break so that the slaughterman has to bring the animals up the ramp himself by any means he can. Lairage facilities are often old and of poor design; the races leading to the stunning pen can cause a good deal of congestion. After being shot in the pen, the animal will be shackled. During shackling it frequently gives a violent kick as a result of muscular spasm. Cattle will then have their throats cut one at a time. They are then hoisted up onto the bleeding rail where there will be probably six, maybe eight, animals hanging over the bleeding trough. The carcasses pass on down the line for dressing.

Sometimes two small animals are put into the stunning pen together, in contravention of the 1958 regulations (as mentioned above). In Canterbury abattoir Mr Whiting has witnessed cattle being stunned one after another until there are four on the floor. If by chance one of those animals has not been properly stunned, it could begin to regain consciousness before its throat is cut when it will clinically die from loss of blood.

Stunning equipment is required to leave the animal with its heart still beating in order that the blood shall pump from the body to produce meat which has a minimum of blood in it. This is why animals are always bled.

At present, stunning equipment is not maintained by qualified engineers who would be able to ensure that it was kept 'in proper repair' as required by law. Abattoirs are fairly complicated places with very hot water, high voltages, electric winches, lighting, ventilation and drainage problems. These things are usually looked after by semi-qualified staff. The equipment is potentially dangerous; guns easily become both dangerous and *inefficient*. It would be in everyone's interest to ensure proper maintenance as the law requires.

[1] Report of a Seminar held by the Ammerdown Group, April 1980, on the Transport and Slaughter of Farm Animals.

Pigs, Goats and Sheep

Pigs, goats and sheep are treated differently from cattle. In some abattoirs sheep are on a conveyor-belt system and are shot with captive bolt pistols on the top of the head which can be 'humane'; but very often electrocution is the preferred method and this can have horrific results.

'I have seen the most terrible atrocities in some abattoirs where sheep are never stunned, because the electric tongs are never used,' states David Whiting. Electrical stunning is used for calves, sheep and pigs in the UK.

Sheep are herded from the lairage into the stunning area and because the sheep is docile, the slaughterman just pulls it up by the hind leg, slips the chain shackle over the rear hock and then puts it on the elevating hoist. It takes about twenty seconds, while it is lifted live, fully conscious, upside down by its ankles – the chain now biting and causing some discomfort – onto the bleeding rail. When seven or eight animals are on the bleeding rail, it will then go on from the stunning area into the clean dressing area, where the slaughterman will hold the muzzle of the sheep in his left hand and slit its throat with his right. *This is completely against the law as laid down in the Slaughterhouse Act 1974.* When stunning is carried out in accordance with the law, there is often a problem caused by the use of low-speed elevators where there may be a 20–40 second interval between stunning and sticking.[1]

The abattoir in Leicester in which David Whiting observed this process, *is killing 2,500 sheep a week and has been doing so for years.* He was there to demonstrate a particular kind of captive bolt pistol on cattle. The slaughtermen say that electrical stunning does not work on sheep because the wool on the sheep's cheeks and temples prevents a good electrical contact and therefore just gives the animal a nasty shock without actually stunning it. They feel, therefore, that it is better to put the sheep straight onto the shackling process.

Sheep and pigs are usually stunned by electric shock applied to the head, but this is often not done efficiently because of 'throughput requirements'. For 90 volts, 50Hz, the current must be applied for a minimum of 7 seconds or for 70 volts, 9 seconds. (High frequency equipment is being developed to

[1] As stated in the Ammerdown Group's Report.

reduce these times.) David Whiting states that he has never seen stunning tongs held across the temples of a pig or sheep for any longer than 4 seconds, and Brian Parkinson of the Humane Slaughter Association, gives no longer than 5 seconds. When working on a line Mr Whiting said he could give no longer than 5 seconds himself because he could not keep up with the pace the slaughterhouse required, even when someone else was putting the shackle on for him – a job which requires some skill but which is usually done by the man who tongs the animal.

'Not less than 7 seconds' was stated as the correct time by F.P. Lawton of Manchester Abattoir, who also stated that the weakness of electrical stunning is the ease with which it can be misused.[1]

A large pair of tongs sends voltage through metal cups at the end of which are pads which must be kept saturated in salty or soapy water (electric current does not flow through water but through the impurities in the water). But salt tends to corrode the contacts which can make the equipment less efficient if it is not constantly overhauled.

Lower-voltage alternating current is used for safety reasons and if the animal is sweaty and wet, a large part of the stunning current may go over the animal's skull, and not through the brain and out the other side – fat insulates. This means a nasty shock, but not necessarily unconsciousness. The animal goes down partly electrocuted and paralysed. For pigs this is very relevant as they are not easily shackled. If a pig is kicking, the sharp hooves can hurt the operator, and so it is in his interests to get the animal immobilized on the floor as quickly as possible. The animal drops heavily and lies rigid and quivering, its legs outstretched, by which time the shackle can be put around it. Once the weight of the animal is pulling against the shackles, it is placed onto an elevator and then it can't do very much about it even if it regains consciousness, and his problem is over. But the stunning process is all too often not very effective. After twenty minutes or so of tonging pigs, a man would feel quite exhausted. The heavy tongs easily slip over the animal's neck instead of its head *which paralyses it, but does not make it unconscious*. Most of the pigs go to the bleeding rail still conscious of pain.

Stunning can work effectively as required by law but to produce full unconsciousness (after paralysis) the time

[1] UFAW Symposium 1971, Humane Killing and Slaughterhouse Techniques.

required to keep the electric tongs on the animal's head produces severe muscular contraction which often leads to unacceptable amounts of haemorraging – blood splash – which devalues the carcass. It is therefore in the interests of the slaughterhouse to only partially stun or paralyse the animals for handling convenience and for the maintenance of carcass value.

Even if rendered unconscious by the time they reach the bleeding rail, several animals are hanging there and will be stunned in batches – perhaps half a dozen or more – then they will be bled in a batch. Then another man – who is also working as quickly as possible to get his bonus – will take over the next job of plunging the animal, if it is a pig, into the scalding tank and debristling it. This is a semi-automatic process. It is not infrequent for pigs, and sometimes sheep, though they are much quieter, to kick so violently that they jerk themselves off the bleeding rail, fall to the ground, regain consciousness, and run amock among carcasses, offal, blood and fat. Naturally they feel aggressive and afraid and can be dangerous.

Low voltage stunning doesn't work effectively and demands for such huge quantities of meat make the slaughterman's job one which is almost impossible to render humane. High-voltage stunning could be more effective. High voltage/low frequency stunning ($>240v/50HZ$) is already being used in Holland. Under this system sufficient current passes through the brain to ensure complete insensibility within one second compared with up to 7 seconds for low voltage systems. But this would have to comply with the regulations under the Health and Safety at Work Act.

Pigs are sometimes stunned by CO_2 (carbon dioxide) but it has been amply demonstrated that this is not a stress-free method. Studies by Dr Cantieni and Dr Dodman at the University of Glasgow indicate that present methods of pre-slaughter stunning using CO_2 'appear to cause the pigs great distress'. Mr Leach, formerly of the Meat Research Institute, Bristol, believes that further research is required:[1] 'It seems to me that the crucial question is whether pigs are insensible when they exhibit convulsions in atmospheres of about 70% CO_2 and 30% air.'

[1] From Pre Slaughter Stunning Methods and Slaughterhouse Operation in British Abattoirs. Submitted by FAWCE to the MAFF September 1979.

A closing comment in a report to the EEC[2] is worth noting: 'In order to comply with the law a 'stunning appliance' must be used, whereas success – in the sense of actual stunning – often remains doubtful.'[1] In addition the Ammerdown Group reported: 'Although common in some parts of Europe, in the UK there is very little stunning of pigs with CO_2. It is a controversial subject, but there is considerable evidence that stunning by this method is stressful procedure.'

Poultry

The ritual killing of poultry sold live to customers in a side street off Petticoat Lane is allowed to continue because of a loophole in the law. The laws governing poultry are not as good as those for cattle.

> From our experiences in testing electrical low-voltage hand stunners on domestic fowls, turkeys and ducks, it does appear that some of the manufacturers, most of the users, and probably some of the inspecting officers are not really aware of the differences between electrical paralysis and electrical narcosis [state of sensibility].

Under the 1967 Act, ministers approved stunning instruments of the following kind:

> An instrument which passes an electric current through the brain of the bird sufficient to render the bird instantaneously insensible to pain. Doubt remains as to whether the phrase 'instantaneously insensible' is being interpreted correctly under field conditions . . . it may well be that inspecting officers also have difficulties in differentiating electrical paralysis from electrical narcosis.[2]

In 1975, David Whiting investigated what was then the world's fourth largest chicken plant, 'The Rainbow Chicken' complex in Durban, S. Africa. The conditions in which the chickens are

---

[1] Review of Pre-Slaughter Stunning in the EC (Commission of the European Communities Information on Agriculture no.30 March 1977).
[2] W.N. Scott, MRCVS, UFAW Symposium.

reared is very bad indeed. Not only there, but at the Brake Brothers factory in Ashford, England and in the Matthews turkey empire in Norfolk (the largest of its type in Europe) he looked at the slaughtering process. *Mr Matthews is killing some 6,000,000 birds a year* and the cruelty, Mr Whiting feels, centres very much around the way in which the birds are loaded onto lorries when they are caught to go to slaughter when many wings are broken and also in the time they are left hanging upside down on the conveyor belt. In chicken plants the electrical stunning baths cannot cope with birds in a state of panic, flapping their wings, their heads swinging about. They tend not to make good contact with the stunning machine, and therefore either come out of it unstunned or regain consciousness before their throats are cut. The staff at packaging points have even complained on occasion that the birds are still apparently alive after they have been through the scalding tank and then through the de-feathering machine. What they see may be merely muscular reflex, but there is a possibility that this awful suffering could occur. Such huge numbers of birds are involved, that even allowing for only 1 per cent error millions of birds will be tortured to death. It is calculated that *seven million* poultry a year are killed while fully conscious.[1]

Poultry are stunned either by high- or low-voltage electrical devices – in both of which 'misses' occur – or by being dipped into live water. But in all cases the birds are hanging head downwards as they are sent along the electrocution lines.

After an interval, a bird will regain consciousness after being electrically stunned. A FAWCE report[2] stated: 'In a recent test of significant size one third of the birds emerged dead from the water bath, and another third were unstunned'. This, despite the finding of UFAW that the electric water bath stunner is 'certainly the most effective and humane device' which has been investigated by them.

This is in contradiction of the laws which safeguard the handling of poultry – which does not come under the 1974 Slaughterhouses Act. There are also problems with automatic neck-cutting machines which are meant to cut the neck automatically of the bird which is not properly stunned. The

[1] The Vegetarian Society UK Ltd.
[2] Pre-Slaughter Stunning and Methods of Slaughterhouse Operation in British Abattoirs, September 1979.

knife can miss, sending birds alive into the scalding tank. As every engineer knows, there is always a failure rate with machinery. It is at the point of breakdown or failure that cruelty will certainly occur and a maintenance engineer, a technician, a slaughterman, a food-packing processor, is not an animal-welfare adviser, and therefore his understanding of the problem and method of dealing with it are not geared to relieving the animal of as much stress and suffering as possible. This is understandable because a huge number of birds are being dealt with on a very expensive, automated production line. Regardless of how many birds are reared, they are killed on a normal conveyor-belt system which is similar to the ones on which motor cars are built. If 20–30lb turkeys are being 'processed' at the rate of six million a year, as was the case with Matthews' turkeys in 1980, the plant is running twenty-four hours a day, for fifty weeks a year and there is no time for delay should something go wrong. Huge articulated trucks constantly arrive with thousands of turkeys stacked eight to a compartment. There are problems with insufficiently trained operators and mechanically and electrically unsound devices.

The turkeys often reach the slaughterhouse with a good deal of bruising and general body damage. They will then be pulled out again by the legs, hung upside down by the ankles, and shunted along on a conveyor belt probably half dazed with fright. Hopefully the sheer mental overload of absolute terror blackens their minds. After the stunning bath, throat cutting, and scalding tank, the softened skin goes through rubber to pull out the feathers – 'This looks gorey,' David Whiting says, 'but one hopes that by then the birds are no longer live creatures.'

Ritual Slaughter

Having explored the situation in slaughterhouses so far, we might think that those in glasshouses should not throw stones, yet ritual slaughter methods cannot be ignored.

Under the terms of the 1911 Act, both Muslim and Jewish slaughter, along with slaughtering methods generally used in Great Britain, are against the law. At present many Eastern countries accept meat for Muslim consumption which has been pre-stunned. A committee set up by the Director of the

Research Institute for Islamic Studies in Pakistan, issued a statement as follows: 'If new means of slaughtering are more quick and sharp, their employment is a more desirable thing. It comes under the saying of the Prophet Inna: "God has rendered us to be kind to everything".'

The immunities in the present legislation derive from the first Slaughterhouse Act in Scotland, 1928, which were put there expressly to protect the position of Lascars, members of the crews of ships in Scottish ports, yet fifty years later, it has become big business. Religious minorities have remained exempt from the rules of the 1974 Act which requires pre-stunning.

The Humane Slaughter Association stated in its 1979–80 annual report that it had been urging local authorities to withhold licences unless humane stunning was practised, but according to the law as it now stands, they cannot do this. The environmental health officer of a borough council can only go by the rule book, for under the 1974 Act ritual slaughter is legal.

Mrs Fenner of the Ministry of Agriculture stated in the House of Commons[1] that slaughterhouses do not require special licenses to carry out ritual slaughter. Local authorities are responsible for abattoirs and it is for them to determine the degree of inspection required and that ritual slaughter may be carried out in any slaughterhouse with a normal operating license. No specific records are required to be kept on ritual as against 'humane' slaughter.

Here is a quote from Dr Linzell, physiologist and veterinary surgeon:

These results led me to wonder about the sincerely held belief of the Jews and Moslems that unconsciousness supervenes instantaneously after the throat is cut and my interpretation of Dr. Baldwin's and my own experiments is that it will be at least 10 seconds. I am well used to working with sheep, cattle and goats and their reactions to pain. From what I have observed in life and on film of the animals' behaviour after the cut, I believe that since, as we have seen, very little blood can maintain consciousness, in the head down position, flow by gravity probably maintains consciousness for 30 seconds or even longer in slaughter by

[1] Hansard 11 March 1982.

the Jewish and Moslem method. In my opinion this is far from instantaneous.[1]

There is a growing amount of ritual slaughter and the commercial demand for the export of Halal or Muslim killed meat. Thousands perhaps millions of carcasses are going out of the country as new slaughterhouses open up. There are now two clauses in the 1974 Slaughterhouses Act which allow meat to be killed for the consumption of Muslims or Jews, the latter by 'Shechita', put there to protect the interests of religious minorities. But the time has come when the spirit of the law, if not the letter, is being stretched beyond all reasonable limits. The law never did intend large-scale slaughter of animals without humane pre-stunning to meet an export market. It is, without doubt, better that animals be slaughtered as near to the point of origin as possible in this country, rather than be transported live overseas to an even worse death and better that we should let the animals be killed here in a manner acceptable to the religious communities destined to eat them, but the situation could be ameliorated.

The problem often lies in the interpretation of the Koran by various religious leaders, remembering that the Prophet himself was a compassionate man. The animal should be rendered insensible before it is put into a casting pen and turned upside down, for that in itself is very distressing for the animal and sets up a good deal of fear. The Ammerdown Group's report states that 'the Weinberg pen in which the animal is rotated onto its back is an extremely stressful method.' It should preferably be put into a restraining area, then stunned and then rotated.

Gods change as people change, but man-made dogmas die hard. Some otherwise Orthodox Jews are of the opinion that Kosher killing is maintained simply for reasons of exclusivity. They must be listened to. As we have seen, so-called 'humane' methods are not truly humane, but a good deal of religious law was made for the benefit of humans and not at all for animals.

The Jewish method

The 'shohet' or man entrusted with performing 'Shechita' is

[1] UFAW Symposium 1971, Humane Killing and Slaughterhouse Techniques.

apparently 'a man of learning', 'frequently the local minister' and often also a 'teacher of religion'.

Bernard Homa, Chairman of the Shechita Committee stated: 'The taking of an animal's life is carried out with the full knowledge and realisation that we are concerned after all with one of God's creatures, and that it is being done by Special Divine Sanction'.[1]

Mr Homa also stated that an animal is *not* distressed when in the vicinity of another of its kind being slaughtered or eviscerated, nor is it disturbed by the sight of blood, that those who cannot agree are guilty of 'anthropomorphism' and 'false sentimentality', but he thinks it preferable that an animal should *not* witness the activities of an abattoir or endure the sight of blood!

An animal killed by the Jewish method has its neck cut by a large, sharp knife in one swift blow, which, he says, 'is absolutely painless', that 'It is well known that when one cuts oneself with a sharp knife, no pain is felt at the time.' But Dr Linzell said that, in his experience, when he had cut himself with a microtome it had indeed hurt.

Homa says that the animal is put in a casting pen – 'the Weinberg pen' already mentioned – and rotated onto its back 'where it is fully relaxed'. His opinion is contrary to that of the Ammerdown Group who found this to be 'extremely stressful'.

An environmental health officer who had recently worked as a meat inspector in the City of Belfast abattoir, where ritual slaughter of sheep and cattle was carried out on a regular basis, told David Whiting that the animals were heavily goaded to persuade them into the Weinberg pen and struggled violently while the crush was being tightened against them. They would kick violently while the pen was being rotated, and also afterwards. He occasionally saw animals break their legs during their struggles and in one case, after the animal's throat had been cut and it had been pulled clear of the pen, it got up and ran around the slaughter hall for a little over a minute.

The RSPCA should take a new look at this problem as it gave its approval to this type of casting pen some years ago.

While we must *never* confuse legislation for humane treatment of animals with racism, which is only another form of

[1] UFAW Symposium.

violence, it is a great pity that Lord Somers withdrew his
Slaughter of Animals Bill in 1962 (a Bill supported by Lord
Dowding) having been persuaded that it might give rise to anti-
Semitism.[1]

The Muslim method

Muslims also believe that theirs is a divine method given them
by the Creator. G.M. Khan, MB, BS, DLO (Lond.) of the Shah
Jehan Mosque, Woking, defended Muslim slaughter in much
the same way as his Jewish counterpart.[2] While we have to
admit that the Christian Church is hypocritical in not
abhorring murder for food, that same self-justification arises in
the Muslim religion. Just as Christians go in for the wholesale
massacre of turkeys at Christmas and lambs and turkeys at
Easter, so do Muslims 'sacrifice' animals to celebrate the
sacrifice Abraham offered of his son Ishmail each year.

The Muslim kills his animal by a cut in the neck, severing the
major blood vessel while it is cast on its side. He is careful to
drain the animal's body of blood as much as possible – for
human health reasons, as with Jews and Christians. He
believes that blessing the animal before killing it – which at
least shows some respect for the poor creature – means that
killing it will not be a sin. In other words, he thereby admits his
own inadequacy, which a Christian does not!

But when Mr Khan states: 'Muslims cannot be emotional on
any subject'[2] does he deny sensitivity? He goes to great lengths
to inform us that animals do not feel pain as acutely as human
beings, but this is open to infinite question. His arguments
appear convenient, but dubious – that the animal brain is less
appreciative of pain (one can only hope that this is true), that its
skin is less pain-sensitive, that immediate unconsciousness
produced by rapid blood loss from a quick, clean cut is the least
painful method of killing.

[1] Hansard 3 December 1962: Lord Somers:

> I must say that I am not in the slightest degree convinced by the arguments in
> favour of this form of slaughter. But in the light of the statement by my noble and
> learned friend, the leader of the House, that if we were to pass the 2nd Reading of
> this Bill it might throw a light of anti-Semitism upon this House – a thing which at
> all costs I want to avoid – there remains only one course open to me, and that is to
> beg leave to withdraw my motion.

[2] UFAW Symposium.

Mr Khan plays with words: that we call ritual slaughter 'cut throat', he says, evokes gruesome images, whereas 'carotoid section' creates no feeling at all, and that in any case people can get used to the sight of blood!

He does admit that animals sometimes stagger about after slaughter by 'carotoid section' – either because the knife wasn't sharp enough and therefore did not cut the vessels, but nicked them, in which case it may have to go through the process more than once, or because it is doing this by 'subconscious reflex'.

He ends by saying: 'In respect of the feelings of those who sincerely find it distasteful, techniques and devices can be found to *eliminate audio-visual impressions of cruelty*' (my italics). Is this the way to hide further from the truth of the matter?

But Dr Linzell[1] states that in his experience of the distribution of nerve endings in the necks of goats, sheep, cattle and pigs, they give every sign of feeling pain; that the vagus nerve carries pain fibres, that its section might be painful in the conscious animal. He also has doubts that rapid severance of the neck is necessary to obtain complete bleeding.

But there is continuing government apathy on this issue. In reply to an eminently sensible question put to the House of Lords by Lord Houghton in June 1981[2] regarding the need for control in face of the escalation of religious slaughter, Earl Ferrers, Minister of State, Ministry of Agriculture, replied that it was 'correct to make such exemptions for the purposes of those religious minorities who require them . . . and it is not the Government's duty to seek to influence either the increase or restriction of this method of slaughter.'

The basis of tolerance and good manners is sensitivity to others but those two supposedly English qualities are made shameful when the pretended sensitivity excludes millions of sentient creatures.

Inspection

The laws are obviously not being adhered to, mainly because it is practically impossible to enforce them.

Local authorities own some and control all abattoirs and are

[1] UFAW Symposium.
[2] Hansard 26 June 1981.

responsible for their condition. They tend not to bring prosecutions under the law, even though they are responsible for licensing and enforcement of the law. Not a very satisfactory situation. People are usually not allowed into abattoirs for hygienic reasons and also because they are mostly private property, though you have a right to request entry to municipal slaughterhouses as a ratepayer, whereas you do not have the right to enter experimental laboratories run on taxpayers' money. In New Zealand, for example, an SPCA (Society for the Prevention of Cruelty to Animals) has right of access to any property where animals are being dealt with and, in fact, has powers of arrest for cruelty to animals which equal the powers of the police. In England, we can only call for police co-operation and they do not even know the relevant laws.

Inspectors do not do their job very well. Ministry employees often do not stay in a job long enough to get to know it well. This has been particularly the case with the half dozen or so inspectors who have been dealing with the transport of live animals by air. Government policy is for Ministry department employees to have a general grounding within their departments rather than a specialist grounding. This provides for wider experience, but it mitigates against animal welfare and its attendant problems.

In respect of slaughtering conditions in this country, we have a great disrespect for the law; quite simply we have well-intentioned laws which are not implemented.

Apart from the animal-welfare aspect, which is obviously in desperate need of attention, it is in the interests of slaughterhouse employees to have properly stunned animals. David Whiting managed to achieve improvements in a pig abattoir in Calcutta on hygienic grounds.

Slaughtermen are inadequately trained. In 1970, the World Federation for the Protection of Animals emphasized the need for training:[1]

Given the basic requirements of building facilities, the handling of animals by personnel is of the greatest importance in ensuring the success of measures to obtain freedom from stress. The training of abattoir personnel, the enforcement of discipline and the consequent raising of

[1] WFPA Report No.7, Welfare of Animals Slaughtered for Meat.

morale is a subject which should receive attention, even where modern facilities are not immediately available.

FAWCE, in its paper to the Ministry of Agriculture, suggested that slaughtermen be upgraded by introducing day-release training to City and Guilds standard, coupled with the present practical training within the slaughterhouse, that satisfactory completion of courses and examinations should be mandatory before the issuing of a licence. FAWCE would like to see an Institute of Slaughtermen similar to the Danish Institute at Rockilde.

Dr Linzell said that 'he and his scientific colleagues frequently had reason to visit slaughterhouses to collect material for their work and what they saw revolted them.' He felt it was clear that what was done when an inspector was present bore no relation to what happened at other times. He cited instances of sheep being kept for days without water; pigs stunned in batches of four or five, long before being stuck and obviously conscious again when this was done; cattle being caused great distress by being driven on a slippery floor to the slaughter point; and sheep not stunned at all.

The slaughtering industry is looking for maximum throughput (that is, maximum killing), maximum economic viability; humane considerations come last. But it is the consumer who is responsible. Will the meat eater go to enormous lengths to support his habit – even after learning the truth about slaughtering? Such kindly ideas as tranquillizers as a humane device are rejected as they might affect the quality of the meat – the *consumer* might be affected. The consumer becomes all important as against the unimportance attached to the enormous daily suffering in the meat industry.

Licensees convicted of cruelty in the way in which they slaughter horses have been allowed to continue holding their licenses and have even been allowed to extend their premises, according to Eileen Bezet, a well-known authority on food animals.

It appears as though a good deal of 'experimentation' has gone into the discovery of humane slaughter methods about which one can only speculate.

Those who serve the meat-eating public in professional and scientific capacities pride themselves on being 'scientific' and 'unemotional'. Is this just another way of saying, uncaring, unfeeling and brutalized?

Henry Thoreau said, 'I have no doubt that it is a part of the destiny of the human race, in its gradual improvement, to leave off eating animals, as surely as the savage tribes have left off eating each other when they came in contact with the more civilised'. But those 'more civilised' today see that time as so very far away.

Source material: David Whiting, written and aural material, backed by his photographic evidence.
Brian Parkinson and the Council of Justice to Animals and Humane Slaughter Association.
Report of the Ammerdown Group's seminar, April 1980, 'The Transport and Slaughter of Farm Animals.' Paper on 'Pre-Slaughter Stunning Methods and Slaughterhouse Operation in 'British Abattoirs' submitted to the MAFF by FAWCE, supplied by Clive Hollands.
UFAW Symposium, January 1971, 'Humane Killing and Slaughterhouse Techniques' with particular help from David Whiting and Peter Roberts.

Journey into Hell: A testimony – for turkeys

'. . . here their prison ordained
In utter darkness and their portion set
As far removed from God and light of Heaven
As from the centre thrice to the utmost pole.'
(John Milton, *Paradise Lost*)

The predecessor of our modern turkey was a native of the Americas where it lived wild and free, until about 400 years ago it was domesticated and brought to Europe because humans liked the taste of its flesh. The wild version is probably extinct in America; the amiable farmyard version no longer waddles or trots.

Jenny Gridley took a temporary job on a turkey farm. This is her testimony.

'I wanted to know about the turkey farm because I have always felt very strongly about the live export trade of animals and I don't ever want to be accused of talking about something of which I don't really have experience.

'I went to the factory in Hereford and saw them being unloaded from the lorry. They were put on conveyor belts, strapped upside down; this was the first time the birds had seen the light of day. When I went there, it must have been a coffee break, because the siren went and everyone disappeared leaving the birds suspended, on a huge conveyor belt, from where they go through some doors to be electrocuted. There are girls there to do something to the ones that get missed. That was Sun Valley, in the middle of Hereford. It was terrible. I burst into tears. I was so upset. I thought they had had such a raw deal. A man came up to me and said, "What's the matter, is it too much for you?" I couldn't say anything.

'No one was affected. The birds just weren't alive to them. It was just money.

'I began at the end where the collectors come to take the turkeys away. They cram them into boxes. I can't remember how many went into a box, but you can see the lorries any day – with all the feathers flying out. I've seen two already this morning. The boxes are piled one on top of the other, and they are taken off to the factory where they are loaded onto the conveyor belts.

'After they had gone we had to clear out the sheds. Everything had to be disinfected and sprayed. Then we had to prepare for the chicks. Apparently they know just how many chicks they will have on a certain day in three years' time. It is all worked out. The chicks arrive from breeding units, in vast boxes. The men unload them from the lorries and just throw these tiny little balls of fluff down, I know that when I worked there, the mortality rate was a lot lower than it had been before, because I was gentle when I unloaded them. The men just throw them out of the boxes. Apparently, they expect to lose 5,000 out of the 30,000 chicks just because of the way they are handled.

'The stench in these sheds is horrendous. When they are adult, they're so big, so fat, so pumped full of hormones and antibiotics they can't move. It's pitch black. They are always in the dark and never have the smallest amount of light. If you happened to leave the door open, an incredible noise would start up. They get excited at light because they can see each other. You have to wait as long as five minutes for your eyes to get adjusted before you can do anything. The darkness is to keep them quiet. They are only one day old when they arrive and are killed at three months, or even two. I imagine it depends upon the time of year – whether they are Christmas or Easter turkeys. They are produced the whole year round. Sun Valley supply *Marks and Spencer*.

'There were days when someone would come round to give them drugs. I don't know how many injections they have in the three months of their life. They are all inoculated before they arrive. Their food is in hoppers which move around the shed. The birds don't move, the hoppers do. When they are really fat, they can't move anyway. They are loose in the shed, but packed like sardines in a tin.

'When they are tiny, they are in circular wire enclosures, with a lamp which acts as a mother. Of course, they all crowd around it. Hundreds die of suffocation, because there are layers and layers. They are craving for warmth and huddle close together, one on top of the other. It is nothing to walk along one of these buildings and pick up twenty or thirty dead chicks. You simply weed them out. Any weak ones have their necks broken. They are put into incinerators, sometimes on the premises.

'I can only say it was like walking into the bowels of hell.

'Life is so meaningless. They just pull their necks. If they had a bad leg or some other thing wrong, they just screw their necks, put them in the incinerator, or chuck them on a pile somewhere. It is incredible to think that it's a life.

'I worked there for three months. I would never do it again. Every supermarket now has turkey rolls, turkey pies, turkey this and turkey that. Perhaps some of them find their way into cat food.

'They all live in hell, all the time that they are alive. And no one cares.'

Battered Lives: The Battery Tragedy

'The first time I ever entered a battery house I thought it was the entrance to Hell' (Violet Spalding, on visiting Lord Nugent's hen battery)

Go smash an egg? It came from a battered hen. Nearly 600,000 tons of broiler chickens and 1,300 million dozen eggs are produced annually in Great Britain.

The Protection of Birds Act 1954 makes it an offence to keep any bird in a cage which is too small for it to spread its wings. But poultry are exempted. Why? Because the farmer wants a large profit.

Life has the most incredible tenacity. It is so precious that it maintains itself in the most adverse and terrible conditions. Man can torture creatures – or humans – to the brink of death, yet they will cling to those tortured bodies and if later placed in natural conditions, many will recover reasonable health and normal functioning.

End of lay battery hens who have never known life outside a dark and dingy overstuffed cage where they cannot move, either purchased before slaughter or picked up off the road where they have fallen from the lorry taking them to death, if placed in natural surroundings will grow lost feathers, teach themselves to walk and gradually revert to hen behaviour – dustbathing, scratching for parasites and grain and so on.

There are about 50,000,000 laying hens in batteries in Great Britain. Less than 5 per cent of our hens are free-range (Ministry of Agriculture). In the European Community some 242 million layers are in battery cages – approximately 80 per cent of the total EEC flock (1982 figures).

In hatcheries where birds are bred for egg laying, all the male chicks are exterminated at a day old. About 50,000,000 'surplus' cockerels are slaughtered every year. The usual method is to cram them into polythene bags and gas them with carbon dioxide. The British Veterinary Association has expressed concern over the practice; Honorary Secretary, Jim Allcock told a press conference that because of the huge number of chicks pressing down on top of each other, the theoretically 'humane' gas often failed to penetrate and that instead the chicks frequently suffocated.

Sometimes late hatching chicks are found amongst incubator waste. Chicks may hatch from discarded eggs in dustbins, only to suffocate, starve or be eaten by insects.

At about sixteen weeks, hens are placed four or five in a cage 20in x 18in, 15in x 19in or 16in x 18in – sizes vary. The recommended cage size is 15in x 19in for four hens.[1] But some

[1] Code No.3 for Domestic Fowls (Misc. Provisions) Act 1968.

European countries have even lower standards; France is especially bad – stocking densities are said to be as little as 300 sq.cm – in England the Ministry recommended density is 464 sq.cm. It is to such 'welfare' codes that Ministries of Agriculture refer when they say that all possible welfare recommendations are adhered to and that nothing more need be done for poultry.

The cages are metal, with a sloping wire floor which has a minimum gradient of 1 in 5 – this allows eggs to roll down for collection. The hens are given minimum headroom and cages are stacked in tiers – the lowest are often in darkness. Droppings are conveyed to a 'lagoon' where they remain at least until the annual turnout or into a 'deep pit'. Feeding and watering are automatic.

Hens would normally start laying towards the end of winter when the days begin to lengthen. In the late 1940s, many farmers began keeping poultry for winter in deep litter houses – barns strewn with about 2ft of straw. Then they realized that by increasing the length of day with electric light, hens could be induced to lay out of their normal season.

Various different methods are now used to promote optimum laying – sometimes there is a bright light for 16 hours or 18 hours out of 24, sometimes lighting is dim. Laying is connected to hormone activity and hens lay more in summer outside and so a type of artificial summer is sometimes created but most batteries still have small 40 watt light bulbs and so the light is very dim, creating a very gloomy atmosphere.

Some captive hens at the North of Scotland College of Agriculture, Aberdeen, were subjected to a 28 hour day – all daylight excluded – with a time clock to switch on and off electric lights on a 28 hour cycle, giving longer, but fewer 'days' a year. The researchers claim they get less work at weekends and bigger eggs. Although the hens lay fewer eggs, better weight grading means *higher profits*.[1] The hens may stand for their 'day' on sloping wire and crouch down on the same wire floor during the remaining hours of darkness.

Battery houses vary in size – one battery house may contain 20,000 hens, a not unusual figure. The National Farmers' Union say that most hens are collected at about 25 weeks – the

[1] AG, September 1981.

first eggs at 22–3 weeks are considered too small. The imprisoned hens spend 70 weeks in lay and produce about 260 eggs over a 52 week period – they may lay for up to 60 weeks. When asked why the hens are killed at about 14 months one factory farmer said, 'They could be molted and put on a second lay but that is uneconomic.'

However, many hens are kept for a second lay which means that they are false moulted. All lights are turned off and food and water is withdrawn for 24 hours. Food is kept away for a further 24 hours and then the hens are given a tiny diet for another fortnight. All of their feathers drop off. This is shock treatment. These creatures then face another year in the same environment. The eggs are bigger in the second year. A hen's natural lifespan could be 12 or 14 years.

The common condition of battery hens is debeaked (a painful process in itself), raw neck, few feathers left, deformed feet. One hen, not specially chosen, rescued by Chickens Lib, had a 'grossly distorted hock joint' and was found to be suffering from arthritic changes to the joint as a result of a previous dislocation: 'One can but surmise that it was broken when first stuffed into its cage, and she then stood on one leg until the hock joint had set at a peculiar angle.'

There is no seclusion for egg laying in a battery. Professor Konrad Lorenz, animal behaviourist, has described the frustration experienced by hens who must lay their eggs with no privacy as being the worst torture to which the battery hen is exposed, comparing the hen's reluctance to lay publically with the instinctive reluctance felt by civilized man to defecate in public.

One Ministry of Agriculture official from Leeds told Chickens Lib that in her experience the main cause of death in layers at the present time is associated with egg-laying problems – internal egg laying is one of these. Does this bear out Lorenz's theory on public egg laying?

Under intensive conditions hens cannot fulfil any of their innate behavioural instincts – they cannot perch, fly, scratch the ground, dustbathe or spread their wings. If they can move at all, it is from one side of the cage to another, but overcrowding will probably prevent this. Such conditions create feather pecking and cannibalism because of boredom. The only remedy is debeaking and the reduction of light.

Some academic research relates feather pecking to tugging at young plants in nature and it arises in stress conditions such as intensively lit or overheated or badly ventilated houses, monotony in the absence of litter and high occupation density; lack of certain vitamins and amino acids may also contribute. Yet it has been found that in the social order, aggressive birds are usually good egg producers. 'All things considered, the paradoxical conclusion may be that the most productive birds are least suited to intensive husbandry with its frustrations consequent on density of occupation.'[1]

The escalation of this cruel form of egg production has been terrifying. In 1961, the battery system accounted for only 19·3 per cent of British egg production. In 1981, it accounted for 95·8 per cent.

The conditions under which these chickens live is extremely stressful, yet some are subjected to the cycle of battery laying to slaughterhouse more than once.

Transportation to the slaughterhouse is appalling. Every year approximately 350,000,000 chickens are transported to slaughter. One observer wrote:

There was still the inevitable foul stench, the morning pile of rejected dead birds, lorry loads of live chickens waiting for a considerable time by the slaughterhouse, limbs and feathers sticking awkwardly out of crates, dead and dying birds clearly visible from the back of lorries, rows of birds hung upside down to begin the conveyor belt trip to death, and the sight and noise of the mixer churning up the unwanted feathers.

Often birds fall from the overstuffed lorries – there have been accidents in which their live cargoes have spilled across the road.

When Violet Spalding and Claire Druce of Chickens Lib visited a slaughterhouse in search of battery hens for demonstration purposes, they were directed by a nearby farmer who advised them not to take his hens as they would be 'no good'. He had bought them up cheaply the previous year from a

[1] 'Health & Welfare Problems of Current Animal Husbandry Systems', Animal Health Trust, September 1980.

slaughterhouse and they were then at the end of their second lay.

They managed to convince him that they would like the hens – which were in very poor condition with extremely deformed feet. They eventually went to a good home, and although one or two of them died in particularly cold weather, the rest regrew their feathers and are leading happy, healthy free-ranging lives.

After slaughter these hens are all used in such products as baby foods, pastes, stews, curries – many are used in the restaurant trade – or in any guise where their terrible condition will not be noticed.

Chickens Lib have obtained written confirmation from the Ministry of Agriculture that 50 per cent of hens are given antibiotics – in order to keep them at what is called 'optimum level'. 50 per cent of all egg-laying hens are given antibiotics to counteract diseases and as a routine food additive to encourage optimum egg laying.

In addition, battery houses are bombarded with antipest sprays. Said Claire Druce: 'It is impossible to exaggerate the horrors of the system; you go into a battery and you can hardly breath. The air is so foul. I felt like fainting. I'm not the fainting type, but I really had to pull myself together. The stench was horrific.'

One of the jobs in the battery house is to pick up the dead every day until there are enough for the incinerator. Nobody knows what the hens die from. Some are pushed to the back; they are weak and cannot reach the food.

It is impossible to carry out the law as laid down. If a 20,000 bird battery were inspected properly, it would require staff to be present all day long, looking thoroughly. No one could work in such conditions and the farm workers union have stated that on the whole, their members do not like working in such places – they are hot, dirty, dusty, smelly and unhealthy. If the law were implemented, there would be no one willing to carry out its requirements. They would probably require breathing apparatus and moreover, would suffer extreme boredom.

On 1 January 1979, a law came into existence, entitled, 'The Welfare of Livestock (Intensive Units) Regulations 1978'. It states: 'The livestock shall be thoroughly inspected by a stock keeper not less than once each day to check that it is in a state of wellbeing.' In a battery house, where thousands of animals are kept in tiered cages – some very low, some very high – often with dim lighting and extremely unpleasant working conditions, and the usually very small workforce looking after these, it is plain to see that the law is generally broken.

On 8 January 1979, the UK ratified the Council of Europe Convention for the Protection of Animals kept for Farming Purposes. Article 4 of the Convention states:

> The freedom of movement appropriate to an animal having regard to its species and in accordance with established experience and scientific knowledge, shall not be restricted in such a manner as to cause it unnecessary suffering or injury. Where an animal is continuously or regularly tethered or confined, it shall be given the space appropriate to its psychological and ethological needs in accordance with established experience and scientific knowledge.

In the light of this evidence, and the fact that the convention was ratified, is Britain now acting illegally in continuing to support and encourage its huge battery-egg-producing system? We have to ask just how a 'state of well-being' can ever be for a battery hen?

The West German High Court of Appeal has ruled that battery cages constitute cruelty under Federal Law. However, 200 prosecutions against farmers using the now illegal system have been 'held over' pending EEC action. (The RSPCA in Britain successfully prosecuted a Dorking battery farmer under the 1978 Law concerning daily inspection.)

The British House of Commons Agriculture Committee reported in July 1981 (HMSO 406–1) and recommended among other things that battery cages should be banned throughout the EEC in five years' time, but the Minister of Agriculture has rejected this advice. The committee stated: 'Our conclusion is clear: we have seen for ourselves battery cages, both experimental and commercial and we greatly dislike what we saw.'[1]

Since 1981, the establishment of new battery units has been banned in Switzerland. Existing units must cease production by 1991. Meanwhile eggs must be marked 'regular' (battery),

[1] 1st Report, Para 149.

'deep litter' or 'free range'. A special fund was set up to help farmers change their production methods.

While the Council of Europe considers the rights and wrongs of batteries, the European Economic Community exists to protect economic investments and now finds the convention embarrassing.

No agreement about battery cages has been reached by the EEC and the British government is using this to avoid action in Britain. What is more, we are aiding the export of this gruesome egg production method. *Farmers Weekly* recently carried an advert for a hatchery manager to take responsibility for the production of 230,000 day-old chicks each week and the plant is to double in size within six months. The advertiser is Sharkia Poultry (UK) Ltd – the job is in Egypt.

The International Finance Corporation, Washington, finances huge poultry projects in many countries – Turkey, Egypt, Mexico, The Philippines, Haiti, Trinidad – and provides technical and legal expertise so long as those countries keep buying livestock, pharmaceutical drugs, equipment and buildings from developed countries.[1]

All of these imprisoned birds will eat huge amounts of much needed grain to provide a poor source of food.

Alternatives

There are several acceptable alternatives to the battery system:

(1) Free range – which should mean a system where the hens run free on grass at a stocking rate of about 100-150 hens per acre. Hen houses are provided for egg laying and shelter and for security at night.

(2) The straw yard system as demonstrated in Cambridge by Dr David Sainsbury at the School of Veterinary Medicine. This uses a covered, weatherproof building with the south side open to daylight and sunshine (but netted to exclude predators) and deep straw litter on a concrete floor. Perches and nesting boxes are provided. A stocking rate of 3 sq ft of floor space per bird is essential to its success and for the hens' well-being.

(3) The aviary/grass run system. This means a henhouse which provides several levels of slatted floors for the hens which

[1] AG No.72, September/October 1983.

reach them by ladder. Litter on the ground provides for scratching in bad weather, but hens also have daily access to outside grassruns, regularly alternated to keep the ground fresh. This system makes for good land use as it is relatively intensive, but the birds have a choice of environment. Egg collection and grading may be automated.

(4) The fold unit system, suitable for limited egg production, if well managed. The fold unit is a hen house and run which is moved, preferably daily, onto fresh ground.[1]

The levy collected from chicken production by the Eggs Authority amounts to about £3,000,000 a year, most of which is spent on advertising to persuade us to buy more eggs.

Eggs are not particularly good for you anyway: 'Doctors are beginning to realise the harmful effects of eating too many eggs. Eggs cause putrefaction in the intestines because of the high sulphur content; their high cholesterol content is another good reason to eat them only occasionally,' says Eunice Farmilant, writing on macrobiotic cooking.[2]

Nutritionists may differ in their opinions on eggs, but battery eggs usually taste bland, have thin shells, watery whites and pale yolks: watery whites are something the farmers will not admit to but according to the Annual Report of the British Egg Marketing Board 1968: 'No one has ever discovered the cause of this problem, but we believe it may have something to do with infectious bronchitis among the laying flocks or with the age of the layers.' The numbers of second quality eggs have been rising steadily year by year. Infectious bronchitis is apparently the most likely cause of the problem – it has been suggested that some of the amino acid components are modified which upsets the protein structure of the albumen.

The Ministry of Agriculture states that battery eggs are 70 per cent lower in vitamin B12 than free range eggs, and 50 per cent lower in folic acid, both substances vital for health.

Research by the University of Texas under nutritionist Dr Roger Williams, has shown battery eggs to be 'significantly inferior' to free-range in constructional food value.[3]

---

[1] Information given in Chickens Lib Fact Sheet 1, January 1982.
[2] *Macrobiotic Cooking*, Signet, USA, 1972.
[3] Reported by the Farm and Food Society.

The Dairy Industry: The Milk of Human Blindness

'If they do this when the wood is green, what will happen when it is dry?' (Luke, 23.31)

I resent the Cadburys tanker hurtling down the narrow road that leads to our Herefordshire home disturbing the green stillness. Things aren't what they used to be for cows. Gone is the caring hand milking on small homely farms. They are now part of an enormous industry. Many people now feel that the production of dairy products is even more cruel than the production of meat. Dairy farming in Britain has not yet reached the awful intensive proportions that it has in the USA where the cows no longer see green fields and are tethered in stalls,[1] but we could be moving without protest towards the increasingly unacceptable.

A total-confinement dairy setup consists of only two buildings: the mechanical milking parlour and the holding barn. . . . Other farmers prefer to keep their cows stationary in tie-stall barns and move portable milking machinery in to them. These cows remain in stalls for months, chained at their necks.

Most people are unaware that cows must go through yearly pregnancies in order to yield up their milk, cream and cheese. Hardly any cows in dairy herds are allowed to suckle their calves for more than three days.

'Separating the calf from the mother shortly after birth undoubtedly inflicts anguish on both. Cattle are highly intelligent and attachment between the calf and the mother is particularly strong.'[2]

'The modern dairy cow leads a hell of a life. Each year she hopefully produces a calf which means that for 8 months of the year she is pregnant. And for 9 months she is milked twice a day. For 6 months she is both pregnant and lactating,' said one writer in the *New Scientist*.[3]

Peter Roberts, the founder of the campaigning organization Compassion in World Farming was once a farmer who became increasingly concerned about the amount of cruelty involved in

[1] See Jim Mason and Peter Singer, *Animal Factories*, Crown, New York, 1980.
[2] Report of the Brambell Committee. HM Stationary Office, 1965.
[3] 13 January 1972.

his occupation. He and his wife Anna worried over the bull calves born to their cows, and about the cows who inevitably became barren. Their destiny was the slaughterhouse, before which they had to be transported, and perhaps exported. He reached a point where he could tolerate this no longer.

A cow lactates for ten months after producing a calf, but she comes back into heat three weeks after calving. Not on that heat, but on the next one, six weeks after calving, she will be served once again by a bull, or she will be artificially inseminated. When her milk dries, it will only be six to eight weeks before she is calving again. If, because of her age, or for some other reason, she becomes barren, her productive life over, yielding no monetary gain, her life will be taken from her. Barren cows eat, rather than produce profit and no farmer can, or will stand for that. Peter Roberts had a herd of about thirty-five cows. In that size herd, the barreners steadily grow in numbers and it would be easy to end up with a non-productive farm.

He took his cows to market and noticed agents buying up for Paris abattoirs. Both he and his wife were horrified at the thought of their cows taking that terrible journey.

He said, 'You form a bond of attachment to the cows when you're milking twice a day and attending to their wants and needs. When some poor old girl becomes non-productive, you would have to turf her out, and that just wasn't on as far as we were concerned.'

His solution would be to wait until he had about three barreners and then he would ring the abattoir and ask for them to be slaughtered in his presence, so that he could see them 'safely dead'. Farmers do this quite often, he said, but stay only to see the meat weighed out, so that they won't be cheated.

'There are occasions when animals are terrified in a slaughterhouse,' he said. 'Mine didn't seem to be afraid because they trusted me. I broke that trust, if you like. I didn't want to go home and eat meat afterwards.'

He and his wife became vegetarian twenty-three years ago, although they were still producing milk – and meat – at the time.

But livestock farming lost its appeal; the separation of the calf from the cow was particularly gruelling. They would moo at each other for twenty-four hours, sometimes more: 'The motherhood bond is so strong, it has to be broken with violence. It keeps you awake at night.'

Some of the calves will go to slaughter almost immediately. Rennet, used to make most commercial hard cheeses, has to be taken from the stomach of a newly born calf, despite the fact that this is unnecessary. Vegetarian cheeses are available in health shops – which taste just the same – made without the use of animal rennet. Or they may be reared intensively for the white veal market – one of the cruelest forms of factory farming.

Surplus calves from dairy herds are often sent to market at about one week old and will be bought up for intensive beef units, especially Fresians. They will be fed for twelve weeks on a largely cereal diet, and will be encouraged to overeat, while being kept closely confined, then slaughtered.

Female calves considered suitable to join the dairy herd are removed as soon as possible after the birth so that 'the cow may settle down again in the herd'. Sometimes fed on milk substitutes, the calves' development is artificially encouraged so that at 18–24 months, a cycle of continuous pregnancies may begin.

Separation in any case must come within the first week after birth. If they are not separated, the cow will hold her milk – she will not give it to the human. The presence of the calf causes the let-down of the milk. It is an hormonal action. If the calf is taken away and the human then attempts to take milk from her, the cow will very often hold it. This is why the calf is taken away very early while she is still so full that she cannot hold it. But within three to four days, the motherhood bond has grown very strong.

The calves are reared on buckets. For those fed with milk, six gallons may be taken from the mother each day and one gallon of that given to the calf. The cow has been stimulated to give far more than the calf needs. If the cow is allowed to hold her milk, her natural reaction will be to produce less. If milk is not taken from her, she will dry up.

Peter Roberts feels that there is in fact more cruelty involved in milk production than in beef production. One of the procedures he finds very objectionable is 'steaming up'. As soon as a cow goes dry, there will be the 6–8 week space before she calves again. In this time, she will be given steaming-up ration, a concentrated cake which contains minerals, protein, carbohydrates and vitamins. This is a complete concentrate food, given first in small quantities, then built up quite rapidly, so that she is on a very high nutritional plane just before she calves. As her stocks build up, the udder becomes very hard and distended and very painful to her. The more she's 'stocked up', the better she'll milk. If a farmer stocks a cow well enough, he'll get 2,000 gallons in a lactation, which is considered very good. After three or four lactations, at that level, the ligaments which hold the udder in shape begin to give. She gets a dropped udder which swings as she walks. As she brings her leg forward, she can't avoid kicking her udder.

Our demand for milk and cheese creates deformed, uncomfortable animals. A cow may not be able to keep up with such demanding levels for too long. But worn-out cow meat is not popular in Britain. The cow who was forced to give her best for your bar of dairy milk chocolate may well be sent off on an horrendous journey to a slaughterhouse, perhaps overseas.

Source material: Peter Roberts of CIWF and the Vegan Society

What You Can Do

Slaughter

* Make as many people as possible, by any means possible, aware of the true facts about meat. Dispel the delusion that slaughter in Britain is humane. If you are able, go and see for yourself.
* Support organizations campaigning for the welfare of farm animals and humane slaughter. Support the Vegetarian and/or Vegan Societies.
* Become a vegetarian and spread compassion and non-violence by example.
* At least initially cut down meat consumption.
* Deluge the Ministry of Agriculture with letters asking why their apathy on humane slaughter issues.
* Supply your MP and your Euro MP with information on the present inhumanity of the meat industry and demand that he takes action.
* Write to local newspapers with the information you now have.

Urge the RSPCA to take up this very important issue.

The dairy industry

* Support Compassion in World Farming.
* Support the Vegan Society.
* Cut down on dairy products as much as you can or, better still, cut them out of your diet.
* Protest to MPs and EuroMPs about the gross wastage involved in this industry – butter mountains and milk lakes.
* Arrange showings of *What Happens to the Calf*, a film made by the Vegan Society.

The battery system

There is no reason why the British government cannot implement a phasing out of the battery system in Great Britain. It is up to the British public to press for it:

* Eat fewer eggs and buy only free range.
* Support CIWF, FREGG and Chickens Lib.
* Complain to the Trading Standards Department in your area if you see eggs misleadingly labelled.
* Write to your Euro MP asking him to support the abolition of the battery cage.
* Write to your MP.
* Write to the RSPCA encouraging them to make more prosecutions against battery farmers, stating that it should be under the *1911 Act*.
* Spread CIWF and Chickens Lib posters and literature to counter the £3,000,000 egg promotion.
* Offer some of CIWF's small labels – designed to conform with the consumer protection law to retailers selling battery eggs. Armed with these, the consumer can label the retailer's produce 'Genuine battery eggs'.

Organizations to Join

Farm Animal Welfare Co-ordinating Executive (FAWCE)

FAWCE is a joint body of farm-animal-welfare societies, which arose from Animal Welfare Year (1976/77) and the 'Put

Animals into Politics' campaign (1978/79).

It was in April 1977 that Animal Welfare Year wrote to all societies concerned with farm animals, inviting them to attend a conference to discuss how progress might best be made in that area. The Food Animals Conference held in 1977, under the chairmanship of Robin Corbett, MP, resulted in the formation of the Farm Animal Welfare Co-Ordinating Executive with Robin Corbett as Chairman.

It had been felt that there were enough interested societies to set up a joint body so that they might work together with their common aim. Such a body was felt to be valuable for the exchange of ideas it would bring, and the consolidation of viewpoints, as well as being available to give advice. Such a body would also have direct access to the relevant minister, something which an individual society finds hard to achieve. FAWCE now represents about a dozen societies, together with some independent members.

FAWCE's terms of reference state that 'the committee shall discuss, investigate, review and make recommendations upon matters relating to the improvement of conditions and/or protection of animals, birds and fish used for the production of food or farmed for other purposes.' The functions of the committee are set out as being:

1   To encourage and facilitate the exchange of information between member organizations.
2   To discuss, review and recommend legislation and regulations concerning food animals and their welfare.
3   To monitor, study and inquire into trends in methods of farming and alert member organizations and the public where action is needed to give further protection to animals.
4   To initiate campaigns or to co-ordinate campaigns of member organizations whether directed at the public, press, Parliament or the industry.

FAWCE was very active in the campaign to abolish the export of live food animals for slaughter or further fattening; it published an excellent report on Pre-Slaughter Stunning and Slaughter Methods which was submitted to the Minister of Agriculture. Since its submission, slaughter has been included in the remit of the government's Farm Animal Welfare Council. FAWCE has also been invited to comment on sundry proposed pieces of legislation and has done a good deal of work in publicizing the Council of Europe Convention on the Protection of Animals kept for Farming Purposes.

The Minister of Agriculture gave a firm undertaking that it was his intention to comply with the principles of that Convention. Such an undertaking given to Parliament is binding, whatever party is in power, unless and until it is formerly revoked. The aim of the convention is described as being to 'secure conditions that shall be in conformity with the physiological and ethological needs of the individual animals'. As Damaris Hayman, secretary to FAWCE, has said:

> Clearly pressure is going to be necessary to ensure that the government abides by its undertaking and FAWCE is urging supporters and the public in general to do all they can to stress the obligation to phase out extreme systems such as battery cages, veal crates and sow stalls, which are not in line with the Convention. This phasing out will, we hope, eventually cover all the EEC countries, which should also ban imports from countries employing such unacceptable methods.

The societies currently comprising FAWCE are: Anglican Society for Animal Welfare, Animal Welfare Trust, Catholic Study Circle, Compassion in World Farming, Dartmoor Livestock Protection Society, Farm and Food Society, FREGG, Friends' Animal Welfare and A/V Society, World Society for the Protection of Animals, RSPCA and the St Andrew Animal Fund.

Compassion In World Farming (CIWF)

In 1967 ex-farmer Peter Roberts together with like-minded people, founded the campaigning organization Compassion in World Farming. He, his wife Anna, Grace and Ivan Cook and the solicitor who helped them to form the public trust decided that, although vegetarian themselves, the organization would not be for promoting vegetarianism, but would call for support from a much wider section of the public. In a society which demands milk and meat, they knew that they could not make the changes they wanted overnight, and so would campaign for 'a square deal for animals'.

The first thing published was a broadsheet, which spelt out short- and long-term aims. The long-term aim was to seek an alternative to meat:

> Meat eating [said Roberts] is so ingrained in the population, we thought that if we could give a non-cruel substitute, we could cut down on the amount of meat eaten. To reduce meat was a definite aim. For example, that people might have a free-range joint at the weekend, and soya for the rest of the week.

Eventually, CIWF asked for marketing rights in Britain for a soya substitute made in the USA – 'Protoveg' which became the first soya protein on the British market. And so CIWF, itself a charity, also has a marketing company attached to it. Set up with a loan, the company now helps to keep the charity running.

CIWF is concerned with the agricultural aspects of the total environment. It seeks to introduce non-violence into our relationship with farm animals, wildlife, the plant kingdom, and the soil itself.

In the short term, it campaigns against cruelty of factory farming, and it calls for mandatory standards in order to get a square deal for the livestock during their rearing, transport and slaughter.

The long-term programme calls for less reliance on animals altogether and makes the point that this will release available food resources to a greater number of people, particularly the Third World. CIWF have suggested that the best agricultural land should be switched from animal feed production to the growing of crops for direct human consumption.

CIWF's campaigns are really twofold: pressure-group activity and educational work. The pressure-group activity is aimed at arousing public demand for improvement in the protection given to livestock by the laws of this country and of the EEC. Its educational work is carried out by visits to schools and by providing audio-visual material through the educational circuit.

They have also produced two documentary films and teaching kits, and in addition, a bi-monthly newsletter, *AG* is sent to a considerable number of secondary schools. A new film has also been produced which is specifically for use in junior schools.

An important leaflet, 'The 10 Mandates' which sets out 'an eclectic summary of requirements for intensive animal farming applicable to creatures kept for food and clothing' produced by CIWF, could productively be distributed among friends and neighbours. It helps make known the plight of the factory-farmed animals to those who remain unaware of the tragic lives of the animals the law neglects.

CIWF has had some successes. The largest veal producer in Great Britain who owned a considerable number of veal farms was the target for a good deal of CIWF propaganda. In 1980, he began taking out his veal crates and rearing calves in a loose system. He stated that CIWF was his severest critic and invited Peter Roberts to a press conference in which he said that the market for veal in this country was held back by the stigma of cruelty. Only when rid of this stigma, could veal be sold. He introduced new straw pens with twenty calves to a pen and took on no new veal crates.

He confirmed better results with the new system and also found that a sick calf, put in an isolation pen for fear of the spread of infection – that is, into solitary confinement – invariably meant that it would die, despite infra-red lighting and straw. He then began to pen sick calves next to the others who were milling around. They began to survive. A calf needs the companionship of its own kind. This was a staggering thing for a farmer to admit, because the Ministry of Agriculture, veal producers and the NFU officially say that calves must be reared separately because of disease. But Peter Roberts says that it is non-ventilation which makes calves sick. One wall of their housing should be taken out and replaced by netting. Calves were not designed to live in centrally heated houses. The same can be said for pigs. CIWF argues that outdoor pig keeping is in no way less profitable than indoor, but pig farmers seem hard to convince.

CIWF is also campaigning for straw yards and an aviary system to replace the battery system. It is hoped that European legislation will eventually lead to the phasing out of the battery cage.

But the fight is hard and long. The last people to admit they are wrong are the Ministry of Agriculture. Says Peter Roberts:

Because of their name, the Ministry of Agriculture has responsibility for the science and practice of agriculture in this country. They hold the land in trust. There should not be maximum exploitation of animals. But in fact they advocate exploitation. The present situation has grown up out of greed.

Compassion in World Farming is an excellent, steadily campaigning organization which is well worth supporting for its humane principles and constructive work. The newsletter is always informative and factual.

Compassion in World Farming (CIWF), Lyndum House, Petersfield, Hants. GU32 3JG.
Also Mail Order meat substitute products from:
Direct Foods Ltd., Petersfield, Hants GU32 3LT, or shop direct from The Bran Tub Wholefood Shop, 20 Lavant St, Petersfield. 15 per cent discount cash and carry from Direct Foods' Petersfield Warehouse.

The Farm and Food Society

The Farm and Food Society attempts to work constructively in the field of farm animal welfare and 'to encourage a feeling of responsibility for the lives of the creatures who serve us'. Founded in 1966, the Society declared its wish 'to establish a voluntary organization which would work for farming which is humane to animals, wholesome for consumers and fair to farmers'.

The Society states that it 'recognises the essential part which agriculture plays in the national economy and in the whole ecological movement'; its work is educational, but it is actively involved in trying to create a 'social climate which will enable farming to combine the best traditional methods with wise use of technology . . . towards a non-violent system of farming in harmony with the environment, with as many people as possible involved with the land.' This would, it is felt, in turn 'improve the quality and safety of food and the living conditions of stock, while providing employment for people of all standards of intelligence, reducing pollution and conserving an attractive way of life now threatened with extinction.'

Such eminent people as the late Dr E.F. Schumacher have been patrons of this society.

It aims to back those producers who farm in accordance with its principles by helping them to market their produce and make efforts to safeguard them from unfair competition. Action is also taken to protect consumers against misleading advertisements, and pressure is exerted for better food quality.

It works politically, by maintaining contact with MPs, the press, and government departments, and is affiliated with other organizations – the International Federation of Organic Agriculture Movements and the World Federation for the Protection of Animals. It is represented on the Farm Animal Co-ordinating Executive (FAWCE), the Humane Education Council, and the Animal Welfare, Scientific Development and Health Committees of the National Council of Women.

The Society produces documents which are exchanged with the Council of Europe and the European Commission and other international bodies. It keeps up a steady contribution of letters which are published in the farming and veterinary press and has supplied background material for various articles and radio and television programmes. It publishes a quarterly newsletter which contains useful information. Some informative literature has also been produced, which is extremely readable and factual.

These two booklets should be purchased from the Society: 'Environmental Pollution by Modern Methods of Livestock Production' and 'Agriculture and Pollution'.

Membership is open to the public. Any donations go towards a fighting fund which 'maintains constructive work'.

Farm and Food Society, 4 Willfield Way, London NW11 7XT.

Chickens Lib

Chickens Lib is a pressure group campaigning for the abolition of the battery cage for egg-producing hens; pressing for legislation which will outlaw this system.

Violet Spalding and her daughter, Claire Druce, first became aware of the plight of battery hens in 1973. They had no intention of starting a society, but a pressure group developed which now has over 1,500 supporters throughout the country, with many contacts in other countries and the support of several MPs.

Chickens Lib is a direct action group totally against violence to achieve its aims. A newsletter and factsheets provide subscribers with a wealth of reliable, up-to-date information, and projects to hit specific targets are mailed to supporters three times a year.

Chickens Lib now believes that legislation currently in existence is probably adequate to protect egg-laying hens, but this remains unimplemented on the most grotesque scale. It works for the rights of hens in co-operation with FREGG and Compassion in World Farming, to get these rights taken up in Parliament and to bring information to the public, while bringing pressure to bear on large companies – such as Goldenlay and Marks and Spencer – and the Church, the latter to acknowledge and express concern about the cruelty of battery egg production.

Supporters are kept regularly informed and are encouraged to take an active part in campaigns.

Chickens Lib has managed probably more than any other organization to awaken public awareness to battery hens. Its single-mindedness and constructive action tactics are effective and encouraging.

Chickens Lib, 6 Pilling Lane, Skelmanthorpe, Huddersfield.

Free Range Eggs Association (FREGG)

FREGG is an association of farmers, shopkeepers and anti-factory farming enthusiasts who have decided that they want to do something practical to decrease the sale of battery eggs.

Many people do want to purchase free-range eggs, even if they cost a little more. The government's weary old argument about the public not being willing to pay higher prices is entirely suspect: in 1978, the Egg Authority asked for government and EEC approval for the killing of 2,250,000 hens with the object of increasing the price of eggs (FREGG newsletter, January 1979).

Although about 90 per cent of eggs are now produced from batteries, many people dislike this form of egg production. FREGG makes the point that we cannot yet advertise as in the

United States 'Fresh from the Cage'. The slightly less blunted sensitivities of the English prefer to be duped into half believing that jolly hens are clucking happily in green fields. School children are the especial victims of the egg industry's purposeful deceit tactics. 'Fresh Farm Eggs' is the best known great deceiver – a common sign in the English countryside. Some retailers are not even sure how their eggs are produced and may be victims of deception from producers.

FREGG consists of a group of volunteers – whose activities are unfortunately severely restricted through lack of finance – who wish to promote the sale of free-range eggs by inspecting genuine farms and putting them in touch with retailers who then receive the FREGG sign – a hen's head in a yellow triangle – which can be displayed with the eggs. A contract is signed when the display is handed over to the retailer in which he undertakes not to use the sign to promote any egg sales other than those approved by the Scheme, to return the sign to the Scheme on request and not to pass it on to any third party.

Farmers applying for inclusion in the Scheme are asked to fill in a questionnaire as to their methods of husbandry and to sign a contract confirming that they do not mutilate the birds, feed routine antibiotics or hormone supplements, that all their birds have access to outside runs, and that they will keep stocking density at a moderate level. They undertake to inform the Scheme of any changes in their methods of husbandry and agree that violation of this contract makes them liable to forfeit £50. Contracts are renewable every year and FREGG inspects farms every 12–18 months. Genuine free-range farmers are put in touch with shops, but there are apparently far more shops wanting free-range eggs than farmers to supply them.

FREGG supplies members with a list of recommended farms and shops, but these are never included unless they have been visited personally by a FREGG representative. Keeping a check on producers and retailers must be a formidable task, especially for such a small association, and to a certain extent the farmers' and shopkeepers' integrity must have to be relied upon, yet it is hoped that the FREGG Scheme encourages that virtue as their cause is based on moral principles rather than the immoral ones of the battery farmer.

FREGG produces a newsletter for members in which, it is good to note, it supports, publicizes and endorses the activities of other organizations fighting the anti-battery battle.

FREGG needs a human battery of helpers. Membership subscription is minimal.

FREGG, 39 Maresfield Gardens, London NW3. Hon. Secretary, Mrs M. Battcock.

Protect Our Livestock Group (POLG)

POLG is a small pressure group based in Cheltenham dedicated to the abolition of Live Food Animal Exports. Founded in 1973, it has worked steadily to collect and disseminate facts and has printed three informative, illustrated booklets, 'The Moral Point', 'Humanity Zero' and 'Illgotten Gains' together with a few newsletters and bulletins. POLG has worked hard to distribute these throughout the country and all of its literature has been sent to every government department, to MPs, religious leaders, trades union leaders, chambers of commerce, butchers, farmers, dealers and more. By 1980, POLG could state that it had 'completed an umbrella-coverage of factual information to every section of the community.'

Farmers, long-distance lorry drivers who carry animals and even some dealers have voluntarily expressed their disgust to POLG at the suffering involved in the export of live food animals: 'it will be a good thing when this filthy business ends and we can return to the carcass meat trade,' one farmer admitted. During an exhibition in Cheltenham where POLG had a stand, many of their visitors came to make confessions about the inhumanity of their own trade.

POLG takes its mobile stand around the country, collects signatures for a petition against live exports, takes part in demonstrations and continues to bring pressure on MPs and the Ministry of Agriculture. It clearly states that so long as the live export flourishes POLG will continue to publish the facts and figures, 'and will ensure that this protest is distributed on behalf of the electorate throughout the corridors of power.'

As the government made £90,813,074 from the sale of 1,030,803 animals to foreign slaughterhouses in 1982, there is an enormous battle ahead. In 1975 combined pressure from the public and all animal welfare organizations brought the government to a so-called 'free vote' in the House of Commons on the Live Exports Issue. The decision to continue with the trade was taken on a relatively small majority of votes. Those MPs who voted against the ban must carry the responsibility for the suffering of millions on their long journeys to death.

Protect Our Livestock Group, PO Box No. 255, Cheltenham, Gloucestershire GL52 6QH.

The Council of Justice to Animals (CJA) and Humane Slaughter Association (HSA)

This society began as two organizations which amalgamated in 1928. The Council of Justice to Animals was formed in 1911 to promote humane methods of slaughtering animals for food and to provide for the painless destruction of cats, dogs and other animals when necessary. The work of the Humane Slaughter Association is revealed in its title.

After the two had joined together, the society campaigned at national and local government levels for the use of humane pre-slaughter stunning methods, including electrical systems for poultry, for the abolition of special exemptions based on religious grounds, for the provision of purpose-built livestock markets and the prohibition of the export of live animals for slaughter abroad. It has also worked 'at ground level' giving practical help such as financial aid in the building of new sidings and cattle pens at Merklands Wharf, Glasgow, for handling animals imported from Ireland. It has also demonstrated the use of the captive bolt pistol both here and abroad and has sent equipment to many other countries.

In addition, it has provided financial assistance as well as advice for improvements to livestock markets and has made short training films demonstrating various methods of slaughter.

In 1979, it sponsored a symposium on 'The Humane Treatment of Food Animals in Transit' and, in 1980, gave financial support for the Ammerdown Group Seminar on 'The Transport and Slaughter of Farm Animals'.

It pursues its conviction that all food animals should be rendered insensible to pain before slaughter. To this end, it demonstrates humane slaughter methods in abattoirs, investigates the treatment of livestock in markets and lairages, and in transit, provides financial support for research and development of improved stunning or slaughter equipment and of transport vehicles used for animals, and advises government, the Farm Animal Welfare Council, the industry and local authorities where it can, on the treatment of animals for slaughter.

Brian Parkinson, its current Secretary, is not a vegetarian, but a licensed slaughterman, an ex-RSPCA inspector, and joined the Society in 1975.

The Society provides a yearly newsletter, sent out in the spring and publishes an annual report and accounts in September, which is sent to all members and associates.

Convinced vegetarians may not think this organization is for them, yet many supporters of humane slaughter are vegetarian, simply because they face the reality of the current tragic situation. About 90 per cent of the population of the Western world still eats meat. It is also as well to bear in mind that conditions in slaughterhouses abroad are often even worse than our own, and those who travel, as does Brian Parkinson, along with others, trying to convince people in other countries to adopt more humane methods, are doing valuable work which idealists as well as realists would want to see done. The 'humane' slaughterman is the lesser of two evils in what, for the slaughtered, must be an evil world.

CJA & HAS, 34 Blanche Lane, Potters Bar, Herts EN6 3PA.

The Vegetarian Society of the UK Ltd

Vegetarianism was not organized in Great Britain until the nineteenth century. In 1807, Reverend William Cowherd, founder of the Bible Christian Church in Salford, began to promulgate the idea of not eating flesh foods. Two of his colleagues and followers together with others, sailed for America and formed the nucleus of the American Vegetarian Movement, while Joseph Brotherton, MP, also a follower of the Reverend Cowherd, became a president of the Vegetarian Society and his wife published the first vegetarian cookery book. Vegetarian societies grew slowly during the next 150 years.

Towards 1969 there was a strong urge within the vegetarian movement to create an umbrella society which would unite all fields of animal welfare under one organization. But such an ambitious plan never got under way. However, the two main societies in London and Manchester did merge and also managed to bring in a number of smaller autonomous vegetarian societies by giving them branch status. The ideal still has not been achieved as there are many smaller vegetarian societies which still remain autonomous, but which are listed in 'The Vegetarian' (the society's bi-monthly magazine). Since the 1969 merger, however, national membership numbers have more than doubled.

The Vegetarian Society is an educational charity which sees its teachings as the basis of the solution to all animal welfare/ rights issues. Logical, if oversimplified, the argument runs that if we were all to become vegetarian then we would straightaway eliminate the cruelties of factory farming and slaughter. In turn, people would be far healthier and research on animals would not be needed – for drugs, pesticides, food additives and so on. In addition, there would be less money spent on the Health Service. The food shortage problems of the Third World would be solved and there would probably be less violence in our society.

The facts are that it takes 3lbs of grain to produce one pound of poultry or 10lb for one pound of beef. In Eastern countries about 90 per cent of the cereal crop is consumed directly for food. The average for the world is 40 per cent, in Britain and Western Europe it is 30 per cent and going down, while in North America, it is only 14 per cent.

We import cereals, soya beans, other oilseeds and fishmeal as sources of protein to feed food animals from countries which are already short of food. Further protein imports come from North America which in turn makes for a dependency on American policies. Starving *Africa is actually exporting beef to Europe* as is Central America to the United States. There would be enough food to feed the world if the demand for animal products were reduced. There is no necessity for either factory farming or for the huge amounts of chemical fertilizers and pesticides we use or for deforestation, all of which impoverish the world for all of us.

To eat meat we are not only slaughtering millions of innocents, but we are downgrading the quality of our lives, we are making ourselves more unhealthy and we are robbing poorer nations of their daily bread.

The work of the Vegetarian Society is divided into three areas: animal rights and welfare, food reform – or promoting the use of whole, organic, rather than processed foods – and helping the food problems of the Third World. It is a 'non-aggressive' society which 'hopes to educate the public to a better way of living' and feels that if vegetarianism is correctly followed, it is the complete answer.

The Society is solid rather than sensational, and tends to aim at education rather than propaganda but realizes that to a certain extent it has had to update its image and thinking, releasing itself from the traditions of its nineteenth-century origins.

In the animal-rights field it is advancing step by step – several symposia have been held since 1979 and also in that year came the first of the annual marches to Smithfield which attracted a good deal of media attention.

The society now has an official research section and a cookery section, both of which are extremely active. On the educational front it produces a great deal of reliable literature and 7–10,000 free information packs have been mailed to enquirers each year. In 1976 food charts were prepared in response to the demand from schools and colleges and in 1977 weekend courses were introduced for instruction on specialized food topics. In 1979, three seminars for teachers were held in Exeter and London and the Youth Section that year designed a mobile display which visits libraries throughout the country. A basic information sheet is available for teachers and students which publicizes the encouraging fact that vegetarianism is now being studied in Britain's schools, and that it is one of the topics set in the Food and Nutrition examination for the Scottish Certificate of Education at A level. (Special packs for home economics teachers and schools are available.) In addition, the society's Campaign for Real Bread has promoted consumption of wholemeal bread in place of white – which they hold to be an adjunct to the meat industry as food animals are fed what is taken out of the flour to manufacture white bread.

The Research Section of the society is extremely active and has sponsored many important projects in recent years covering such issues as the nutritional values of certain plant foods, health (or lack of it in vegetarians) including an investigation of alternative agriculture systems based on plant foods at Aston University, a project at Oxford University dealing with the links between meat consumption, heart disease and cancer of the colon (the first results were published in the Lancet in 1979), co-operation with studies at London University on liver metabolism in vegetarians and co-operation with Oxford University for a ten-year study to compare the health of vegetarians and non-vegetarians. Member volunteers are co-operating in tests relating to vitamin B12 and there are further tests in London University on volunteers for the essential amino acid taurine, to find out whether vegetarians are synthesizing their own. Support is being given to Oxfam which is sponsoring a vegetable gene bank which helps to keep stocks of plants with different attributes. These are only some of the projects with which the society has been involved. The former semi-voluntary cookery demonstrations have been organized and given continuity through the food and cookery section: in 1981, regular residential courses aimed at professional caterers were introduced at the Manchester headquarters, Parkdale.

A national organizer for cookery courses was appointed in 1982 and evening classes are held in the Marloes Road premises in London. The foundation series of courses leads to the Cordon Vert Diploma 'in recognition of a thorough knowledge of the principles of vegetarian cookery'. Course instructors are of a high standard and include professional caterers, teachers, television demonstrators, cookery writers and nutritionists who will also demonstrate at all kinds of functions and events.

In addition to its ongoing activities, the society's scientific advisor, Dr Alan Long, has produced some excellent hard-hitting papers including the 'Green Plan' which was submitted to the government in 1978 in preparation for its White Paper 'Food from our own Resources'. Here is an extract from its introduction:

The original Green Plan was launched in February 1976 after much thought and discussion, but with little effect, during the late Sixties – the spirit of 'you've-never-had-it-so-good' overwhelmed its thrifty ideas: however, in the early Seventies buying of grain by the Russians accentuated the precariousness of the world's food supplies, so other organizations and writers, as well as ourselves, began to be heard. The message was reinforced by increasing concern in the affluent West over the diet-induced diseases. Rather than the all-too-familiar shifts and turns of spatchcocked agricultural programmes, Green Plan set forth long-term proposals with the intention of involving consumer and producer in feasible and worthwhile reforms. Moreover, the public was showing signs of dismay over intensive farming ('If it moves, kill it; if it doesn't, spray it') and the slaughter at least of endangered species of animals, so the time was ripe to embody the traditional compassionate reasons for vegetarianism in practicable suggestions for living well with dwindling consumption of meat and dairy-produce. This represented a fulfilment of the Vegetarian Society's slogan 'Live and Let Live'.

In 1979 the *British Medical Journal* published an article by three eminent nutritionists suggesting a 'Prescription for a better British diet': it bore some similarity to the proposals of the Green Plan, which was considered in the ensuing correspondence. The nutritionists prescribed, among other reforms, a reduction by 15 per cent (equivalent to a meatless day in each week) in the consumption of meat. Adoption of this change would reduce the slaughter of animals by 55 million a year.

All the factors prompting the original development of the Green Plan have increased in importance, although Britain's peculiar role as the world's major importer of feed and food (and thus its appropriation of foreign acres) is still taken too lightly; yet it takes a dock-strike of barely a week or two to precipitate a state of emergency, with our farming our most vulnerable industry. Britain certainly should heed the Green Plan's injunction to producers: grow food, not feed, for need not greed! If our manufacturing and service industries fail to yield funds for imports, our food supplies will be precarious. In 1979 Britain was spending £4,000 million (net) on imported food and feed.

The last paragraph of the Green Plan sounds a hopeful note if only governments could take both an humane and longsighted look at the future:

After a period of much reduced livestock-production, as

described for the first phase of Green Plan, it will be possible to live well in the vegan way, exploiting no animals. This would realise the Vegetarian Society's motto 'Live and Let Live', and its function would cease – except perhaps to assist the few remaining slaughtermen who would be looking for new work.

The Vegetarian Society welcomes new members, especially active ones and responds with information to those just beginning to think about the issues.

The Vegetarian Society of the UK Ltd., Parkdale, Dunham Road, Altringham, Cheshire WA14 4QG.
The Vegetarian Centre and Bookshop, 53 Marloes Road, London W8 6LA.

Sources: Information on history from Maxwell Lee, 'The Vegetarian View'. John le Grice, Deputy President, Vegetarian Society.

The Jewish Vegetarian Society

The Jewish Vegetarian Society was founded by Philip L. Pick in 1976. His daughter Vivian was attending the Royal Academy of Music at the time and became interested in the number of vegetarians she found at the college. Concerned that the Jewish religion had lost sight of its original teachings and feeling that the greater part of cruelty to animals was to do with the eating of flesh, Mr Pick established the Jewish Vegetarian Society, affiliated to the International Vegetarian Union.

He is of the opinion that the Jewish religion has been corrupted into becoming a faith ruled by the stomach. He has set down his views, with good evidence taken from the Old Testament and the Talmud, in an excellent and informative paper entitled, 'The Source of our Inspiration', copies of which are obtainable from the society. He maintains that before Noah and the Flood, it was a capital offence to kill an animal, that animals were given equal status. He provides interesting pieces of information such as the fact that Orthodox Jews have blessings for all life's benefits – all kinds of food, new clothes etc. But there are no blessings for meat – something slaughtered cannot be blessed – and no blessing may be made over furs or any animal skins. You cannot destroy creation and then bless the Creator for providing.

The Society exists to:

* make known the many beautiful Jewish teachings in which the non-carnivorous way of life is advocated and to emphasize that the eating of animals involves the individual in a cruel and obscene traffic;
* advocate living on the pure and wholesome foods provided by Nature;
* foster the concept of respect for all life as a link between peoples of every creed and nationality;
* organize cultural, social and other activities, and to provide information as to vegetarian facilities on culinary, health, travel and other matters;
* advance the cause of vegetarianism as being the only solution to ensure sufficiency of food production for the world's population, and for restoring universal peace and harmony;
* keep close contact with the Movement in Israel with its vegetarian villages and its high proportion of vegetarian population.

The society now has a flourishing branch in Israel and hopes that Jerusalem will eventually become the headquarters.

It produces a quarterly magazine *The Jewish Vegetarian* which contains some very informative articles. An anthology of these articles is available as a hardcover book, *Tree of Life* from the society.

Full voting membership is open to practising vegetarians and to those who are in sympathy with the work of the society. Associate membership is available.

The Jewish Vegetarian Society, Bet Teva, 853/855 Finchley Road, London NW11 8LX.

The International Vegetarian Union

The International Vegetarian Union holds biennial conferences at which vegetarians from all over the world have a chance to meet together and exchange ideas. The Vegetarian Federal Union was formed in 1889 to bring together all vegetarian societies – local, international and foreign. Until

1950 all of the IVU work was done by honorary officials, but through the generosity of Mrs Clarence Gasque of California, permanent headquarters were established in London with a paid full-time secretary and the international movement now has affiliated centres in many countries.

International Vegetarian Union, Mr Maxwell Lee, Hon. Sec., 10 Kings Drive, Marple, Stockport, Cheshire SK6 6NQ.

World Vegetarian Day

1 October is now World Vegetarian Day. 16 October is World Food Day dedicated to the implementation of the vegetarian ideal. 24 October is UN Day:

> UN Day is perhaps an occasion when we should stop and give thanks for our freedom from war. A time to consider those people who know nothing of lasting peace, who starve, who are oppressed and are exploited. The International Meat Trade is a wasteful trade; where people need grain for their own consumption instead this is fed to animals, which in turn satisfy the craving of meat-eating man in the affluent areas of the world. By adopting a meat free diet, we boycott the international meat trade, and help ease social injustice throughout the world. (The Vegetarian Society of the United Kingdom)

The Vegan Society

The Vegan Society was formed in 1944 by a group of vegetarians who realized the cruelty involved in milk production. Its first secretary, Donald Watson, took some time to find a name but finally chose vegan – which has now been absorbed into the language and appears in Websters International Dictionary – from the first two, and last three letters of vegetarian. This is quite appropriate, for as he said, veganism sprung from vegetarianism and was taking it to its logical conclusion.

A few people suffered health difficulties at first, for it was not until 1948 that vitamin B12 was isolated. The body should manufacture its own B12 in the intestines – only a few people find difficulty in producing this vitamin in their own bodies because of human dependence on animal foods for so many hundreds of years.

B12 taken as a vitamin supplement is not synthetic, but is made from bacteria. Vegans take B12 grown on a plant base in a laboratory. Once the B12 enigma was solved, nutritionists had to agree that a vegan diet can be very healthy, providing a wide variety of nutrients.

There are now second- and third-generation healthy vegans of which the society can be justifiably proud.

The Vegan Society is steadily growing; it has gained over 1,000 new members in 1983 and now has members in 42 countries, while there are 54 local contacts in Britain, each with their own group. Their journal *The Vegan* has a circulation of 5,700.

The society's main objects are to further knowledge of and interest in sound nutrition, to promote veganism as a way of life, by promoting the vegan method of agriculture and food production which will be of physical, moral and economic advantage to mankind.

It has worked towards the abolition not only of foods from animals, but also of commodities, especially those coming from slaughterhouses. To this end, many Vegan Trade Lists, information leaflets and recipe sheets have been issued over the years. The society has also helped to promote and support manufacturers of wholly vegan products, such as Plantmilk Ltd, who have often experienced difficulties when introducing new products onto the market.

The adoption of veganism could solve the world's food problems as well as creating an humane new world.

Information: The Secretary, Vegan Society, 47 Highlands Road, Leatherhead, Surrey.

4 Animals in Entertainment

Cruelty to Animals in Films and Television

It probably does not occur to most people that there have been hundreds of animal victims sacrificed in the name of entertainment. A few become stars whom the public take to their hearts and are protected by their fame. The stuntman chooses to play with death, the animal victim is drawn into something which has nothing whatsoever to do with him.

From the earliest days of the film industry, little attention was paid to the wellbeing of the animals used. They were regarded as 'props', used to produce immediate impact.

The reports of some films show that we have not much progressed beyond the days of the Roman arena in all its brutal agony:

> The production unit was singled out for its apparent complete indifference to the suffering inflicted on the animals it used. This is particularly true of the 'sunken road' sequence in which 'French cavalrymen' are supposed to tumble down a steep embankment. 'Variety' reported on . . . ditches . . . clogged with dead horses.[1]

This was Columbia's *Waterloo* (director, Sergei Dandarchuk, producer, Dino de Laurentis, with Orson Welles, Jack Hawkins, Virginia McKenna, Christopher Plummer and Rod Steiger — it must be said that not all actors necessarily know what is happening in scenes in which they do not take part).

'A total of five horses were killed – one was literally blown up

[1] ISPA Report: 'A Case for the Statutory Control of the Use of Animals in the Motion Picture Industry.' London, June 1976.

– and four others destroyed as a result of injuries – a steer had its throat cut and there are scenes of illegal cockfights in the film.' So reported the *Standard* in May 1981. That was Michael Cimino's $20,000,000 *Heaven's Gate*.

Irresponsible producers and directors and actors whose world too often seems to end at the outer layers of their epidermis will sometimes use animals as if they were cheap and disposable. There *are* honorable exceptions – James Mason turns down any film which might possibly involve any suffering or distress to animals, Clint Eastwood will allow no cruelty whatsoever and David Carradine has a special clause in his contracts that all animals must be treated according to AHA (American Humane Association) standards. Too many others remain shamefully silent.

However, many people working in the film industry are quite unaware of (a) the situation and (b) the problems.

Apart from the various forms of violence to animals which filmgoers see on the screen – and it can be argued that even simulated gruesome scenes of violence just shouldn't be shown – the most common form of abuse involves horses, cattle and buffalo.

Four obnoxious devices have been commonly used for fall effects. These are:

1   The 'running W'. This is a nasty arrangement of cables attached to a hobble on the animal's front legs. It will be put, or scared, into a full gallop. At the desired point, its legs are swept from under it, precipitating a heavy and unexpected fall, often with the full weight of the animal, and its rider, being taken on its head and/or neck.

2   The 'pit fall'. This is used for the same effect. A pit is dug and refilled with soft earth and/or sawdust. The animal is galloped at full tilt into this, bringing it down again heavily.

3   The so-called 'unsupervised fall'. An untrained horse is pulled over and down by the skilled rider throwing his weight from the saddle and pulling violently on the reins.

4   Hidden trip wires are also used to produce similar effects. Horses are very sensitive, highly strung animals. A properly trained horse ridden by a skilled stunt rider will fall onto its side. A horse which falls artificially may somersault and therefore suffer from shock, very likely injury and possibly death.

In the growth years of the early film industry, animals were increasingly used in scenes of violence in which the viewer was unable to distinguish reality from simulation. Not all producers and directors were using cruel methods, but there was enough obvious wrong-doing to bring public pressure to bear on the industry. In 1940, the Motion Picture Association of America accepted a Code of Self-Regulation. This outlawed the use of such fall devices as those mentioned above, and prohibited the infliction of suffering or abuse of any kind on the animals involved in film production (along with cruelty to children and questionable morals). It also made provision for inspection by an independent body. The American Humane Association, then the largest national animal-welfare organization, was given specific permission to have an observer present during all filming where animals were involved. If an animal was obviously injured during production, the code review board could order the sequence deleted.

But in 1966 Hollywood put a stop to the censorship system of the Hays Office and the animal-welfare guidelines were dropped at the same time. Voluntary compliance was to be put in their place.

The old Code was replaced by a new, much more lenient one. The result was disastrous for animals – and the uncooperative directors refused to submit scripts to the AHA for scrutiny. Now there is a rating system; films are rated from X (objectionable material) to G (for general audience). There is no restriction on activities during filming, and only to a certain extent on what appears on the screen.

An article in *The New York Times* entitled 'They Kill Animals and They Call It Art' by T.E.D. Klein said that screen shocks didn't bother him, but misuse of animals did – 'their corpses fill the screen,' he wrote. The attitude of the 1960s film makers was 'shoot for real' or go for 'spectacular footage' and never mind what the animals suffer.

The situation today has become like that of 1939, which provoked a public outcry. It came to a head then with a scene from *Jesse James* in which Tyrone Power as Jesse James, pursued by a posse to a cliff edge, had to jump into the river below. For this, horse and stuntman were put on a greased plank rigged to trip them over the cliff. The stunt man survived, but the horse did not. An article by Michael Satchell in the American magazine *Parade*[1] stated that both on- and off-camera, ill treatment of both domestic and wild animals is increasing again. It ironically calls our assumption that injury or suffering to animals on screen is merely trick photography 'only another Hollywood illusion'.

Satchell disclosed that many horses are being killed or 'subjected to bone-crunching falls' by running W's which are again becoming popular. It also says that 'dogs have been strangled, shot or tormented, that exotic, even rare animals, from a giraffe to a rhino, have died through stress, ignorance or poor handling.' Wild animals which would naturally avoid each other have been forced to fight. Live chickens have been strung on nooses and dangled in front of big cats, rabbits have had their rumps rubbed raw, then splashed with turpentine to make them run fast. Terrified dogs have been staked down as bait for wildlife scenes in which big cats stalk prey. Docile wolves and bears have been beaten to make them ferocious.

Ingmar Bergman wanted to kill a horse on a set; when one of his actors, David Carradine, protested, *Bergman had it killed off the set and used the still warm carcass. He said he had also killed two other horses, burned a horse and had a dog strangled.*

Although the American Humane Association (AHA) maintains a Hollywood office and publishes lists of films stating whether animals have been treated humanely or not, directors have not been obligated to admit or heed their requests until very recently. However, in June 1981, good news came from Carmelita Pope, Director of the AHA Hollywood Office. She wrote:

In the recently ratified Screen Actors Guild/Producers Agreement, AHA was able to strengthen the language in the 'Cruelty to Animals' clause. It is now compulsory for the producer to notify AHA on use of animals, supply scripts of the action and allow us on *any* set. It is a great victory for us! Since the censoring Hays Office was dissolved in 1966, we have had no real authority. Although censorship no longer exists in this country, we shall at least be allowed on all the sets to supervise the animal action. There will still be problems, however, since we must educate our producers to

[1] Parade Magazine, *Chicago Post-Tribune*, 26 April 1981.

the fact that the clause does exist and must be enforced. It's a daily battle.

It is, however, more difficult to obtain cruelty prosecutions in America as their laws are more obscure and vary from state to state. (Most cruelty prosecutions in Britain are brought under the 1911 Cruelty to Animals Act.) However, in the new 1980 codified agreement devices such as the running W are not specifically outlawed and there are no definite sanctions if directors or producers ignore the contract clauses. Fines mean little to big-time directors and people who witness cruelty on the set are often afraid to speak up for fear of losing their jobs.

Another phenomenon of the 1960s was the amount of filming that took place in countries where there was absolutely no legislation to protect animals. If it existed, it was ineffective.

All the old malpractices were extended, particularly by the 'free expression' producers with excesses beyond the threshold of 'pain pornography', described by the American Veterinary Association as 'obscene', when it called for the total condemnation of what it called 'cruelty for pleasure'. The new freedoms of the sixties had both positive and negative results. Even now, when Spaghetti Westerns, for instance, tend to be filmed in Spain, obtaining information is difficult and it still tends to be less expensive for American films to be made outside America.

Certain films must remain forever condemned because of the outrageous callousness of their directors.

* Schaffner's *Patton*: In World War II two mules blocking a vital supply bridge were shot. In the interests of 'truth' this was duplicated for filming – the two mules were hobbled then given bungled injections which took a long time to take effect and from which they eventually died. In addition a donkey was clubbed to death, two calves were killed, a horse was killed by a small explosive charge tied to its chest, after being left injured in agony while the film unit took its lunch break.
* *The Mountain Men*: A Martin Ranshoff production for Columbia Pictures written by Fraser Clark Heston and starring his dad, in 1979. An R rated film, it involved some terrible horse somersaults with the use of toe-traps and running W's.

* *Tom Horn:* a Weintraub–Solar Production for Warner Bros starring Steve McQueen (1980). A horse was tripped with cables for a forward somersault fall and another horse was sedated to simulate a killing, but the AHA was not there to ensure that a vet did the job.
* *The Legend of the Lone Ranger:* a Martin Starger Production. Starger was extremely uncooperative to the AHA and personnel from the Santa Fe Animal Shelter were not allowed access to ensure the safety and protection of the animals. After certain pressures, two scenes were cut from the script, but some tripped falls were left included.
* *Heaven's Gate:* (already mentioned) a Partison $20 million production, distributed by United Artists, starring Kris Kristofferson, Christopher Walken, John Hurt, Jeff Bridges and Isabelle Huppert. The AHA was not allowed onto the set, Cimino ignored their requests, and it has a thick dossier of alleged cruelties. There is a law suit against the writer/director Michael Cimino, producer Joanne Carelli, and veteran Hollywood head wrangler, Rudy Ungland – a man with a nasty reputation for the way he treats horses – for permanent psychological damage and injury to the lead horse. Cimino was forced to eliminate two hours from the original script, but the inhumanity that has already occurred cannot be eliminated. At least five horses were killed, running W's were used and Cimino wanted real blood.
* Francis Ford Coppola's *Apocalypse Now* starring Marlon Brando (live water buffalo hacked to death) and *The Missouri Breaks* with Brando and Jack Nicholson (a horse drowned, tripwire stunts and a rabbit brutally killed).

Television films in America have also come in for criticism. In one wildlife film giraffes died from stress and poor handling. A cable TV channel in New York showed a nasty film of a small dog tied to a stake and shot to death with a rifle. 'The 30 second sequence was repeated for 30 minutes and presented as conceptual art . . . the "artist" had partially funded his *Shot Dog Film* with a grant from the National Endowment for the Arts' – a federal government agency which gives tax money to cultural projects.

Some other films mentioned in the World Society for the Protection of Animals' report were *Furtivos,* produced in Spain, in which a dog was trapped and beaten to death while being snared and half submerged in a waterfall.

QBVII: this film contained a shooting pigeon scene in which birds with clipped wings, unable to fly, were thrown in the air and shot at with blanks. Later, Bedouins clubbed the birds to death with rifle butts. This was in violation of the Israeli Cruelty to Animals Ordinance, but the remote location made it impossible for action to be taken until it was too late.

Apache: this film, made in Spain, used the 'unsupervised fall' a good deal. An eye witness reported noting one horse that did not get up again.

Pat Garrett and Billy the Kid: trip wires were used and so were 'pit falls'. Many horses were killed, or suffered injuries, such as broken legs, so that they subsequently had to be killed. Live chickens were buried to their necks in sand and used for target practice.

The WSPA has stated that it has 'no reason to doubt the veracity either of evidence or source' used in its report.

The British film industry is so small that there is little to worry about, but the RSPCA did successfully prosecute in the case of a film called *The Great Train Robbery* about the 1800s in which gambling with rats and a terrier was depicted with real fights.

A 1937 Act of Parliament forbids the distribution of a film in which animals are killed or injured or seriously ill-treated so that many films are cut. If the British Board of Film Censors is in doubt, it consults the RSPCA. This does have an effect, but it comes too late. The British Film Producers Association does have a code of conduct resulting from discussions with the RSPCA. This guide, circulated to all its members, states that experienced handlers and trainers must always be present when animals are used, but the code is, of course, not enforceable by law.

The RSPCA has made approaches to Equity and hopes that a sub-section might be created for animal handlers and trainers so that a proper standard could be set up and maintained. If Equity insisted then these would be used on all TV programmes and in all films involving animals. The trainers and handlers would have to be of a certified standard.

Dorothy Steves, well known showbusiness dog trainer and owner of Radar who starred in *Softly Softly*, would welcome handling and training to be given specific professional status. It would improve the standards of trainers and the conditions in which the animals perform.

The way in which animals are used in television filming is the responsibility of individual producers and if not cruelly treated, they are often misused. In the filming of the series *Anna Karenina*, a horse was given a dangerous drug called immobilon when it was anaesthetized so that it could be seen lying on the ground after a jump. It does have an antidote but, being highly toxic, can produce side effects and has caused death in some horses. It is lethal to humans. (One vet died accidentally, having pricked himself with the needle while using this drug on a horse and one vet committed suicide with this drug some years ago.) The RSPCA is totally opposed to its use other than where necessary in bona fide veterinary practice.

The popular series *All Creatures Great and Small* used two veterinary advisors – one of them said to be 'notorious'. While the series did in some ways aid public awareness of animals, certain effects were produced in very questionable ways. Immobilon was used during the making of the series. The vet involved let the crew film an operation, stating that he had a portable surgery with him, but the RSPCA considered this prostitution of the profession. David Williams, a veterinary officer with the RSPCA has confirmed that many series are produced in a similar manner.

People are eager for their pets to appear on television. A dog or cat left in the studio all day can be shut up in a basket for hours on end with no food, water or consideration – which amounts to negligence. Stress and fright during the actual studio appearance are potential hazards, which can be avoided if special provisions are made.

To avoid such eventualities there should be a code or a law, whereby a producer must consult the RSPCA before making a programme which includes animals.

Equity in Great Britain should press for contracts to contain a clause about animal abuse of any kind and we are hoping to work within the Writers Guild to persuade British writers to play a part in changing attitudes to animals, both in feature films and on television.

In America, the AHA has been giving PATSY (Picture Animal Top Star of the Year) Awards since 1951 to recognize noteworthy performances by humanely trained animals in motion pictures. The awards signify skill and ability in animal handling and mark compliance with AHA Standards in the treatment of animals. These are intended to call public attention to the value of kindness to all animals – one rat, named Ben, twice won the award.

The main weapon against unthinking, insensitive and even sadistic directors, and the producers, film companies, actors and crews in their train, is publicity. The American Humane Society would like to see its 'unacceptable' list reaching the mass-movie audience, not just its 2,500 branches, some local film councils and the PTA so that sweeping decisions could be made to boycott films in which cruelty has taken place.

One *New York Times* writer wrote:

Whatever the eventual effects of such carnage upon our psyches and our society, it may be worth reminding ourselves that Hollywood's bullets are blank. But for the animals, the bullets and the knives and the blood *are* real; and more and more directors are using the deaths of innocent creatures to provide shocks their films might otherwise fail to deliver.

Let us hope the day is not too far off when, after every film which includes animals, the words will be put on the screen: 'No animal was killed or mistreated for the purpose of making this film.'

Source material: ISPA report 'A case for the Statutory Control of the Use of Animals in the Motion Picture Industry', 1976.
Information given orally from David Wilkins, RSPCA veterinary officer.
Additional information from the American Humane Association, Los Angeles Office.

A Pandora's Box of Nasty Tricks: The Circus

Stefan Ormrod (RSPCA wildlife officer): I presume African elephants stand on their heads in the wild.
Dick Chipperfield (circus proprietor): Yes, of course they do.

The circus, in various forms, has been with us for a very long time. We can look back to ancient India, as far as 3,500 BC when Indian princes would stage performances for the public by both men and animals. The circus remained in India and is still a popular form of entertainment today. Later, Assyrian and Babylonian kings began to show off their menageries, especially the trained lions which were used in battle. In such shows, as many as a hundred lions might be let loose on crowds of Bedouin victims. Such was their circus.

The ancient Egyptians had a rather more gentle approach towards animals which they revered in their culture and religion. They tamed and trained wild creatures, but held them in greater respect than some of their more barbaric neighbours.

The glitter and superficial glamour of the popular show of today still hides an element of darkness, both real – for the animals – and hoped-for, imagined, as the human performers exercise their 'daring' skills. Is it not a very similar crowd of people that likes to watch a man among half a dozen supposedly savage cats and watches the tightrope walker with baited breath?

Those feeling hearts who already have the gist of my meaning can, however, be comforted. The circus as we know it is going into decline; its disease is deteriorative. The symptoms are seediness and withering caused by lack of nourishment and rejection. Many former benefactors have penetrated to the darkness behind the lights and their testimony is spreading. The death will be quite painless and the gap left will be so small as to hardly be noticed. The passing will leave many hard-pressed animal-rights workers a little more time to get on with other very urgent matters.

I hadn't visited the circus since early childhood until the Spanish Circus came to Hereford in 1982. This is a desperate attempt by Robert Bros, English circus owners, to attract publicity. The performance, mostly by English people with an apparently Italian master of ceremonies, was so third rate as to discourage the most enthusiastic child. The seats were two-thirds empty.

We can only ignore the abject misery it causes its animals so long as we are unaware of the true facts.

The elephant is a much-used circus animal. In his book about elephants, *The Dynasty of Abu*, Ivan Sanderson, FLS,

FZS, FRGS, botanist, geologist and zoologist, says of these creatures: 'In the face of the Abu we stand before one of, if not the, greatest of God's creatures – ourselves not excepted.' He mentions the age-old belief of the orient that elephants have their own primitive religion – that they worship the sun and the moon. He tells how many wild creatures can be seen standing silently every morning and evening, usually around dawn or sunset, whether the sun is visible or not. He describes the overpowering maternal instinct of elephant mothers and the altruism displayed by these extremely intelligent creatures when one of their fellows is trapped or wounded.

Let us wander mentally for a moment to the rising heat of the African bush in the midst of Nature's abundance, where creatures – when not being hunted by two-legged predators – rejoice in their existence. And then let us return to a grey, damp evening on Clapham Common; a muddy car park, an oversized tent looming up in the twilight. Walk around to the back of it, to a smaller, unlit tent and peer inside. There, chained to the ground, gently rocking from side to side, you'll see two or three oversize prisoners of man's perverted sense of fun. They don't tear at their fetters or exercise their might, but in their natural surroundings they would be walking slowly for many miles each day for their exercise. The swaying simulates the slow gait natural to them. Their only exercise now is when they are pushed into the ring, forced to perform to a timetable, and pushed out again. Fear has bound their minds about as surely as if they were locked into a steel cage.

About sixteen circuses remain in Britain and it can cost £10,000 a week to keep one on the road – a figure quoted recently by Dick Chipperfield.

Circus owners maintain that they rely on animal acts to bring in their audience, yet there are circus people who feel that the show is just as good, if not better, without these poor imitation humans. With television we now have ample opportunity to see wild animals: their presence in the circus should be a thing of the past.

It was the lifelong ambition of Tamara Hassani, daughter of Coco the clown, to have a circus of her own, using only human skills and now we have the Hassani Circus, which was initially subsidised by the RSPCA. It is a success and is now self-sufficient.

There are three other circuses which do not use any animals – the Circus Oz (Australia) which toured England in 1981, the Great Circus of China and the International Circus Competition held in London annually.

In January 1975, Bexley Heath, Kent, banned performing animal acts. A petition of 1,200 signatures was presented to councillors supporting the ban which stated: 'We are doing an injustice to our children to let them watch these magnificent animals degrade themselves by performing unnatural tricks.'

A survey was carried out in four junior schools of the older children up to age eleven. 420 children were asked 'Do you like performing animals in circuses?' More than two-thirds of them preferred trapeze artists and clowns. The children said they preferred to see wild animals in safari parks where they could move around in natural conditions. Many thought there was cruelty to animals.

Dick Chipperfield, a traditional circus owner, obviously sees his animals as money-earners: he stated on television that 'people do not come if you don't have animals'. We must, therefore, judge the rest of his argument for the use of animals in the ring in the light of his basic monetary interest. He maintains that during training he bridges the gap between man and animal, that he establishes a 'relationship' with his animals. But we must surely bear in mind that a relationship can mean a bond of anything from love, indifference to hate. He says he breeds his own animals, that he is 'preserving more animals than all the conservation societies put together'. (Note that lions are an abundant animal at present. He owns quite a few of those). He conveniently forgets that circus animals are living in a totally deprived environment, that because of the stressful existence many captive animals who are representatives of dying species do not breed. But, to quote David Hancocks (*RSPCA Today*):

It is impossible that the activities of circus animals can ever achieve any worthwhile goals in either education, research or conservation. They must always rely on a show of man's dominance over the animal, and will inevitably always present a distorted view of wildlife. Therein lies their futility.

Despite being bred in captivity, the drives and instincts which have taken so many millions of years to evolve cannot simply disappear in one or two generations. What is the point, we must ask, in preserving animals simply in order to make them look rather ridiculous? At the turn of the century groups of 'sane' ordinary people were paying a penny to go and look at the lunatics in asylums for their Sunday entertainment. . .

Dick Chipperfield also maintains that there 'has to be a commercial place for an animal in the world today,.whether as a tourist attraction, performing in a circus, on view in a zoo' etc. To that we must ask *why*? Why must humans see *life* solely in terms of economics?

A major consideration is the degree of confinement endured by captive animals. A beast wagon (a lorry trailer open only on one side) 20ft x 8ft x 6ft may house seven polar bears, one 30ft x 9ft x 5ft may hold thirteen lions. In these, the animals will not only travel but will spend most of their lives, apart from perhaps two short performances a day.

Apart from the confinement, indignity and deprivation suffered by these performers, aspects of overt cruelty during training must be considered. It has been admitted by a spokesman for the Association of Circus Proprietors of Great Britain (not an independent body) that cruelty can, and probably does take place in training but not, it is claimed, if the circus is a member of the Association.

In training for circus acts, sticks and goads with spikes or nails concealed in them are known to be used. It is impossible to prove whether they are in regular use or not, but many circus animals regularly show fear, rather than compliance. I myself watched animal keepers/attendants at the back of the ring in the 'Spanish Circus' in 1982 jab at the elephants' hind quarters with a nasty spiked stick as they paced around and as they left the ring, despite the fact that the poor creatures were behaving perfectly. It looked suspiciously like an act of gratuitous violence designed to endorse fear and the master–slave relationship.

Moreover, circuses can engage acts for just one season and it would thereby be impossible for the Circus Proprietors Association to be aware of all methods used in the training of these animals. It is also impossible for their officials to be aware of what happens to the animals twenty-four hours a day. Performing acts are interchangeable internationally and, as

well as the question of transportation, it is not possible to vouch
for training methods used in other places.

One RSPCA reporter wrote:

> I sat near the animals' entry and exit tunnel cage, however,
> and he (a magnificent tiger) was prodded viciously in the
> belly and ear by the well-armed attendants who were lined
> up to move animals quickly on and off. This is now a scarce
> animal, I thought, and this is the use to which we put him. . .
> The largest tiger was drawn up to a height of about 11m (35')
> on a swinging, lonely platform amidst the flashing arc lights,
> then lowered again. It seemed a pointless exercise.
>
> There were lions (rather young-looking), more young
> tigers and a cheetah. All performed their well-learned tricks
> and afterwards the audience cheered, but it occurred to me
> that the applause had been louder and longer for the white-
> faced, baggy-trousered clowns.
>
> A lonely bay horse galloped round the ring and skipped
> over blazing stakes – its legs among the flames. This
> beautiful animal had to crown its indignities by kneeling in
> the centre of the ring. . . . Next came what was, for me, the
> saddest and most tragic thing of all. There were 5 elephants
> and the biggest one had to climb onto a tub. He didn't
> particularly want to, so an attendant tugged on his ear (a
> very sensitive organ) so hard that he was almost hanging
> from it, while another was busy striking at the hind legs of the
> other elephants to get them to kneel . . . then walk forward on
> their knees. . . . We should be kneeling to you, I thought, to
> ask your pardon.[1]

Pointed sticks used to be used as goads and sometimes still are,
but nowadays you will often find blunt-ended sticks which look
harmless, but are electric and designed to give a shock when
jabbed under the tails of large animals. Such things are used to
keep up the strictly timed flow of a performance, but are often
decorated with ribbons or flowers in order that their real
purpose be hidden.

All kinds of provocation are used to make animals perform in
the way their masters wish. One *Daily Star* reporter saw a

[1] 'On with the Circus', leaflet printed by the RSPCA.

kangaroo being slapped in the face for ten minutes to make it 'box' before it was taken into the ring to fight a clown.[1]

Bears – which should be roaming the Arctic wastes – are often to be found in circus rings. (Dick Chipperfield told the above mentioned newspaper that 'animals like these don't need exercise'.) These creatures have a tender spot on the nose and short lead-bodied weapons are always held at the ready to exploit this fact. Irene Heaton of the Captive Animals Protection Society remembers visiting Smarts Circus at Bristol on a *hot summer day* where she saw nine polar bears with absolutely no water. They were licking each other's saliva in great distress. When she asked the attendant why they hadn't any water, he replied that 'they had a hose over them once a day and that was quite enough'.

The *Daily Star*, which to its credit, often takes up the animals' cause, claims that one of its investigators who managed to get himself temporarily employed in the Circus Hoffman, saw lions and a tiger jabbed in the face with a sharp steel-tipped instrument, lions beaten on the paws with a heavy steel rake, other caged animals hit in the eyes with the sharp bristles of a yard brush, bears confined in a 'tiny dark cage' and animals left unwatered and unfed for days, their attendants seeming to take some kind of sadistic delight in their behaviour.[1]

Whips and goads are but one part of the harsh training process. Obviously the trainers are not going to injure or damage their assets to an undue extent as they would no longer be an asset to them. But according to RSPCA experts, 'baiting, luring, triggering of escape and aggression impulses or direct physical force are used to make the animals perform the required movements repeatedly until eventually all that is required is the appropriate "trigger". Methods and degrees of force depend on the species being trained.'

Fear can be ascertained by such things as variation in blood pressure and heart rate, ear and tail movements, facial expressions, body postures and vocalization. Large cats can often be seen in the ring, crawling, their bellies almost on the ground – rather like a cowed dog – ears flattened, sometimes snarling loudly. All these signs indicate one thing – fear. An ignorant audience may mistakenly admire the trainer's daring

[1] *Daily Star*, 28 April 1980.

when it sees a lion or tiger pawing at the whip, but aggression –
as in humans – is an immediate response to fear.

Anyone who has studied the basics of animal behaviour will
know that a threatened animal – including the human animal –
has what we call a flight response. If the 'attacker' comes within
the flight distance of an animal, it will attempt to run away, but
in circumstances in which this is made impossible for it – that is,
confinement, it will show fear and make a 'low intensity threat'.
If the attacker/intruder continues to approach once that point
is reached, then the distance becomes critical and the animal,
feeling very threatened, will find itself with no choice but to
attack.

Animals born in captivity have the smallest flight distances,
as they are used to human contact, but they will never really
lose those instinctive responses, just as we humans have not lost
them. Some animal behaviourists distinguish between 'wild'
and 'tame' by referring to 'secondary flight distance'. The tame
animal may allow its keeper to touch or stroke it, but faced with
unusual situations, it will react just as it would were it still wild.

The following is an extract from an interview I had with
Richard Waller, African and Indian wildlife expert and
photographer in which he makes this point quite clear:

> Pre World War II people tended to look upon all wild
> animals as very dangerous and savage. But no animal is.
> They would certainly never kill a man of which they're
> practically all frightened except in certain situations where
> man gets himself far too near . . . I lecture widely on tigers
> and always point out that no animal is dangerous unless man
> makes it so – by wounding, by intent to kill, or just by being
> stupid and going too near. As we approached one tiger in a
> tiger sanctuary in Central India, she could smell humans,
> but was anyway aware that something was annoying her,
> when she was wanting to go to sleep. She was growling. We
> were 40–50 yards away. As we approached, nearer, the growl
> intensified and if we'd gone even nearer, she would have
> snarled and become much more ferocious. Eventually it
> would have become a roar, when she would either have gone
> right off, or a 50–50 chance, she might have charged, but if
> you allow an animal to do that, you only have yourself to
> blame. They speak as plainly as we do with human speech –

'get away'. The elephant will do the same – put its ears back and trunk up, and so on. You should not go near these animals until you know their language.

Richard Waller not only explains very clearly about flight distance, but he also gives a picture of wild creatures living their own lives their way, in their own territory. Imagine how it must be for such magnificent creatures to be imprisoned, goaded, oppressed, forced, and all for a few silly tricks. By what right do we steal the freedom of the wild for a few cheap laughs?

In their wild state, many species would never soil the places in which they sleep and eat, yet in confined conditions, they are forced to do so. In addition, they are deprived of their family and tribal life which they would enjoy in their natural state.

Before an animal is trained, it must be tamed. There are two ways of taming animals – which Ivan Sanderson calls subjugation and tantalization, but he feels that there is only one way of training - by the reward method. It is said that a combination of 'stern discipline and pain combined with sentimentality and over-indulgence' is the only plain method clear to animals being trained. Moreover, 'in training mammals, discipline is not enough; you have to be brutal; otherwise the discipline will not be understood . . . you have to hurt it so much (without doing bodily harm) that it comes to fear you and to such an extent that it never forgets just how brutal you can be.'

The trainer is forever telling his victims *we have ways of making you perform*. In his book *Zoovet*, David Taylor wrote:

At first hand I have seen bears encouraged to move from travelling box to circus ring by lighted newspapers thrust beneath them, and I have heard the regular sickening thuds as a chained African elephant was beaten systematically with bamboo rods by two keepers to break it by literally torturing it until it collapsed. The most repellent feature of the process was the calm clinical way in which the keepers administered the beating. It was a job, just like grooming, which called for a repetitive movement for long periods of time. Of course when the police arrived the men were indeed grooming an elephant. Bamboo rods applied with all a man's might across the rib-cage of an elephant leave no marks. . . .

The audience marvelled at the obedience of the little apes and smiled as the trainer fondled their hairy heads. It was all in the fondling. The man showed me his thumb-nail, which had been allowed to grow long and then filed into a vicious point. It was strong and horny and he used it with cruel skill to gouge and twist the sensitive flaps of the chimpanzee's ears. It was really a display of brutal sleight of hand carried on in full view of the public. I was to find that this method of controlling chimps by their delicate ears was commonplace in the world of chimpanzee training; even mature specimens were subdued by the agony of a quickly applied hold.

Stefan Ormrod, wildlife officer with the RSPCA stated that he

bathed the cuts on some young elephants that were undergoing 'subjugation' – being acquainted with the feel of chains about the feet and being taught to obey the commands of a human master. I even saw one of these 'masters' beat an elephant about the head with an iron bar simply because it was slow to understand that it must sit on a pedestal.

Circus animals undergo a good deal of refresher training and it is this which MPs and other investigators are invited to see, *not* the initial training. Such sessions are, moreover, always strictly by appointment only. Many RSPCA inspectors have attended performances and have reported suffering in circus animals over a period of many years, but 'unnecessary suffering' as stated in the law (1911 Protection of Animals Act) is very difficult to prove in this case and trainers defend their treatment of the animals by pleading necessity, the law being totally inadequate to cope with the situation. This makes a ban on performing animals an absolute necessity.

We know that for an elephant, being made to stand on the front legs amounts to cruelty. For 'liberty horses' necks pulled down by tight reins and prolonged walking on hind legs causes pain and strain on the muscles, tendons, ligaments and skeleton. The horses are often kept tightly tethered outside the ring.

Smaller performing animals often live in their owners' caravans and lead a rather better life than the larger beasts, but most of them are controlled by the same kind of discipline as the larger animals. They too, may suffer deprivation, being confined for the larger part of the day. Life can sometimes be just as bad for them as it is for the wild animals, however. *Daily Star* reporters saw two large poodles used to ride on the backs of ponies, imprisoned in cages less than 4ft high and 2ft wide.

The Performing Animals (Regulation) Act 1925 deals mainly with the licensing of trainers who are not required to specify how or by what means their animals are trained. The law safeguards circuses from spot checks by local authorities and the police, and this would also include animal-welfare societies.

This law includes nothing about cage sizes in which the performing animals must live and nothing about the conditions under which they are transported. It takes absolutely no account of the mental or emotional suffering and stress undergone by circus animals, something now widely recognized by zoologists and animal behaviourists.

The Captive Animals Protection Society states: 'Therefore it is impossible for us to bring a successful prosecution on the evidence of cruelty that we have in our files.' The RSPCA has managed to bring only two successful prosecutions against circus owners in recent years.

The above mentioned 1925 Act was the outcome of a Select Committee Report in 1922 set up after a Private Members Bill was introduced which reflected the then growing public concern over the treatment and exploitation of animals in circuses. This committee recommended that all persons who train animals, as well as the places in which they are trained, be registered and that powers of inspection, without previous notice, of such places of any exhibition, be granted to certain individuals, local authorities and the police (not, however, the RSPCA). Various other powers were proposed but also not incorporated in the Act.

Sixty years on, many of those recommendations remain on the shelf and the legislation is still upheld as holy writ, despite growing public concern against circuses and increased specialist knowledge.

It is also strange to note that under the Zoo Licensing Act 1981, zoos are under an obligation to keep their animals in regulated conditions, whereas circuses remain unjustly exempt and continue to house their animals in intolerable conditions.

RSPCA prosecutions taken under the 1911 Protection of Animals Act are concerned with physical suffering and obvious cruelty. Mental and psychological cruelty, deprivation and stress are not included.

It is not only immensely difficult for investigators and animal-rights workers to gain up-to-date evidence, with two witnesses and a veterinary surgeon present, but what is and is not cruel is far too open to arbitrary opinion. Mary Chipperfield, for instance, does not object to anyone seeing her bring a horse to its knees by ropes being pulled on either side of it to make it collapse. In her opinion, this is not cruelty.

The main provision of the 1925 Performing Animals (Regulation) Act was that 'No person shall exhibit or train *any* animal unless he is registered in accordance with this Act.'

This distinguishes a performing animal from a household pet, but the Act itself *protects* the *cruelty* rather than the animals.

It is interesting to note the following from the 1925 Statutory Rules and Orders (No. 1219) on Performing Animals: 'Form of application for a Registration Certificate to Train and/or Exhibit Performing Animals'.

Column 8 Describe briefly the general nature of the performance or performances in which the animals are to be exhibited or for which they are to be trained, mentioning any *apparatus* which is used for the purpose of *performance*. The description . . . need not give details which would divulge any professional secret.

Note 'any apparatus which is used for the purpose of the *performance*'.

It can be seen from this that props, utensils, instruments or weapons need not be divulged, nor seen or examined by the authorities.

During a reading of the 1965 Bill, it was said that 'there is no definition of cruelty'.

To prosecute a person using a goad, for instance, that person actually using the instrument must be prosecuted. By the time the case comes up in court – which could be a six months' wait – the man may have left the circus, or his colleagues would close

ranks and state that he had left and it would be quite easy for
him to disappear.

Miss Irene Heaton of the Captive Animals Protection
Society tells how a former employee of Smarts Circus who
looked after the fifteen-strong elephant troupe gave her
interviews on the cruelty he had witnessed. First employed as a
driver, he was then asked to take care of the animals during
their winter season. He told how many a time he had to take a
bucket of Jays fluid to wash the wounds of elephants as they
came out of the ring. He also told how he had seen circus
performers literally beat an elephant around the ring in their
spare time just for sadistic amusement while the circus was at
its winter quarters. After eighteen months, he was so sick of
what he saw that he left.

David Taylor, the Circus Proprietors' Veterinarian,
published his book *Zoovet* in which he condemned most
circuses, before he accepted this post. He stated that most
circus people were quite adept at deceiving RSPCA inspectors.
Now that he is employed by the circus, he has changed his
opinion and condemns only what he calls the 'tatty, smaller
circuses', and goes to local council meetings to argue in favour
of the circus against the campaigners.

This man may now be doing his job as well as he can, but on
his own admission, he visits circus owners twice a year on
average and spends 70 per cent of his time overseas, working in
zoos, so it is impossible for him to oversee all the members of an
association.

Jim and Marjorie Sutcliffe, officers of the CAPS, have done
their best to investigate circus cruelty over many years. Twelve
years ago, the Moscow State circus went to Bellevue in
Manchester. There, they found bears confined in individual
wooden crates in what was nothing more than an old garage
with no windows and no space for moving about. The bears
were making a distressful noise because they had been hit.
When they wrote to the noted impresario, Victor Hochhauser,
who had put on this particular show, his reply was that nothing
illegal was happening.

In 1982, a Russian circus, appearing in Monte Carlo, *boasted*
that its bears had been caught in the wild.

Miss Heaton saw chimps in Smarts Circus in Bristol in
empty cages obviously experiencing psychological deprivation.

The mother chimp sat pathetically hugging her baby to her.

Beneath Blackpool Tower, there are dungeons with no windows. It is there that many circus animals spend a great deal of their time. The public were formerly allowed to view them there – they can no longer do so. It is unnecessary to ask why. . . .

There is a fair amount of comment from veterinary surgeons available and especially interesting are remarks made in 1981 by John McKenna, MVB, MRCVS, who was called to Dick Chipperfield's circus when it visited Cheltenham in 1980:

> Apparently the elephants suffered burns in a fire when the circus was based at Weymouth and several had nasty burns – wet ulcerating sores exacerbated by the flies during particularly warm weather at this time. One elephant was recumbent and had the worst blemishes and I attempted to treat her but she unfortunately died after a few hours.
>
> The circus had been here several days when veterinary help was summoned and I was amazed both at that fact and also at the apparent lack of basic animal welfare that was so lacking in the management of these unfortunate elephants and their burns, eg. being tethered outside with no shelter from flies and no annointing of the wounds with fly repellent antiseptic applications.

One veterinary surgeon, G.W.R., B. Vet. Med., MRCVS, whose full name cannot be published for professional reasons, wrote the following in July 1975 after visiting a well-known British travelling circus. We have no reason to believe much has changed in the interim:

> The animals I found contained in a makeshift 'Zoo' attached to the 'Big Top', the 'Zoo' itself being open to the public on payment of a minimal entry fee.
>
> As a qualified Veterinary Surgeon, and as one whose objectives have always been to prevent or relieve suffering wherever it may apply to the animal kingdom, I can honestly say I was literally made to feel quite sickened by the disgraceful conditions and total debasement which the majority of the animals were subject to.
>
> I was particularly concerned about the trailers housing

the big cats and the bears. The absolute confinement of these once proud creatures, the inhumane and quite unbelievable conditions in which these creatures were housed and the physical appearance approaching malnutrition I found quite atrocious.

I am aware that certain minimal requirements are in operation for the housing and rearing of the majority of those animals intended for slaughter and ultimately human consumption and feel that where totally wild animals are brought from absolute freedom into captivity they should at the very least be allowed certain exercising facilities with adequate food and water rather than the extreme confinement for what must be 23 hours a day combined with barely a maintenance ration. I would also be interested to know to what extent veterinary treatment is available for these animals, as from purely casual examination, I noticed 3 animals with lesions in need of attention:

A polar bear with acute keratitis of the right eye in danger of losing that eye altogether unless treatment was instigated without delay.

An elephant with an abscess on its trunk.

A Himalayan bear with a large purulent abscess.

In conclusion I can say I would wholeheartedly support any formal investigation and would be quite prepared to stand by my observations and comments at any time.

Dr Desmond Morris, author of *The Naked Ape* has written:

Many animals are so tenacious of life, so desperately flexible that they can survive in minimal conditions, but bare survival is not enough. There was an excuse for it once, centuries ago, when we were ignorant of the fascinating details of animal life and looked upon animals simply as brute beasts provided for our pleasure. But we have come a long way since then and the mediaeval menagerie should not be more than a memory, an historical record, an ancient monument.[1]

England now leads in the protest against performing animals in

[1] Desmond Morris, 'Must We Have Zoos? A famous zoologist answers Yes. . . But', *Life Atlantic Magazine*, 9 December 1968.

circuses – as far as we know, there are few protests in Europe. Conditions in other countries are even worse than they are here. We are in the vanguard of the movement against this albeit minority, but needless, suffering. Because the circus is now gradually dying and because the public are becoming aware of the true facts and more and more local councils are banning circuses with animal acts from their lands, the circus owners are worried. Until two years ago, their newspaper, *World's Fair* published an itinerary of appearances, but they have now reduced the publicizing of appearances because they are afraid of demonstrations. More and more people who have been, and are, against circuses are emerging, asking what they can do to help. In 1957, when CAPS started its campaign, not a single local council was interested in their arguments. Now over fifty councils including eleven London boroughs have refused the use of their land to a circus containing animals. The case is sometimes hard to put – sometimes our task is akin to that of Amnesty International. Torture cannot always be proved. But the fact of imprisonment can.

The Labour party claims that it will ban performing animals if and when it comes into power.

If the performing animals circus is banned, the animals can be suitably taken care of and proper provision should be made for them, no matter the cost. The circus owners should be legally made to pay. There are not too many of them – there are probably not more than thirty elephants in all. After the kind of service they have given, the animals deserve a decent retirement. They certainly do *not* deserve to be put down and I do not believe we are in a position to judge whether death would be the better alternative for them. Most important of all is the fact that no more of these animals should be born or taken into a life in which their only future prospect is one of degradation, unbearable confinement and abject despair.

Virginia McKenna has commented on the circus:

An animal is a beautiful part of the world in which we live, with more natural dignity than man can perhaps ever now attain. As self-professed champions of a free society let us allow animals their natural expression of life within a natural environment. What gives us the right to do otherwise?

Source material: Miss Irene Heaton and Mr and Mrs J Sutcliffe, oral material backed by documentation.
RSPCA Today, Winter 1980/81. *Daily Star*, 28 April 1980. *Anglia Reports* (Anglia TV programme on circuses). 'Animals in Circuses' (RSPCA leaflet). 'The Case Against Performing Animals' (CAPS leaflet). *On With The Circus* (RSPCA publication). 'Performing Animals' (RSPCA leaflet). Ivan T. Sanderson, *The Dynasty of Abu*. Richard Waller interview with Rebecca Hall. David Taylor, *Zoovet*. Particular help given by Miss I. Heaton and Mr and Mrs Sutcliffe of CAPS.

What You Can Do

Films and television

* Write to Equity and press for a sub-section for animal handlers and trainers to be formed in Britain, also for contracts to contain a clause outlawing animal abuse of any kind.
* Complain to the BBC or other television companies should you suspect that cruelty has occurred in the making of any programme.
* Write to the Writers Guild of Great Britain asking that British script writers include a clause in their contracts outlawing cruelty to animals in filming.
* Write for the black list to the American Humane Association, PO Box 77, Hollywood, Cal.90028. (The Association will also pass your views on the subject to the Motion Picture Association of America and to the major Hollywood studios.)
* Flood Hollywood with letters of protest – to directors, studios, actors.
* Organize pickets and boycott films in which it is known that abuse has occurred.

Circuses

* Join CAPS.
* Write to your local council giving informed objections. Ask them to lay the letter for the chief executive of the next council meeting or write to each individual member of the Council yourself. Ask them to refuse the application next time the circus wants to come to town.

* Write to your local newspaper whenever the circus is about to pay your area a visit and state your views clearly.
* Distribute leaflets from the RSPCA and CAPS.
* Go to the circus site and demonstrate.
* Do all in your power to influence the people in your area to boycott the circus.
* Some campaigners put stickers over the circus posters saying 'cancelled'. Some take the posters down, but that is a matter for individuals. CAPS does not tell its supporters to do this.
* If you are a teacher or on a PTA, discuss the matter. Children are both vulnerable and often very sensitive to the suffering of the animals once they know what is happening.
* Complain if the circus appears on television.

Organizations to Join

Captive Animals Protection Society

The CAPS was founded in 1957 by about half a dozen people who felt that the cruelty involved in the circus was hidden from the public by the glamour of the Big Top. CAPS, although a small society, gradually grew and in 1965 promoted Lord Somers' Bill (to safeguard circus animals and prohibit completely the use of many species), which was only narrowly lost in Parliament. From that time support came from groups throughout the country and from abroad.

CAPS, working together with other organizations, keeps up the pressure on the declining circus, with demonstrations, approaches to local authorities, exposure of circus cruelties and contact with the media. It is also in contact with hundreds of children who show increasing interest in the animals' welfare, giving advice to any who write asking what they can do to help ban animals from the circus.

CAPS, The Hon. Secretary, 17 Raphael Road, Hove BN3 5QP.

5 Horses

'One can only surmise why Patricia should be the leader, but perhaps it is because . . . in all her fifteen years [she] has never had a bit in her mouth, a saddle on her back, or carried a human being. Maybe the other horses recognise her free, unbroken spirit, her proud head and unbowed back. . . . My only regret is that I cannot throw open the Sanctuary gates and give her and her precious herd the Freedom of the world, to go where she will, to fulfil a natural destiny.' John Bryant, *Fettered Kingdoms*.

It was a daring and ambitious mortal, Bellerophon, who was the first man to mount Pegasus, the immortal steed, embodiment of the spirit of the horse. Bellerophon temporarily possessed him, but when he finally decided to ascend Olympus upon the horse's back, he was flung back to earth when the outraged Jupiter sent a gadfly to sting Pegasus, causing him to shy. Bellerophon was blinded by the fall; not only was he prevented from reaching the home of the gods, but never again could he mount the heavenly horse. Is there a lesson in this myth?

The horse has played a prominent role in the development of the human race and we know that the ancient Egyptians used them to pull their chariots as far back as 1700 BC, but asses were probably used by ordinary people centuries before. Since those ancient times when the horse was hitched to the chariot of war, it has been a forced partner in man's pugnacious activities and there are many stories of the bravery and intelligence of horses in the two world wars. But man soon forgot. . . .

Today, the suffering of horses, ponies, mules and donkeys is increasing and very little is being done about it, except by the few organizations and individuals who make it their concern.

Not only are they maltreated, neglected and bullied by ignorant owners, but they are victims of money-greed on the race course, the steeplechase course and in the showjumping arena; they are fed to madness, forced to make sometimes impossible jumps, pushed into danger and often inevitable injury for man's vicarious thrills and fed drugs like the notorious Butazolidin to keep them going when pain might otherwise have stopped them. Many a time, the injured, instead of being given long and caring treatment so that they might regain health and perhaps be released into rest or retirement, are immediately despatched by the bullet – the easy way out. Retirement has to mean care in suitable conditions, with warm, comfortable stables available; an old arthritic horse which has been used to stabling will be miserable if left in a cold wet field. Perhaps even worse is the enormous world-wide meat trade, not to mention horses used in cruel experiments. And remember the fuss over poor Sefton? At the Ferne Animal Sanctuary in Somerset, you can see an old military horse who would have been sent to the knacker's yard were it not for a few wrens, who bought him at the eleventh hour.

There are probably now more horses and ponies in Britain than there were at the beginning of the century as increased affluence has brought horse and pony ownership within the reach of more people. But irresponsible ownership and lack of knowledge about horses' needs has created a good deal of suffering.

The horse-meat trade is now big business – frozen horse meat exported from Britain in 1982, mainly to France, Belgium, the Netherlands and Italy, brought in £10,401,264. The tragedy is that there are now very few private buyers at commercial horse sales, yet still owners continue to breed.

Dartmoor ponies – which all belong to someone – are allowed to breed but the foals are taken at four months to sales and slaughter. It is estimated that 98 per cent of the ponies sold at the Annual Sales on Dartmoor have been slaughtered for consumption in this country.[1] Horse meat almost certainly goes into beefburgers, meat pies and of course, pet food. New Forest, Welsh and Shetland ponies are also rounded up regularly for

[1] Annual Report, 1982, Bransby Home of Rest for Horses.

slaughter – foals are often sold illegally as 'veal' in British butchers' shops. Mr Hunt of the Bransby Home for Horses, who attends many horse sales, saw one particular horse slaughterer buy 2,000 in one week. On average, this man kills 600 horses and ponies weekly. He sends horses surplus to his requirements to his brother to be killed elsewhere.

After a good deal of pressure from the National Joint Equine Welfare Committee, which is composed of twenty societies, the Ministry of Agriculture did issue a code of conduct for the treatment of horses destined for slaughter. But that code, although bringing slight improvements, has been largely ignored. Horses do not enjoy the same protection under law as farm animals which, as has been stated, are treated atrociously (see p.62).

As there are only four EEC-approved slaughterhouses (besides the many pet-food knackeries) for horses in England, they are often forced to travel long distances after being sold and this can result in much unnecessary suffering.

In addition, there are 'guinea hunters' who make money by buying at one horse sale and reselling at another so that these horses endure the extra stress of additional journeys but meet the same end.

Horses, ponies, foals and donkeys of all shapes and sizes are crammed into lorries with too few or no partitions. It is illegal for shod animals to travel like this, but it is done all the same. Consequently foals or smaller animals and tired or old ones get trampled, crushed and badly injured. This means nothing to the meat men, however, as they are still worth the same as meat.

It is now supposed to be illegal for horses to be exported live for slaughter from England but this still happens. To export horses, it is necessary to secure a permit but those exporting for an undesirable purpose can easily make a false statement. Until the Ponies Act was passed in 1969 – after several attempts – boatloads of ponies and foals were travelling quite openly from England.

New ponies up to 14·2 hands must not be exported unless they are over the minimum value rates but individual investigators have strong suspicions of a clandestine trade. There are no minimum values set for horses over 14·2 hands. It remains to be seen whether current suspicions will be proven and the criminals caught.

The story continues around the world. According to John Hoyt of the Humane Society of the USA, about 6,000 horses are transported and slaughtered for food each week in America.[1]

They endure terrible journeys in poorly fitted and designed vehicles – by rail, lorry and ship. In the rough, overcrowded conditions, injuries are an everyday occurrence – bruises, breakages and cuts. With no air conditioning they suffer extremes of heat and cold in addition to carbon monoxide pollution in the lorries and the stress of being forced into vehicles with strange companions with no previous acclimatisation. The horse's highly strung nature further contributes to his own suffering, for, when confined, he will panic and kick and bite, damaging himself and his companions.

In the last ten years horse slaughter has risen 2,000 per cent in the USA – about 17,000,000lbs are exported annually, mostly to Canada, France, Belgium and Japan. Horsemeat in America goes into pet-food, mostly for greyhounds.[2]

A federal law banned the export of live horses by water from the USA and so they now travel to the Canadian border before export overseas, with no regulations to cover their conditions in transit.

500,000 live horses, donkeys and mules pour into Italy each year from Greece, Romania, Yugoslavia, Poland, Russia (contracted to supply Italy with 180,000 horses annually) and also formerly from Uruguay until this was banned after a public outcry, in August 1983, only after there had been many deaths on board. Some already sick and injured or very old, are forced to endure journeys of hundreds of miles on rough roads in ramshackle vehicles and overcrowded ships, roughly handled and thoroughly abused. Chris Larter, a professional horse transporter, has done a great deal to bring the iniquities of this sordid trade to light, having herself followed consignments, watched their treatment and witnessed their condition. There are photographs of miserable horses, sick, weak, broken, being driven up the ramps. The Italians and the French, the Belgians

[1] WSPA Biennial Conference Speech, London, 1982.
[2] John Hoyt.

and the Dutch all consume large quantities of horsemeat as do those who in Britain gobble preserved sausage and salami into which those mangled bodies are pressed. However, English horses are now being flown via Shannon to Italy for meat and Irish horses go from Waterford and Cork to Europe by boat, yet the authorities say nothing. In September 1980 a horse was 'seen swimming strongly mid-channel'. It must have fallen from a small boat.

Because the Italians (minced horse, mule and donkey goes into spaghetti sauce) and French demand fresh horse meat, the animals must endure miles and days of extra agony. Even when vets are present – they mostly aren't – they are not allowed to give painkilling injections as this would make the meat unfit for human consumption.[1] The horses may be days without water and proper food.

Of the 12,000,000 animals conveyed annually to or from European countries, 360,000 are horses (classified as 'farm animals' once they are designated as meat). Of these 230,000 are imported by France and Italy.[2] Spain and Morocco also contribute to the horse trade.

Press reports and television films have had some effect and do worry the dealers, as does international opinion affect the governments responsible for making legislation. A French television documentary about the export of horses from Greece to Italy forced overnight action, so that horses no longer had to be certified unfit – they had previously been purposely maimed and disabled for export sale. This, although only improving conditions for the horses slightly, does demonstrate the effects of publicity.

Writing on her experience at the French–Italian border in 1978, Chris Larter reported:

> In another wagon there was a dead horse, which judging by its position with a hind leg halfway up the side of it, had got cast and been unable to get up. Its head was jammed in a corner and its rope halter had throttled it. By its condition and smell it must have been dead around 2 days. . . In the next wagon we heard a lone horse pawing . . . I discovered it had a completely shattered off hind leg, which was swinging

[1] See *Bunte* (German magazine) reports in 1980 and 1981.
[2] *Country Life*, 24 June 1982.

uncontrollably. When I asked for a vet to come and shoot it, I was told there wasn't one. . . These horses were from Yugoslavia and probably had a further day's journey in the death wagons before what would probably be an agonising death in some Italian slaughterhouse.

She has also seen horses in Australia forced to travel vast distances for up to three to four days with temperatures of up to 115°, often with little or no water. They are then subjected to callous abuse in the markets. Chinese horses go by sea to Japan to join the Japanese horses in a fattening ranch where they are overfed and have little or no exercise which causes laminitis (an inflammation of the feet). Most of them are killed by primitive poleaxe instead of humane stunning apparatus.

Source material: Mr Hunt, Bransby Home of Rest for Horses; Chris Larter, GAWF; Mrs Eileen Bezet, WSPA; ILPH Annual Report, 1978, with particular help from Chris Larter.

What You Can Do

* Write, expressing your opinion in a polite, informed way to the ambassadors at the embassies of the countries involved in the horse trade.
* Support the horse protection societies and the Anglo-Italian Society, the Greek Animal Welfare Fund, WSPA and Eurogroup (RSPCA) who are now all trying to do *something* to stop this traffic.
* Write to the Minister of Agriculture demanding legislation to protect horses bound for slaughter in Great Britain.
* Write to your MP and Euro MP informing him of the need for this legislation.
* If you own horses or ponies do not allow indiscriminate breeding.
* Don't eat Italian sausage; if possible don't eat meat.
* Rescue a horse at a sale only if you have adequate ground or access to grazing and hay, stabling and knowledge of horse care.
* Support the horse rescue homes – every little helps.
* Supply the facts to local radio and newspapers, especially if

you can visit a sale or can take photographs.
* Report all cruelty or neglect either to the horse societies or the RSPCA.
* Write to the RSPCA chairman of the council and ask that the society campaign more vigorously for horses both in England and throughout Europe.

Organizations to Join

Bransby Home of Rest for Horses

The Bransby Home of Rest for Horses has been in existence for some fifteen years rescuing needy equines. At present it has eighty-five under its care – horses, ponies, donkeys and two mules.

In addition to providing sanctuary for these animals, the home is active in trying to improve conditions for the native ponics on Dartmoor (where ponies are left in very poor condition), visiting, reporting on, filing complaints to government about and rescuing from horse sales up and down the country. Many cases of neglect are investigated.

The Home spends a minimal amount on administration and currently has plans for building repairs and the improvement of drainage to grazing fields.

Its London support group needs more helpers: 12 Abbey Close, Pinner, Middlesex.

The home runs an adoption scheme (whereby sponsors contribute to the keep of an individual horse or pony) and additional funds are always needed – the horse rescue problem is growing, *not* decreasing in Britain and thousands are going for slaughter.

The Bransby Home of Rest for Horses, Bransby Saxilby, Lincs LN1 2PH.

The International League for the Protection of Horses (ILPH)

The founder of the ILPH Miss Ada Cole, devoted her life to alleviating the suffering of horses after she visited Antwerp in 1911. There in the docks were line upon line of old and injured

English horses being led to slaughter. Behind those who could walk came others too weak to walk at all and some already dead, this their only reward for a long and strenuous working life.

Miss Cole's compassion was aroused. She joined with a Belgian humanitarian, a M. Ruhl, and followed the horses' journey from landing to death:

> Week after week, month after month, we saw the same terrible suffering. Horses landing injured or dead, falling on the road, trembling with hunger and exhaustion in slaughterhouse stables, screaming at cruel death, trampling, roped together in groups, throughout the night. And more than one a week was sold for vivisection for the instruction of students, where no anaesthetic was given.

Due to her efforts, a law was passed in 1914 by which horses could leave England only via five registered ports and only after they had been declared fit to travel.

After World War I (when she helped British soldiers across the border into Belgium) she continued her work against the trafficking of horses, founding her own society, the International League Against the Export of Horses for Butchery in 1927. She died disappointed and overworked in 1930.

In 1937, with promotion by the League, the Exportation of Horses Act was passed, and the League's name was changed to the International League for the Protection of Horses. It now seeks to promote all aspects of equine welfare at home and abroad.

Among its achievements since the 1937 Act have been: the procurement of various orders to protect horses during carriage by rail, road or sea; it has played a part in stopping the export of horses from the USA to England for slaughter; it also played a part in securing the Horses Landing from N. Ireland and the Republic of Ireland Order 1954, which protects horses imported into Great Britain while landing and in transit after landing; and also took part in the advancement of the Slaughter of Animals (Amendment Act) 1954, the Riding Establishments Act and the Ponies Act 1969. It also pushed for the closure of the notorious Vangirard slaughterhouse in Paris.

It has purchased thousands of distressed horses and where possible has restored them to health and placed them in good homes under supervision of the League. It also has its own homes for horses in Surrey, Norfolk, Bedfordshire and Co. Dublin, and has awarded scholarships for research into equine health and has assisted in blacksmiths' apprenticeships. The League also has branches and connections abroad where similar work is carried out.

The Hon. Secretary, International League for the Protection of Horses, PO Box 166, 67a Camden High Street, London NW1 7JL. Tel: 01-388 1449.

Friends of Bristol Horses Society

The Friends of Bristol Horses Society began in the 1950s when the Railway Authority in Bristol decided to dispense with its heavy horses as it changed over to motorized transport. The younger horses would be transferred to other stations in the country, but for the older horses, it meant a quick sale and possibly slaughter. The carterers were upset at this possibility as was a Miss Mabel Cocksedge, a member of the Railway Authority staff who made moves to start a society which might purchase the horses. Free grazing was offered by a horse lover to start rescue work.

Some years later, grazing land was bought and it was at that time that the society bought fifteen horses in Dublin, awaiting shipment to the Continent for slaughter.

The purchase of Staunton Manor House Farm enabled the Home to be officially opened in 1960. There were then eighteen horses; now there are over one hundred and horses are rescued from all parts of the British Isles, including many retired pit ponies from the Welsh coalfields.

Friends of Bristol Horses Society, Home of Rest for Horses, Staunton Manor House Farm, Sleep Lane, Whitchurch, Bristol BS14 0QJ.

The Horse and Pony Rescue Club

This rescue farm, the creation of Mavis Whinnet, takes in, and buys from sales when possible, horses and ponies. It is a small club, but has done some extremely good rescue work. Visitors and additional support would be welcome.

The Horse and Pony Rescue Club, Hillside Farm, Ashwater, Beaworthy, Devon EX21 5DN.

The Donkey Sanctuary

The Donkey Sanctuary was started by the Svendsons in the grounds of the Salston Hotel, Ottery St Mary in 1968. Its work rapidly grew and by 1973, it had increased so much that it was decided to apply for registered charity status.

The sanctuary amalgamated with Reading Donkey Sanctuary – which then housed 204 donkeys – when its owner Miss Violet Philpin died in June 1974 after thirty-five years of caring for donkeys. With so many new animals to care for, larger premises were immediately needed and so Mr and Mrs Svendson bought a 54-acre farm in Salcombe Regis.

The buildings were made into warm winter quarters and an intensive care unit for the very sick. By 1976, however, the larger premises were inadequate and a second farm of 127 acres with large barns was purchased 6 miles away.

No breeding is allowed at the sanctuary – stallions are gelded on arrival – but many of the mares arrive already in foal. These foals enjoy the full security of the sanctuary. Occasionally unweaned foals arrive from markets and are difficult to rear, but usually survive well on the milk from sanctuary cows.

Some donkeys are re-homed, but people who offer homes are first visited by one of the sanctuary's three inspectors and only the best conditions are accepted, and new homes are regularly inspected once the donkeys are living in them. No donkeys are ever sold – only donations are accepted.

The sanctuary's Donkey Charter gives to every donkey admitted the right of life regardless of age or health and the best possible treatment, care and drugs to preserve its life to the maximum.

In addition, the sanctuary sends educational literature to schools and supports the Riding Establishments Acts Committee in their work and supervision of working donkeys. All reports of cruelty and neglect are followed up and a watch kept on markets.

In addition, the International Donkey Protection Trust was set up to improve conditions for donkeys and mules both in

England and throughout the world, to bring help to donkeys working in isolated areas in foreign countries and to attempt to influence governments to tackle the parasite problem, to give donkeys a healthier and longer life. Mrs Svendson regularly travels abroad working on behalf of needy donkeys.

The Slade Centre was formed to 'help handicapped children enjoy petting and riding donkeys at their indoor riding centre.'

The Sanctuary survives on voluntary donations and can be visited on weekdays from 9am until 5pm.

The Donkey Sanctuary, The International Donkey Protection Trust, The Slade Centre, Slade House Farm, Salcombe Regis, Nr. Sidmouth, Devon EX10 0PL. Tel: Sidmouth 6391.

The National Equine and Smaller Animals Defence League

The National Equine and Smaller Animals Defence League was founded in 1909 by Francis A. Cox supported by Lord Henry Cavendish-Bentinck, MP, John Galsworthy, Lady Pender, Philip Snowdon, MP, George Greenwood, MP, Jerome K. Jerome and the Right Honourable Winston L.S. Churchill (then Home Secretary). The main object then was to work for and secure a reform in the treatment and conditions of pit ponies. This was achieved when the Coal Mines Act was passed in 1911. Since that time, the League has continued to work for better conditions for pit ponies and has called for their withdrawal and replacement by mechanical haulage.

The League's Home of Rest for Horses takes in pit ponies, horses, donkeys and other large animals which need rest, retirement or medical attention.

The League also maintains an Animals' Refuge and Hospital near Carlisle, where animals and birds, both domesticated and wild, are taken in for treatment and fees are minimal for people who cannot afford normal veterinary costs. Stray and abandoned animals are sent to the Refuge by the police, and the League operates a Dog Warden scheme for Carlisle County Council and organizes a humane education programme providing material and lectures for schools, clubs and institutes.

The National Equine and Smaller Animals Defence League, Oak Tree Farm, Wetheral Shields, Carlisle CA4 8JA.

6   Domestic Pets

The Dog

Britain does not treat its dogs as well as it imagines. The stray and abandoned proliferate, living miserable lives and meeting tragic ends. Dogs were domesticated by man in prehistoric times and in the twentieth century, as well as performing what veterinary surgeon, David Coffey, quite rightly calls 'their most arduous task to date' – that of family pet – they help mankind as companions, guards, therapists for the sick or disturbed, guides for the blind and messengers and workers in rescue teams in times of war and peace. Any human who condemns the dog would do well to spend a day in the library of the Imperial War Museum looking through the books on animals in war. They could not fail to be moved. Although dogs are in many ways the helpless slaves of man, man has greatly benefited from this symbiotic relationship. I believe, however, that in an ideal world all animals would be entirely free and have no cause to fear man and therefore would be his natural friends and not have to be tamed or domesticated.

Whatever we may feel about the rights and wrongs of keeping 'pet' animals – and there are many, for pets must suffer untold psychological stress – we are living in far from ideal conditions, and so the dog must be cared for by man. In this context, we cannot, must not, ignore the dog's innumerable good qualities from which we can learn and so enrich our own lives.

We have some five and a half to six million dogs in Britain, up to one million of which are said to be without owners – abandoned, straying, or wandering uncontrolled. Apart from the many dogs who are overtly victimized by man – 13,459 suffered in British laboratories in 1981, many murdered in such crude experiments as the LD50 test – and those that are cruelly treated, beaten, starved or otherwise abused by malicious or inadequate people, and those who, no longer entertaining, or perhaps a burden on their often selfish owners, are taken to vets to be killed before their time – the strays are an indication of the amount of suffering we allow to be inflicted on such a good and long-suffering friend.

It is the ownerless dog population which is now causing most concern among dog and animal-welfare societies. Exactly what to do about the problem has created an area of dissent, where even the most well intentioned are liable to take a managing approach.

Dogs, unlike other animals, have to be licensed. The fee is 37½p (7/6d) and has remained unchanged since its instigation in 1878, but costs approximately £1.20 to collect! Only approximately half the dog population is in fact licensed, if that. Many people don't bother, and the law is not enforced. It is thought that about a million puppies are born each year, about two-thirds of which are eventually destroyed. Some solution has to be found.

Because of the way in which we live, strays do lead miserable lives and are often shot or poisoned (poisoning is illegal) by farmers and gamekeepers, or may be left injured to die lingering deaths. Many are stolen from the streets and sold to experimental laboratories. The laboratories do not mind or care where the dogs come from, in fact former pets are probably very useful to them as they are used to humans, probably very trusting and will handle well. Roaming packs of feral dogs can be a potential danger to humans and to other animals.

Many dogs are never returned to their owners because they carry no identification. The owners cannot be traced. Tattooing is one good solution – thieves or children will easily remove a dog's collar, but tattoos are permanent. It has been found in America that laboratories do not buy in tattooed dogs as it could be proven that they were pets with an owner. Tattooing can be arranged through Valerie Pratt at the Central Dog Registry.

All dogs should be identifiable and all owners traceable. This would discourage owners from abandoning pets. Under the 1969 Abandonment of Animals Act, it is an offence to abandon an animal – even temporarily. Most people are probably unaware of this fact both because the law is not enforced and because it would be extremely difficult to enforce it anyway. An American article on dog population[1] stated that dogs which are owned, but allowed to roam (in America) are an even greater cause of over population than abandoned dogs. If we had a system whereby the guilty humans could be prosecuted, life might be better for the dogs.

Wholesale neutering, now advocated by several animal-welfare societies, would not be necessary if dogs were always kept under proper control. Our nine-year-old bitch was never in danger of impregnation because she had always been carefully looked after. It is far less difficult to control dog reproduction than that of cats. A controlled dog will not get the chance to mate in a haphazard fashion. We accidentally found an ideal solution – a very large bitch and a fairly small dog. He couldn't mate her if he tried, but they were absolutely devoted, he protected her from all other dogs when out walking and would never leave her, so has never attempted to wander as do many male dogs.

Many people are also unaware that they are liable for any damage or compensation in any accident caused by their wandering dog. So surely, we need stricter enforcement of the 1960 Act, together with a system of identification on dogs which makes owners traceable, along with large enough fines to make enforcement viable? At present, all laws relating to animals simply do not carry, or are not given enough weight to produce realistic penalties. Fines for cruelty, for example, are derisory, while owners who shut their dogs out all day while they go to work are never prosecuted. Often such people are intractable, but the more intelligent may be susceptible to reason when the facts are correctly explained. Therefore, education should be a first concern, together with reminders about what is illegal. This can be done by local authorities and animal-welfare organizations. The latter do their best, often quite effectively, insofar as is possible, but official backing would ensure wider coverage.

JACOPIS (Joint Advisory Committee on Pets in Society) feels that a mandatory dog warden service would go a long way, if not eventually all the way, to solving the dog population problem. Although financial restrictions are stopping many

[1] *Dogs*, March 1977, Vol.8, No.2.

authorities from employing wardens at present, JACOPIS
found in their survey that most were in favour of the idea.
However, some, admittedly only a few, were not calling
wardens by that name, but 'pest control officers' or 'dog
catchers'. Such labels place the job in a completely different
light and are quite unacceptable, especially as the warden's role
should be at least 50 per cent educational in the broadest sense
of the word, that is, making a good and useful relationship with
the public and between the public and the authorities.
Wardens, now paid for by ratepayers, are currently more
common in urban areas where complaints about loose dogs –
single or roaming in packs – are quite frequent on larger
housing estates, due always to irresponsible owners.

While wardens are considered by many people concerned
with the welfare of dogs to be a good thing, there are certain
factors which should be taken into consideration: A man on a
possibly small or moderate wage, perhaps working only part-
time as some wardens now are, could be tempted to take offers
from dealers to supplement his income. He would be an easy
person for a dealer to approach as he is involved directly with
the rounding up and catching of dogs. It is possible, in such a
situation, that even dogs with collars and tags would not be
returned home if a corrupt warden were in the employ of any
one authority. It is very important (i) that wardens are
thoroughly screened for their job and required to produce
excellent references; (ii) that the job specifications be made
absolutely clear. A warden would have to have a knowledge of
the law relating to dogs, be extremely sympathetic, be very
good with people and extremely good with animals and able to
handle very frightened and half-wild dogs with firmness and
kindness. He would also have to be pro-life and not pro
'humane' destruction; (iii) there should be some means of
scrutinizing a warden's work, from time to time. Those
scrutineers should be a kind of watchdog body, able to receive
and act upon any possible complaints about a dog warden in
their area. This could possibly be done by a committee from the
RSPCA presuming the RSPCA sees fit to change its current
unacceptable role of dog slaughterer or some reputable local
animal-welfare organization.

JACOPIS states that one of the prime duties of wardens
should be 'co-operation with members of the public, local news

media, veterinary surgeons, local animal-welfare organizations, and other relevant groups,' that this would also help in the passing of bye-laws. The banning of dogs from parks, as happened in Burnley, causing a public outcry, could not then occur. In that case and others, there was no proper consultation or liaison with dog owners, something which is *essential* in a democratic society.

JACOPIS also suggests that the problem of strays be handed over to wardens and taken completely away from the police. This could lead to a possibly dangerous situation. At present, under an Act of 1960 dogs impounded by the police must not be used or sold for vivisection, but a local authority would not come under this Act. In the USA and Canada 1 per cent of dogs in pounds may be fed into laboratories, though this law is now being repealed in some states, but only with strenuous efforts from animal-rights activists. (We should bear in mind, however, that this is a symptom, not a cause, for *no dog* should be suffering in a laboratory, purpose-bred or not.)

Dogs taken in by wardens should be put into local authority kennels, not into subcontracted kennels. It should then be possible for the public to inspect those kennels at any time, especially to avoid situations such as those in Battersea Dogs Home where dogs were allegedly sold to dealers; albeit perhaps unwittingly.[1]

Dogs suffer not only from being sold into experimentation by dealers, but also from bad pet shops and markets such as Club Row – the animal section of Petticoat Lane, commonly known as 'the market of misery', which, after two years' hard and valiant campaigning organized by Angela Walder and her colleagues in CAW (Co-ordinating Animal Welfare), has been closed. The British Veterinary Association would like to see all animal street markets closed. Pet shops vary a good deal. There are good ones and very bad ones. All pet shops are licensed under the 1951 Pet Animals Act which is enforced by local councils. If licenses are well enforced, the worst abuses can be stopped, but in some cases the license only means the payment of a fee which makes the Act and the license nonsense. There is no obligation for veterinary inspection of pet shops. Sometimes the inspector is an environmental health officer who is not

[1] 'Dogs Home "Tricked" by Dealers', *Evening Standard*, 15 May 1980.

necessarily animal orientated and is not particularly worried about the welfare of the animals, only about how they affect the surrounding humans. If you see a badly run pet shop in which conditions are not good enough or where there are too many animals bunched together or any other factors which may be causing discomfort, you should complain to your local council and remind them that they should enforce this Act. If people complain, they will be obliged to do so.

Dogs are victims of man's needs and must be accorded the dignity, respect and right to life which they deserve as friends and companions.

Loved and Hounded: The Problem Faced by Cats

> If a man could be crossed with the cat it would improve man, but it would deteriorate the cat. (Mark Twain, *Notebook*)

If you do not know cats, then perhaps you have not learned to love or admire them, but love them or not, the problems of being a cat in a human world are immense.

Paul Gallico describes those problems so well in his novel about a cat, *Jenny*: 'Homeless waifs, old 'uns and kittens going nervously about the difficult business of gaining a living from the harsh and heedless city.' Little has changed for them in the thirty-four years since that book was written.

Felis sylvestris, the European wildcat which once roamed Europe, its race, a fraction of what it was, now banished to the more remote areas of Europe and western Asia, is a partial ancestor of the domestic cat. *Felis libyca*, the African wildcat, which still lives in Africa, Asia, Corsica, Sardinia and Majorca, is probably a primary ancestor of our well-known fireside *felis catus*. The African wildcat was tamed and deified by the ancient Egyptians as almost certainly was the jungle cat, *felis chaus*, which still lives in Egypt and southern Asia.

It was the Egyptians who truly domesticated the cat; in ancient Egypt it was adored both as a domestic pet and a household god. Although it is not by accident that cats became domesticated, and it is not known exactly how the genetic change came about – whether suddenly or gradually – there is a theory that 'it is quite likely that the cat in effect domesticated itself, walking into people's lives as it were – or (in biological terms) finding a new ecological niche to exploit.[1]

Felis catus, domestic cat, found its place alongside humans but never became totally dependent on them. Still able to survive outside society, cats become feral in huge numbers when stray, lost or abandoned. They gather in colonies and are to be found on many a building or derelict site, near hospitals, in parks, public buildings, wherever there seems to be a constant source of food. Cats would normally live only in family groups, but the necessity of gathering about a food supply creates colonies in which disease can become a problem for them. Such colonies are also often considered to be inconvenient by humans who mistrust or feel threatened by large numbers of animals. Colonies of farm cats existed before World War II, but when cities were bombed, houses destroyed and families evacuated, cats found they had to fend for themselves, and so became feral.

Kittens reared by these homeless cats grew up feral, but humans, as is their wont in England, kindly began to feed them, which contributed to the rise in the feral cat population. Nowadays many other factors add to the stray and hence feral cat problem: families break up or move and city sites are redeveloped; many people have little or no sense of responsibility towards their pets, many of whom will end up 'on the streets'.

Female cats and kittens leaving a home will easily find a place in a colony. Kittens passed to unwilling owners will often leave their new homes and become feral, while female cats may rear kittens in the wild but feed at home themselves. In places where cats have been encouraged as a form of rodent control – factories, hospitals, power stations, for example – they have often bred to proportions which have become difficult to handle. When owners die, family or friends may not take responsibility for the dead person's cats; when cats are abandoned – pregnant females may be discarded, pets are sometimes put out when food is considered too expensive, or when treatment, neutering or holiday boarding costs become inconvenient, or are left when families move to dwellings in which they may not keep them – they become feral. Some

---

[1] *The Book of the Cat*, Pan, 1980.

people are against spaying and neutering but subsequently cruelly abandon offspring. By nature rather nervous, cats sometimes get lost when families move house.

The general public is largely unaware of the extent of the problems faced by our feral cat population. Felines do not enjoy the status of canines and feral cats are treated as vermin to be slaughtered by pest control officers, or worse, inept humans with guns. There have been many reported cases of this happening – at one mental hospital in Essex they were shot by torchlight under a shed and hopelessly maimed. It is illegal to poison them under the Poisons Act of 1962.

Some are treated more fairly – the British Museum has a colony which is officially cared for by a cat officer.

Hospital administrators often panic over cat colonies as they fear the potential population increase, which might bring fleas, smells from the toms, and cat diseases – visceral larva migrans, ringworm and toxoplasmosis. These are in fact no more a danger in feral cats than in pet cats and the real 'danger' lies in direct contact with excreta.

On the other hand, the more enlightened in such institutions see these cats as therapeutic companions with whom mental patients enjoy communicating and thereby derive great benefit.

In England and Wales the owner of the land on which feral cats are to be found, or people who regularly feed such cats, may assume and exercise the rights of ownership. Both the Criminal Damages Act and the 1911 Protection of Animals Act, cover the cat, which is legally assumed to have an owner and so cannot be deemed vermin. In Scotland, however, feral cats are treated as vermin, and so poisoned.

The larger animal-welfare societies have, until recently, concerned themselves with pet cats and mostly ignored the feral cat problem, spending no money on improving their lot. The RSPCA, for example, had a policy of putting such cats down, something which they had to revise after criticism for such indifference. They set up a working party which met occasionally for four years (1977–81), and produced a comprehensive report resulting in the new policy statement which reveals a change in attitude:

> On those sites where the welfare of colonies of feral cats is ensured and their presence is welcomed by the owners of the

site, the RSPCA advocates the sterilisation of these cats, provided that the instructions concerning humane procedures are followed, as described in a leaflet issued by RSPCA Headquarters.

On the whole the RSPCA now advocates stabilization and support of feral cat colonies.

There was little concern or understanding shown for the fact that the problems of feral and domestic cats are very much tied in together. If colonies were controlled nationwide in the best possible way, then their existence would cause neither worry nor inconvenience.

At present some local councils employ pest-control firms which can cost as much as £100 a night. One of the better pest-control operators stated that he had been killing ninety cats a week, humanely. His was but one of many such companies, where people are employed only to treat symptoms, not to eradicate the cause. Some cats will always escape. These will return and fill the vacuum left by their departed fellows with yet more young. That space will also attract other cats from surrounding areas. Sometimes councils will take this mass killing upon themselves without consulting people who actually feed the cats, which of course brings about distress and resentment.

A group was formed in recent years solely for the benefit of feral cats. The Cat Action Trust, still a very small society, with limited funds, aims to stabilise the populations of existing colonies. First the number of cats which may viably be supported in any one place is calculated and the number subsequently kept at that level by spaying and neutering. It has been found that cats which are regularly fed can be caught in specially designed traps. They are taken to a vet and returned as quickly as possible (after the operation) so that they will suffer minimal distress.

If males are left unneutered alongside spayed females they will certainly wander to other sites and father kittens elsewhere. The Cat Action Trust aims to trap both toms and queens, neuter them and return them to the site next day or the day following that. It is now felt that for quick and easy identification neutered cats should have a very small piece taken from the top of the left ear while still under anaesthetic.

This avoids such disasters as females undergoing an operation twice.

Clearing colonies completely is unsatisfactory as other cats will eventually move in and form a new one. Prevention of reproduction has also been attempted by the use of the pill for females. This is not always successful, however, as it must be administered to each queen once a week in food – something which can be very difficult when dealing with wild cats. In addition there can be severe side effects.

In California an experiment was carried out whereby dominant toms were vasectomized. They will still mount the queens and cause a false pregnancy but Jenny Remfrey, veterinary surgeon working for the Universities Federation for Animal Welfare and the Cat Action Trust, does not recommend this method of control.

Ruth Plant, who founded the Cat Action Trust and has great experience with feral cats, feels that once colonies are controlled, feeders must be organized for every site, because some feeders will eventually grow old, ill or move away. She would like to see a Guild of Feeders established, operating from a central office which could send in a locum whenever or wherever the system breaks down.

Local authorities could and should play a useful part in a nationwide neutering campaign for the benefit of feral cats. The RSPCA Working Party advocated a cat licensing system with cats identified by an ear tattoo. Tattooing is an emotive subject, but cat licensing would raise the cat's status to that of the dog.

There is great cause for concern about the use of pest control firms who are not licensed and have no standardized guidelines when dealing with cat colony clearance, which means that standards vary from company to company. In addition they should be liaising closely with welfare societies.

Feral cats are not easy to handle, but special traps are supplied by both the Cat Action Trust and the RSPCA to approved people. These cage-type devices allow the cats to be transported for treatment or re-homing, but their use requires skill and experience.

Where there is a need for rehoming this can be done quite successfully where the new owners are prepared to treat these creatures with understanding and respect. Feral cats fall into three basic types: the shy ones who were once pets, the nervous ones who will be more difficult to handle, having been wild and homeless for a long time, and the wild ones who will fight fiercely during any attempt to catch them.

Very young feral kittens may settle well into domestic life while old cats may or may not do so. Some people are specially gifted in achieving this. Outbuildings or stables are the best accommodation and after four to eight weeks' acclimatization feral cats may settle well into such surroundings, enjoying their freedom while returning to base for food. Some may be distressed at having to carve out a new territory, but will settle best into family groups. To 'rescue' feral cats and then deprive them of their freedom, keeping them imprisoned for years, is not to rescue them at all and must be considered inhumane.

Sources: Ruth Plant. 'Feral Cats in Britain', a paper given at the Feline Advisory Bureau's 15th Annual Conference 27 October 1979 by Jenny Remfrey, PhD, MRCVS of UFAW. 'Feral Cats in the United Kingdom', Report of the Working Party on Feral Cats, 1977–81. RSPCA.

The Destruction of Healthy Animals

It is the most terrible indictment of man, that while he has a rational intelligence which enables him to organize and manage his species, other animals, the plant and mineral life of the planet, he lags sadly behind in real emotional or spiritual development. Even some religious and spiritual leaders and teachers, ignoring the basic spiritual requirement – respect for all life – condone the daily massacre of innocents which is now so vast in scale that we must all be affected by its violence.

Experimentation, which can often mean prolonged torture, is horrific, the slaughter of millions of animals for a food which man can do well without, is cruel and primitive, but just as inexcusable is the 'humane destruction' of millions of healthy animals. They are destroyed only because man considers himself the most important, pushing always to the front of the queue; ignorant of the needs of those he has pushed over, harmed or killed in the crush. Homeless animals are 'inconvenient'; domesticated by man, they are continually betrayed.

Many people can't face the horrors of the death cells which exist in our society, but all that is needed for proliferation of evil is for good men to do nothing.

A veterinary surgeon writing in *Pro Dogs News*[1] stated that killing is addictive, that power over life and death brings a certain thrill. He told of his best tutor, a vet called George Gray who practised reverence for all life and would kill no animal unless he had done his very best to save it first. Mr Gray said: 'That is what happens to a lot of vets. They kill a few dogs, for whatever reason, then they get used to the killing and count it as of little consequence. To some vets it's no longer a life and death decision – it's just another veterinary job. What a tragedy to treat life so lightly.'

When his pupil Mr Smith Baxter went into practice, he was incensed at the number of people who requested the killing of their healthy animals and always refused such requests. He was once sent to attend a destruction clinic at a charity organization and was horrified at the attitude of the staff who were so habituated to the procedure that they remained totally unmoved. Once was enough for him, he did not return.

Fortunately, this vet, who practised his profession as it should be practised, believes that even when dead, animals should be treated with dignity:

> I believe that a dog which has throughout its life given fidelity and love to its owners deserves respect in death. . . I would have the whole business of euthanasia and disposal of dead animals approaching that applied to the human situation, but without the frills.
>
> The legality of 'euthanasia' in veterinary practice has led to gross abuses in life and death discussion and it does make one consider that a similar situation might arise if euthanasia were ever legalised in the field of human medicine.

Given the power, humans will certainly cross that line. The Nazi gas chambers existed only forty years ago.

An incredible amount of money and energy is wasted in our society which should surely be practising humane education, not humane killing. All people should be taught respect for all

[1] 'To Be or Not to Be – One Man's View of Euthanasia', *Pro Dogs News*, Autumn 1981.

life, for that lack of respect which now exists affects the quality of *all* our lives. We have a strange sense of values when we allow a dog to be murdered because it sheds hairs on furniture,[1] or stops us going on holiday.

We have almost six million dogs in Britain and about 600,000 of those are killed every year according to JACOPIS. Just under 200,000 are killed by the RSPCA. In 1979, that organization destroyed 192,478 small animals, a large proportion of which were dogs. (86,988 small animals, mostly dogs and cats were rehomed in 1979 but compare that to the number killed.) 1980 and the recession saw a worsening of the situation. When things get a little difficult the helpless are the first to be cast out.

There are four million stray cats in this country. Although perhaps more able to cope in the wild, or feral state, than dogs, many of them suffer a great deal. Humans, on the whole, are not very kindly towards animals which don't belong to them. When these lost and abandoned felines gather in colonies, the authorities consider them vermin and employ pest-control organizations to rid them of their presence. Jackson and Booth, one of the more caring and reputable companies, kills an average of 92 cats every week. Multiply this by 52 and you have 4,784 for one company alone. Many of these were once family pets. Some hospitals are known to shoot feral cats, leaving many to die hopelessly maimed.

Having a good pedigree doesn't help. 30 per cent of the dogs which arrive in Battersea Dogs Home and other animal sanctuaries are thoroughbreds. Due to irresponsible owners, thousands of cats and dogs are killed by vets, the RSPCA, the Blue Cross, PDSA and other smaller organizations every year.

The Canine Defence League refuses to kill healthy animals, but maintains kennels for unhomed strays. It was called in to help with strays in Northamptonshire a few years ago, but found the problem too big to handle. Approximately 2,500 stray dogs go to the police every year in that county. After seven days they are handed over to a contractor who is paid to electrocute them. His contract is a valuable one.

It is very difficult to find a humane method of killing, especially conveyor belt killing. While certain methods may be

---

[1] This was done by a vet to his own dog.

considered 'humane', there is no method which can entirely eliminate distress. The majority of dogs were always electrocuted, but in 1974, John Bryant and Ruth Harrison – both well-known figures in animal welfare – investigated this method. They found that the electrocution cabinets being used were capable of inflicting ghastly torture. While the animal was totally paralysed and appeared to be dead, it went on suffering to a terrible extent. The use of the machines which were causing that state of affairs was banned only when the *Observer* conducted an investigation and declared that the method was barbaric. Now a new type of electrocution machine is used, because electrocution is quicker and easier than intravenous injection. The latter method can in some cases be more humane, but needs more time, and skill, to be carried out correctly without undue stress to the animal. Finding a vein or dealing with a very excited animal can cause difficulty and great pain if the medication misses the vein.

The veterinary surgeon for Battersea Dogs Home does feel, however, that the electrothamator is 'up to the present time the quickest, safest' and – in his opinion – 'most humane method' of euthanasia, so long as the boxes used are up to the BSI standards and conform to the BSAVA requirements. He says that the new electric cabinets ensure humane death because if the set procedure is not gone through, then the machine cuts out. First a stunning current and then a lethal current is administered. Electrocution is supposed to take 1/500 second: 'Only very occasionally does a dog come round.' Should barbiturates be used in a dogs' home – they are used in private practice – he feels that because of the numbers involved and the uncertainty of the animals, there would be at least 10 per cent which would fail to be dealt with intravenously – the only humane way, which would then mean use of one of the other routes – intraperitoneally or into the heart or kidneys, all of which can be very painful.

With that in mind and also 'greatly increased cost' he would only recommend injection 'under extreme conditions'.

His view on destruction under the kind of conditions that Battersea Dogs Home has to work with is that 'cost and speed of operation are primary considerations; that the problems of training suitable people to perform this obviously unpleasant task must also be taken into account.' Therefore, he feels simplicity of method and approach and an uncomplicated, unemotional attitude are essential.

However, the question *how do the animals feel on being put into the death cabinet?* seems neither to be asked nor answered.

RSPCA inspectors learn euthanasia from the Battersea vet. He teaches them to kill by electrocution and injection.

Detailed description of methods of humane killing make very unpleasant reading.[1] First, we have to understand that we allow and seem to want, mass killing of unwanted animals, and the methods of killing are required to be quick and cheap, also able to be used safely by unqualified personnel and not cause any disturbance to the public who might live in the region of such execution areas. In other words, they must be of optimum convenience for *humans*!

Dogs and cats began to be electrocuted *en masse* between the two world wars, but it was found that cats underwent intolerable suffering by this method. They often made poor contact with the floor electrodes and might be burnt in the cabinets. What is more, a cat's nervous system is such that it may collapse as if dead from the shock, but the heart can restart, so that it is not killed by the first dose of electric current.

A good deal of research has gone into developing efficient electrocution methods. In the words of Phyllis G. Croft, PhD, MA, FRCVS:

> The essential knowledge has been acquired *through years of difficult and often rather distasteful research* [my itals]. This knowledge has led to the development of a safe and humane piece of equipment; but all this can be nullified by those who have neither electrical nor physiological knowledge taking matters into their own hands and altering the essential characteristics of the equipment.[2]

In the USA dogs are gassed with carbon dioxide and carbon monoxide so that they choke to death. They are sometimes put into decompression chambers, not an instanteous death. These are modern 'sophisticated' methods. It is considered by some that shooting is a more humane method of killing a dog.

[1] For more detailed study read UFAW's booklet, *Humane Destruction of Unwanted Animals*.

[2] UFAW Symposium, Humane Destruction of Unwanted Animals, 1976.

Richard Ryder, ex-RSPCA chairman, was shown this in Australia where it is favoured by certain organizations. But there are too many variables involved. Even captive bolt shooting used in the slaughter of cattle does not always work as it should. If the animal moves, if the person is not skilled enough or tired or if the equipment is not in prime condition, disaster can result.

G.W. Annis, of the PDSA, speaking at the UFAW symposium, stated that

> When new staff are engaged it is by no means unusual for these people to resign after only one day's duty because they do not like witnessing animals being put to sleep. And when the shooting procedure was carried out, this attitude was much more frequently encountered. There is no doubt that people who do shoot animals must be mentally suited to the suddenness of death and prepared to accept the messy aftermath.

Chloroform euthanasia is still sometimes used for cats but should not be. It is an irritant vapour and makes the animal at first excited; the procedure is not speedy. If attempts are made to quicken it, the drops of liquid may burn the animal's face and feet before it loses consciousness. A former kennel maid from Battersea Dogs Home who witnessed this method which was formerly used there to kill cats, told me: 'The cats were put into a box and chloroform dripped into the top. This suffocates them. It isn't nice at all. It's horrible. It takes a long time. It can take five minutes and they fight to get out the whole time.'

Judy A. MacArthur, BVMS, MRCVS of UFAW stated that UFAW's findings on chloroform were similar to those of the American Panel on Euthanasia which concluded that both chloroform.and ether are 'effective anaesthetic agents and have a definite place in the euthanasia of pups and kittens. They are not recommended for adult animals.'

Such gases as carbon dioxide are used – they are fed into a closed chamber from a pressurized cylinder which gradually reduces the amount of oxygen in the tissues of the animal. The creature is supposed to become unconscious without experiencing discomfort or pain, but cats do vary in their reaction to it. For some, unconsciousness is not instantaneous.

It is not within the range of this book to explore the technicalities of gassing, but for a more detailed explanation of the use of gases see the UFAW pamphlet.

The other method used for small animals is the injection of drugs. Most of the drugs used are depressants of the central nervous system and many of them are used as anaesthetic or pre-anaesthetic agents. However, this may not work well with a nervous animal or when done by inexperienced personnel. Even an experienced handler may have great difficulty in finding the vein, rendering the process quite distressing. However, injection is favoured by many caring vets. David Coffey recommends euthanasia for the sick animals he has to put down, by overdose of barbiturate. The dog is given an overdose which first puts it into a deep sleep, rapidly followed by death. He writes, 'In most cases the dog is dead before the injection is completed. The method is simple and painless and *if carried out with sympathy* causes the dog little distress'[1] (my itals). In my own experience, many animals appear to know when they are about to be killed, which means they will be in a distressed state.

Certain poisons are used in the destruction of small animals, especially rodents, but some of these are very cruel, causing such symptoms as abdominal pain, diarrhoea, vomiting, excitement, convulsions, coma and haemorraging. Some poisons may take days to kill the animal.

The use of poisons in Britain is controlled by legislation: Protection of Animals Act 1911, Protection of Animals (Scotland) Act 1912, Agriculture Act 1947, Agriculture (Scotland) Act 1948, Animals (Cruel Poisons) Act 1962. These Acts restrict the use of poisons to rats, mice or other small ground 'vermin' including squirrels and permit the use of poisonous gases in holes or burrows to kill rabbits, foxes or moles and enable certain poisons to be prohibited by regulations. The Wildlife and Countryside Act 1981 permits poisonous gases underground to kill badgers under license.[2]

It is a pity that so many animals should be considered vermin because they are inconvenient to man. One factor which must be of great concern to everyone is the effect which destroying

[1] David Coffey, *A Veterinary Surgeon's Guide to Dogs*, Worlds Work, 1980.
[2] See Chapter 2.

healthy animals has upon the humans who carry out that task.

Worried by the whole problem, a radical faction of the RSPCA council pressed in 1979 for a stoppage of the destruction of healthy animals.[1] When this was made known, protesting letters arrived from branches from people who boasted about the number of animals they put down each year and affirming that *they* were not going to stop. Such people probably started with humane intentions, but found they could play God and began to somehow enjoy the ghastly game.

The thinking behind the intention was that the RSPCA should not continue to be a mopping-up operation for the government, for while the killing goes on, the root of the problem is simply not reached. An RSPCA working party, chaired by John Bryant, recommended that the RSPCA state its intention to withdraw the destruction service, this to be announced before the end of 1980. It would give perhaps a year's notice in which the government could set up a dog warden service which in turn would bring control and education, thus hopefully gradually reducing the stray problem. This was passed by the RSPCA council, but the new council under Janet Fookes suppressed the implementation of that decision. It was hoped that spaying and neutering would be carried out in RSPCA homes, but the branches, which on the whole tend to be conservative, said that this was 'too expensive'. Rehoming is not always a priority; sometimes the manpower is not available, sometimes it is simply too much trouble. Education, in regard to the stray cat and dog problem, does not seem to have been a priority in the RSPCA, but considering that society's original humanitarian ideas, it should be. And so the killing goes on . . . and on. . .

The bodies of destroyed animals are not always disposed of as the more sensitive might wish. They may end up on council rubbish tips, sold to companies who use the fur, fat (for such things as soap), bones (for fertilizer), or may be incinerated.

The *Sunday Mirror* published a full exposé[2] of a firm called 'Vetspeed' which collects carcasses from charities such as the

---

[1] The Unwanted Animals Working Party was appointed by the RSPCA council in April 1978 and its report and findings were considered the following November, when the following recommendation was accepted in principle: 'The Society accept a commitment to cease the destruction of healthy animals by the RSPCA and that the date of cessation shall be fixed by Council before 31st December 1980.'

[2] 10 January 1982.

RSPCA and the PDSA together with many private veterinary practices charging approximately £20 a month to do so, and then resells the skins to be used in fur coats, the bodies for fertilizer. The people handing over the bodies seem to have been unaware of what was happening to them, believing them destined for incineration.

Responsible owners who pay to have their animals destroyed should make arrangements for burial, perhaps in their garden, or that of a friend, or in a farmer's orchard, where the body could be given back to the earth undisturbed. Those who are concerned about what will happen to their animal's body should never leave it with a vet for disposal. Some people think it immaterial what happens to a body after the animal is dead, but others believe that dignity must be accorded it. What kind of people are wearing those fur coats (dead animals) anyway? That in itself is a violent act, especially when good alternatives are available.

> But the poor dog, in life the firmest friend,
> The first to welcome, the foremost to defend,
> Whose honest heart is still his master's own.
> Who labours, fights, lives, breathes for him alone,
> Unhonoured fall, unnoticed all his worth,
> Denied in heaven the soul he held on earth.
>
> Byron.

Spaying and Neutering

Many people involved in animal welfare, especially those who witness daily the miseries of overpopulation, advocate the spaying and neutering of dogs and cats. There has been little progress in policy-making on this issue but the Liberal Party's Animal Welfare Group has suggested a higher dog licence fee, with a lower one for dogs with a vet's certificate and/or a freeze mark of spaying or neutering – although the latter should be clear for all to see. (The freeze mark, made on the skin at the top inside part of a leg by chemical freezing is an alternative to tattooing.) It may be a long time, however, before any government tackles the problem unless there is more public pressure and/or willingness to bring about such changes.

Spaying and neutering are necessary evils in the present desperate circumstances, but it is unnecessarily intrusive to neuter a male dog. The veterinary profession are mostly agreed on that point. David Coffey, himself a vet, wrote in his book:[1] 'Sadly some of the animal welfare societies have embarked on widely publicised campaigns to encourage the public to have bitches spayed (removal of womb and ovaries). These campaigns are hasty, ill considered and of questionable morality.' The operation does involve major surgery. The tying of tubes performed on women can be performed on dogs and cats. This prevents pregnancy, but not the sexual cycle. Apparently this operation is rarely done, but seems as if it might be a good alternative. Both dogs and cats (female) can be given a contraceptive pill, but the danger of side-effects remains and administering of pills can be a problem, especially if scared or large numbers of animals are involved. Contraceptive injections can also be given, but there are many unpleasant side-effects. Female dogs and cats do not undergo a true menopause, heats simply lessen with age.

Males can be given female hormones to reduce their sex drive, or are commonly castrated. Of this, David Coffey writes:

The castration of male dogs is . . . an abomination. This opinion is not based on male chauvinism, but on an understanding of the hormone status of both sexes. . . In the male, castration alters the plane of behaviour, permanently. He is reduced to a eunuch. Castrated males are flabby, less active, and altogether different beings. . . Castration of male dogs is quite wrong.

Vasectomy would be a far better idea from the welfare point of view. This would mean that the animal is sterile, but loses none of his male characteristics. Neutering is often carried out for the owner's convenience which is quite wrong, but vasectomy carried out to prevent indiscriminate breeding appears, on the face of it, to present a humane solution. It is surprising, therefore, that it is rarely done, especially on dogs. Male cats are more likely to suffer than male dogs. Wandering for several days at a time, fighting, the stress of competition with other

[1] David Coffey, B. Vet. Med. MRCVS *A Veterinary Surgeon's Guide to Dogs*.

males are all dangers which a tomcat faces, added to which he may spray all over his home, leaving a dreadful smell. None of these would be lessened by vasectomy. Unfortunately for cats, their thoroughly domesticated state presents almost insoluble problems for them which only the neutering of the males can ease. *Most importantly, neutering and spaying help reduce the misery of thousands of unwanted and uncared for cats which are born to die each year.* Even people who claim to love cats will let their females give birth and will then drown or otherwise kill the kittens, abandon them, take them to be destroyed or just place a greater burden on welfare workers already under strain. This is entirely inhumane.

John Bryant, in his book *Fettered Kingdoms*[1] writes that he considers all pets to be slaves, that the dog and cat are unnatural creations – the unhappy results of false breeding imposed by man and he therefore feels they should be phased out of existence.

Horses are severely exploited. Stallions are castrated for human convenience, despite the fact that a truly gifted or caring horseperson will be able to control a stallion as well as a gelding. But this kind of relationship involves time and patience,[2] something which few people are prepared to give, especially those involved with horses to make money.

Farm animals are castrated wholesale purely to make them manageable so that humans can exploit them in the most selfish way. That humans are prepared to inflict on animals something they would find totally abhorrent for themselves is indicative of their dangerously compartmentalized view of life. But again, what he will do to animals, he will do to his own kind when he knows he can go uncensored or unpunished. Sultans and emperors found it necessary to have eunuchs, Juan Batista in Cuba and other dictators have used castration of men as a form of punishment and male surgeons have carried out thousands of hysterectomies, sometimes with less than adequate discrimination.

In an ideal situation there would be no surgery on the healthy. Ideals are lights at the ends of long dark tunnels which must never be allowed to go out.

---

[1] John Bryant, *Fettered Kingdoms*, Ferne Animal Sanctuary, Chard, Somerset.
[2] See the story of Dainty and the views of his owner, Rita Kennett in *Animals Are Equal*.

What You Can Do

* Press for more education of the humane kind in schools, clubs, various community services and so on.
* Press vets to look at the problem from within their profession – they could be powerful in changing the situation if they (a) united, (b) chose to try.
* Join and make your views known to the RSPCA, *and* other animal-welfare organizations. Demand to know (a) how many animals are put down; (b) if adequate efforts are being made to rehome as many as possible. Do not be put off if at first rebuffed.
* Control your own animals – don't allow unnecessary breeding which will mean a few more homeless and unwanted animals. Talk about the problem and help to make others aware of this tragic situation. The well-intentioned are often unaware of the extent of it and allow their animals to breed out of misguided 'kindness'. We do not exist in an ideal situation.
* Ask your local authority how it plans to tackle the problem, emphasizing *education.*
* Provide a home for a stray whenever possible.
* Don't give animals as surprise presents unless you are absolutely sure they will be loved and cared for, for the rest of their natural lives. They could become tomorrow's homeless victims.
* Try to give some time and effort, if you find a stray. After notifying the police, take it in if possible, if you can cope, or try to rehome it with someone who you know will care for it. This will ease the load on welfare organizations.
* Support such organizations as the Canine Defence League, The Cat Action Trust who believe in *life.*
* Most of all, do not ignore the problem and hope that someone else will solve it. While you read, thousands of healthy animals are waiting on Death Row. And *they have done nothing to deserve it,* except become a friend of man.

Cats

* Do not abandon a cat under any circumstance.
* Remember that in the long term it is more humane to have cats neutered and spayed.
* Do not give cats or kittens to people who do not really want them.

* Be careful when feeding an apparently stray cat that you are not luring it away from a good home and creating a potential feral cat.
* Make every possible effort to find a cat that gets lost.
* Write to your MP stating that cats should be licensed and given the same status as dogs.
* Support the work of the Cat Action Trust.
* If you learn of an uncontrolled colony consult the Cat Action Trust so that the correct steps can be taken.

Organizations to Join

The National Canine Defence League

The Canine Defence League was founded in 1891 by the wife of a naval officer who managed to collect together like-minded people and began to rescue stray dogs, looking after them and rehoming them. She secured a sound financial base and opened clinics all over the country. The League began to speak for dogs in Parliament and influence legislation.

Between the wars, the League's work subsided, but was restarted in 1964 and firmly re-established by Col Roosmale-Cocq.

It now has 11–12,000 members and eleven rescue kennels throughout Great Britain, including N. Ireland. It was formerly running free clinics but these had to close due to opposition from vets. The clinics were free, manned only by one vet at a time. The veterinary profession said that a clinic must give a twenty-four hour service, which would mean employing three vets, something which the League could not afford to do. And so, alas, the free clinics were forced to close.

The most important aspect of the Canine Defence League is the fact that it will not put down healthy animals, but sensibly all stray bitches are spayed before being rehomed. Thousands of stray and abandoned dogs are taken into its kennels each year. A large number of the dogs are either returned to their owners, if simply lost, or rehomed if they are stray or abandoned. Those who are extremely old, infirm, or who have certain characteristics due perhaps to a particularly sad life history or to especially mongrel looks, which will make rehoming unlikely or impossible, are kept on in the League's kennels. To help keep such animals, the League runs several schemes, full details of which are available from them. Some people sponsor a dog, if for instance they cannot keep one in their own home. Those who sponsor a dog through this scheme, will be able to get news of the dog(s) at any time through head office or will read news of the animal(s) in the League's newsletters and be able to visit the kennels at any time to meet those they are helping to support. Alternatively, or in addition, it is possible to give, or support a kennel. To maintain a dog in a kennel for one year costs £220. A donation of £250 secures a kennel, which will bear a name plate of the donor's name or any name the donor wishes. One more kennel will give hundreds of dogs the chance to live, or as little as a pound a week will help to support one specific kennel which will house many strays throughout the year. A donation of £18 provides a dog bed.

League kennels offer short-term boarding facilities to all dog owners and the society also meets the cost of dog licences for old-age pensioners who find payments a hardship.

The League is a member of JACOPIS and seeks to alleviate the stray problem through JACOPIS's suggested warden scheme, but meanwhile supplies address discs which have a veterinary guarantee on one side so that the person who finds an injured dog will be encouraged to take it for treatment knowing they will not have to bear the cost themselves. The League then endeavours to recoup the costs from the dog's owners. Many dogs injured in the street are destroyed when the owner is not present to consent to the necessary treatment. The NCDL disc guarantees that costs will be met and so is likely to secure treatment. For a small fee NCDL Lucky Dog Club discs are available to non-League members.

Membership of the League entitles the member to free public liability insurance up to £100,000 against damage caused by his/her dog.

Members receive a free identification disc when joining and are entitled to free advice and general information on dog ownership, care, training, welfare and legal matters concerning dogs and have full voting rights in the affairs of the NCDL.

National Canine Defence League, 10 Seymour Street, London W1. Telephone: 01-935 5511.

JACOPIS – Joint Advisory Committee on Pets in Society

JACOPIS is not an organization open to public membership but was formed in 1974 as a result of a symposium 'Pet Animals and Society' organized by the British Small Animal Veterinary Association in January of that year. The member organizations – the British Small Animal Veterinary Association, National Canine Defence League, Pet Food Manufacturers' Association, Association of Metropolitan Authorities, National Dog Rescue Co-ordinating Committee, British Veterinary Association, The Kennel Club, People's Dispensary for Sick Animals and the Royal Society for the Prevention of Cruelty to Animals – joined together in concern at the increasing pressure on companion animals in this country, and on dogs in particular. The kinds of pressures becoming evident were (1) claims about livestock worrying in rural areas; (2) alleged attacks on people; (3) pet animals causing road traffic accidents; (4) fouling on streets, parks and other public places and the problems connected with this.

Dogs are affected by changes in environment as society changes; they have become victims in the higher density population areas, especially where highrise buildings have replaced older type conurbations. JACOPIS believes that the dogs' problems can be solved while at the same time reaffirming the value of dogs as companions to man.

JACOPIS was formed as a study group to 'examine man's changing relationship to companion animals and to make recommendations as to how this change might best be managed in the interest of the animals, their owners and the rest of society.' It has endeavoured to coordinate the work of local authorities, veterinary surgeons, animal-welfare organizations and petfood manufacturers who have never previously been able to meet together to consider their common policies.

One of the first steps taken was the compilation of a report entitled 'Dogs in the United Kingdom' which was concerned with the conditions under which dogs live in the community. This was published in 1975. The report recommended that the dog licence fee be raised from the present 37½p (set in 1878) and now paid only by one half, or less, of dog owners. It was felt that no adequate system of control could be enforced unless dogs were properly registered and licensed, that all dogs should be identifiable and all owners traceable. This, it was felt, would discourage thoughtless abandonment of animals. JACOPIS feels that every citizen should have the right to own a dog, but that owners must be responsible and to this end, education is very important.

The report's major recommendation was the creation of a national dog warden service (an idea originated by Ruth Plant) to be administered by district councils, that a dog warden should be seen not just as a dog catcher to round up strays, but also a person who would perform educational duties, liaising with the public, local media, vets, local animal-welfare organizations and other relevant groups. That this kind of coordination is very important became evident in Burnley and other areas where restrictive bye-laws were brought into force to ban dogs from parks, something which was not acceptable to the public and which was carried out without proper consultation or education. (Burnley District Council imposed two bye-laws banning dogs from several major parks in the town some years ago, and in consequence found itself fighting an action in the High Court.)

The Department of the Environment also established a working party on dogs, the findings of which were published in 1976. Its conclusions, in many respects, corroborated those of JACOPIS. However, the DOE advocated a high licence fee and suggested a warden system be optional, not mandatory; there was no indication of how such a system would operate, how wardens would be appointed or trained. No government support was proposed.

Because of the more nebulous nature of those conclusions, JACOPIS began to organize regional seminars for environmental health officers and wardens in order to assist local authorities in becoming better informed about dogs and related problems. Those seminars produced the following general conclusions:

(i) that legislation should be introduced as quickly as possible to establish dog-warden schemes;
(ii) that such schemes should be properly financed (for example, by an increase in the licence fee);
(iii) that the current legal situation related to animals in general and dogs in particular was extremely complex and consolidation and updating were required;
(iv) that bye-laws, on fouling, in particular, were difficult to

enforce: the police had more pressing matters to deal with than dogs;

(v)   that wardens when appointed should co-operate with members of the public; try to return dogs to owners where possible and not to be seen in a hostile dog-catcher role;

(vi)   that the recommendation of one warden for 50,000 people (approximately one warden for 5,000 dogs) was too high and that one per 100,000 was probably more appropriate.

As a kind of consolidation of the information produced in the course of these seminars, a handbook for dog wardens – in looseleaf form, for updating and revision – was published by JACOPIS, together with notes for environmental health officers on types of suitable candidates for the post of warden and other points that would be of particular interest to them.

As there was no official support, JACOPIS took the initiative in setting up two-day pilot dog-warden training schemes.

Fouling and all of the problems surrounding it have been causing over-reaction, something which prompted JACOPIS to ask the Institute of Park and Recreational Administration to join a small working party on this issue. The result was the production of two papers, a Code of Practice[1] for pet owners and 'Guidelines for Local Authorities'. The remaining problems, it felt, would be dealt with by a dog-warden service. The Code of Practice sets out in a few brief paragraphs guidelines for the control of dogs in public places. The Guidelines for Local Authorities includes an important statement made by Baroness Stedman for the government in the House of Lords on 14 December 1977 in which she made it clear that the government would not tolerate local authorities imposing total bans on dogs and that those who had already managed to do so had been able to through the existence of a specific local authority Act affecting the districts under their control. The paper also made statistical breakdowns regarding the number of dog owners using open spaces and recommended how much green space should be provided by local authorities. It also suggested that children's areas and possibly sports areas be fenced off, but that authorities should provide receptacles for conscientious owners who pick up after their dogs while putting

---

[1] Pamphlets jointly published by JACOPIS and the Institute of Park and Recreation Administration available from JACOPIS.

up clear instructions at regular intervals in their parks.

Another working party was formed with representatives of the Institute of Housing, the Association of District Councils and other local-authority associations concerned with the problems of pet ownership in urban housing developments, in order to make recommendations to guide local authorities which have to make decisions on these matters.

In March 1980, JACOPIS published a revised statement of policy which forms the basis of a national campaign sponsored by JACOPIS and financed by the RSPCA pressing for legislation to establish a national dog-warden service.

JACOPIS is also undertaking to promote awareness of the value of pets in society, believing that 'the way in which we sensibly relate to companion animals is a reflection of the qualities which we seek to establish in our society'.

Dog wardens   About a hundred dog-warden services – there could be 500–600 under a mandatory system – currently exist, financed by local rates. Some have been in existence for up to eight years. JACOPIS believes that a nationwide dog-warden system should be funded by a universal licence fee (£5 was suggested in 1980) with exemptions for the aged and a form of block licence for licensed breeders and officially recognized multi-dog-owners, to be paid as now, through the Post Office. Dogs would be licensed when they first changed hands or at six months, whichever is the earlier. JACOPIS believes that estimating one warden for every 100,000 inhabitants, it would be possible to provide a financially self-supporting service for five years at the suggested level.

It is felt that existing voluntary societies would probably wish to assist in providing local authorities with the kennelling of strays, but in certain areas local authorities may wish to build their own kennels. In areas where there may be no necessity for a dog-warden service, JACOPIS recommends that an exemption be granted by the Secretary of State for the Environment if after careful consideration, he believes that a particular authority had no need of a warden. JACOPIS believes that responsibility for collection, registration and disposal of strays should be transferred from the police to the local authority and that the law should require all dogs to be identified, possibly by a colour-coded disc and recommends that wardens be given the right to inspect licences. It also feels that should rabies break out in Britain, a warden service would mean less likelihood of it spreading as there would be far fewer strays.

Kerb your dog   Most people are probably familiar with this slogan which marks a campaign – originated by JACOPIS – by Pedigree Petfoods, intended to help dog owners and the rest of the population alike. The programme is aimed at eliminating footpath fouling and ignorance about the responsibilities of pet ownership. While warning signs about fouling are generally on display, the public are given no positive indication of an alternative for their dogs. Gutters are not usually trodden in by people and are regularly drained, so 'kerbing dogs' seemed to be a solution. For this purpose, lamp-post stickers were produced bearing the names of local authorities using 'Kerb Your Dog'.

Educational material is also available; wallcharts, leaflets and films, which explain the basic points of responsible ownership. These are distributed in libraries, schools, health centres, pet shops, civic centres and animal-welfare establishments which wish to cooperate. There are also special project packs for schools. 'Kerb Your Dog' also informs the public about the law relating to pet ownership, through advertising in local newspapers, inviting editorial material, and posting information through letterboxes.

If you agree with the aims and ideas of JACOPIS, then you can support it through your community or you can obtain material from them, especially if you are a teacher or animal-welfare worker.

Address: JACOPIS: Walter House, 418/422 Strand, London WC2. Telephone: 01-836 2843.

Pro Dogs

Pro Dogs is a national charity which was founded in July 1976 by Mrs Lesley Scott-Ordish in order to educate the public, with the intention of re-establishing the position of the dog in our society in order for him to have the regard, care and respect he deserves. Its slogan is 'Dogs Deserve Better People'.

It is a member of the Canine Consultative Council which consists of the British Small Animals Veterinary Association, British Veterinary Association, the Kennel Club, the RSPCA and the National Canine Defence League. It is also a founder member of the Scottish Canine Consultative Council. It has made an agreement with the Home Office to supply local information where new byelaws to control dogs are proposed, has been invited to contribute to many programmes concerning the welfare and control of dogs and has visited over two hundred schools, educating children to responsible pet ownership. Well-trained dogs are taken into schools for demonstration purposes and dog ownership is discouraged unless there is someone at home in the daytime and owners are willing to take time to exercise and train their animals.

Pro Dogs now has a membership of over 25,000 which is steadily growing. Its aims are: (i) to promote higher standards of dog ownership and a better understanding of and attitude towards dogs; (ii) to undertake education programmes directed at specific areas of misunderstanding; (iii) to provide medical and veterinary advice and information on matters of public concern affecting dogs and dog owners; (iv) to publish educational leaflets and booklets and establish a free flow of such information through Pro Dogs branches, area secretaries, dog training clubs and others affiliated by membership; (v) to offer evidence, assistance and guidance in connection with any proposed legislation affecting the dog in society, bearing in mind the welfare of both dogs and mankind.

Address: Pro Dogs, Rocky Bank, 4 New Road, Ditton Maidstone, Kent ME20 6AD. Telephone: Westmalling (0732) 848499.

Central Dog Registry

Valerie Pratt began the CDR after conceiving the idea of tattooing dogs for immediate identification.

An American visitor suggested to Ms Pratt the solution – tattooing dogs with the owner's national insurance number: the owners could be traced via a central registry. As no welfare organizations would take up this idea, Valerie Pratt went ahead with the scheme herself and the Central Dog Registry became a limited company.

Tattooed animals are far less likely to be kept by a dealer as the laboratories do not want to be seen to be taking people's pets, more especially when the rightful owner could be traced. Tattooing can also be useful for lost cats whose ownership might be disputed. If injured in an accident, a tattooed animal would be far more likely to receive veterinary treatment rather than be destroyed.

For those people who are hesitant about the idea of tattooing, the Central Dog Registry publishes a list of questions which are likely to be asked. Tattooing does not hurt. It is done by experienced CDR recommended tattooers who can mark dogs without anyone holding them – though it is preferred that owners are present. The dogs do not need tranquilizers. A dog's skin, even if its fur is black, is never too dark for a tattoo to show. Nervous or 'vicious' dogs will not be a problem to the experienced dog-markers. It is wise to have animals of any age tattooed – an old dog with fading faculties is, for instance, more likely to get lost, even if he is well looked after. Tattooed identification is approved by the British Veterinary Association and The Kennel Club of Great Britain.

If you wish to have your animal tattooed, send for an application form, to the Central Dog Registry. You will then be notified of a tattooist in or near your area. Dogs can be tattooed through the auspices of dog training clubs, breeding and boarding kennels, dog rescue centres, veterinary practices. The tattooist makes a charge for marking the animal.

The tattoo is placed on the inside of the dog's right hind leg, where it can be easily read. Cats can be tattooed with a CDR on the inside of the ear. This does not hurt them and shows up well. It may not seem very aesthetic, but it may save them from a fate worse than death.

Central Dog Registry, 49 Marloes Road, London W8 6LA. Tel: 01-602 4444.

Cats Protection League (CPL)

The Cats Protection League was founded in 1927 for the 'promotion of the interests of cats'. From a small society, it grew to be nationwide and now has branches in Wales, Ireland, Scotland and the Channel Islands, as well as throughout England.

It has aimed from the beginning to rescue stray, unwanted and injured cats, neuter 'all cats not required for breeding' and provide information on the care of felines. A useful series of leaflets on many subjects concerning cats is available from headquarters free of charge. All CPL rescued cats are spayed or neutered before being rehomed. The headquarters office administers a neutering voucher scheme whereby needy people can be helped with the cost of the operation. (One female cat could be responsible for up to 20,000 descendants over a five-year period).

The League has some 13,000 members and is a national charity running six shelters – in Haslemere, Surrey, Battlesbridge, Essex, Bredhurst, Kent, Ryde, Isle of Wight, Crawley Down, Sussex and Spondon, Derbyshire.

The purpose-built shelters provide accommodation for unwanted cats on a temporary basis; some have a section for boarders which helps supplement income and some provide for old and unhomable cats. Some of the latter are kept under the sponsorship scheme – £10 per month enables a CPL member to support a cat. Details will be given to the sponsor who may visit it at its shelter.

The shelters are always full – especially in the summer months – and it is hoped that more can be built. Each one costs in excess of £10,000 a year to run. While every attempt is made to help all cats coming into its care, the CPL says it cannot cope with the sheer numbers and some are inevitably put down. This is always done by a veterinary surgeon – 'presumably by injection'. Central policy guidelines are given out to groups from headquarters, but individual feelings are respected if some groups feel they do not want a single cat destroyed. (The CPL has not attempted to cope with the feral cat problem which requires specialist attention.)

The League operates via a network of voluntary helpers in addition to its salaried staff. Besides rescue work, these people are encouraged to raise and spend money locally as each new group is expected to become self-financing. There are now 115 groups and branches throughout the country.

The CPL feels that it has led in the promotion of cat welfare, but does not stand in competition with any other society. Its main achievements have been to give out information for the 'education of cat owners to their responsibilities'; to distribute, free of charge, cocksfoot grass, especially necessary for housebound cats; it gave the first real impetus to the promotion of the cat flap and has campaigned since the last war for the expansion of a neutering and spaying programme. (In 1982 15,612 cats were spayed or neutered under the auspices of the CPL).

86·2 per cent of the funds going into headquarters and 100 per cent of local funds go directly towards maintaining needy cats.

The CPL has infinite scope for expansion and welcomes all new support.

The Cats Protection League, 20 North Street, Horsham, W. Sussex RH1Z 1BN.

The Cat Action Trust (CAT)

The Cat Action Trust was formed to help feral cats in 1976, by a small group of representatives from various animal welfare societies including the Animal Welfare Trust, the RSPCA and the Catholic Study Group for Animal Welfare. These individuals then made themselves fully independent as a group. Some financial support was given by the RSPCA and their work was researched and proven by the Universities Federation for Animal Welfare.

The Trust aims to control and monitor feral cat colonies by trapping the cats, having them sterilized and returning them to their colonies where people will care for them. Trapping is skilled activity and trappers are trained by more experienced members during two or three sessions. The cats are taken to vets known to be able to deal with feral cats; after the operation they are allowed to recuperate in their cages for two days before being set free.

Mrs Young, treasurer to CAT, was one of the first people to organize the control of a hospital colony – Mount Vernon, Northwood in Middlesex – where she works as a nursing sister. This was seven years ago and her work has proved itself in that the cats are living happily, having produced no kittens for several years.

The Trust's work is so effective and has become so well known that the DHSS has adopted its policy – hospitals with colonies are referred to CAT. Many public-health inspectors and hospital administrators tend to ignore this directive until they are forced to realize that this is the only method which really solves the problem.

CAT's methods have proved both practical and economically sound – the expenditure is non-recurring. While it takes a certain amount of business away from pest control firms, these are usually relieved to be rid of the emotive issue of cats.

Many 'tatty, fighting colonies' have been rendered 'sociable, clean and acceptable' and many hospitals and several naval establishments are grateful for the Trust's work. Over five thousand cats have passed through its hands, which means that a probable 3,500 kittens have been prevented.

The work involves equipment – cages, traps, transport – money for veterinary fees and time, patience and understanding. The Trust now has about thirty-five trappers and seven hundred members who support its work, under the enthusiastic patronage of Brian Redhead. Funding comes from subscriptions and voluntary donations.

It hopes that its activity can become more widespread and that more local groups will be set up with more publicity so that many more cats will be saved from misery and death.

Membership Secretary, CAT, 32 Stylecroft Gardens, Wembley, Middx.

Natural Rearing Products

Natural Rearing Products is a company providing herbal remedies for the treatment of animals. They state that 'natural rearing' is the rearing of healthy animals, developing a natural immunity to disease. It opposes the unnatural use of chemicals and vaccines. These methods were developed by Juliette de Bairacli Levy, a traveller and herbalist. Her book, *The Complete Herbal Book for the Dog*, on which the method is based, has been published in several countries and the company publish many testimonials from satisfied owners who have kept very healthy animals using this system.

While the unsatisfactory nature of harsh drugs and

inoculations is becoming more recognized, especially in vaccination in which germs (often live ones), toxins and their attenuations, mostly derived from unnatural – and often cruel – vivisection experiments are used, their herbal treatments are claimed to be far more satisfactory.

Furthermore, it is stated,

Such unnatural medicine has been the basic cause of a vast amount of new ailments, in its short history of little over half a century. Most significant of all is that CANCER, hitherto almost unknown to the carnivorous animals, has become a very general ailment of the modern dog and cat, killing multitudes.

J.Z. Rhine, an American writer on dogs, stated in his *Dog Owners' Manual*: 'Numerous new ailments owe their origins to the *failure of inoculation*. When it fails a "new" illness must be discovered as a scapegoat. (Hard Pad is now a common scapegoat for modern distemper inoculation failures.)'

Juliette de Bairacli Levy has used her methods for her own dogs for forty years with 100 per cent success.

It is advised that disease prevention will be successful only if the recommended natural raw diet is used, in conjunction with the herbal pills and plenty of daily exercise.

Advice, books, leaflets, diet sheets and price-lists are all available from the company's managers.

Natural Rearing Products, La Normandie, Ingoldsby Avenue, Ingoldisthorpe, Kings Lynn PE31 6NH.

7 Animals Used In Experiments

That every prison that men build
Is built with bricks of shame,
And bound with bars lest Christ should see
How men their brothers maim.

And they do well to hide their Hell,
For in it things are done
That Son of God nor son of Man
Ever should look upon.

Oscar Wilde, The Ballad of Reading Gaol

In its treatment of animals, the human race must be counted as largely made up of inferior people who use their power over creatures as an end in itself. This is especially so in the case of experiments which cannot be defended in a universe planned to work in harmony, where discord brings disease.[1]

The majority of animal experiments are carried out for profit-making and the search for knowledge – albeit often irrelevant and inapplicable to humans. The prime motivation is greed.

Animals in Britain who are unfortunate enough to find themselves in a laboratory are supposed to be protected by an Act of Parliament passed in 1876; the Cruelty to Animals Act. When the Act was passed, there were between 300 and 800 experiments a year – in 1982, there were 4,221,801. Experimenters have licences granted by the Home Office under the Act attached to which are certificates. Certificate A exempts the experimenter from his obligation under the Act to use an

[1] See N. Weeks, The Medical Discoveries of Edward Bach, Physician, C.W. Daniel, 1973; and Fritjof Capra, The Tao of Physics, Wildwood House, 1975.

anaesthetic sufficient to prevent the animal feeling pain. The interpretation of the requirement for anaesthetics has always been open. Many drugs are used which would not be considered adequate for the same procedure on a human, but these come under the Home Office statistics as 'experiments under anaesthesia'.

Under a licence, without a certificate, the experimenter would be required to kill the animal before it recovered consciousness, but if he has Certificate B, he may allow the animal to recover (and suffer). According to the 1982 statistics, only in 20 per cent of the experiments started in that year were animals anaesthetized for all or part of the experiment.

Attached to experimenters' certificates are 'pain conditions' in which it is stated that, if any animal 'is found to be suffering pain which is either severe or is likely to endure' or 'to be suffering severe pain' or 'to be suffering considerable pain', it is only in the case of the latter – if discovered by an inspector – that he may direct that the animal be painlessly killed.

The government clearly admits that experiments are likely to include severe and prolonged suffering and pain; under the Law pain is allowed to go on until 'the main result of the experiment has been attained'.

There were 518 registered places in which experiments were carried out and 11,797 licensees in 1982, yet there were just fifteen Home Office inspectors, three of whom are acting in an administrative supervisory role, to check these establishments and report infringements of the 1876 Act.

When there is no inspector present – and they must rarely be present – discretion as to what constitutes severity and duration of pain is left to the experimenter who will not willingly abandon his experiment.

In addition, there is no definition of pain and there are, then, thousands upon thousands of experiments carried out which the public, if they were allowed to see, would call very painful or distressful (stress is a natural state), but which escape censure or curtailment. The experimenter is often applauded within his profession for acts for which without the protection of the 1876 Act he would be prosecuted by the RSPCA and fined in the courts.

When one visitor to an experimental laboratory asked the vivisector who was joining mice together, 'What is that doing for the mice, or for science?' the reply was 'I don't know what it is doing for mice or for science, but I know what it is doing for me. It is getting me a PhD.'

When a scientist on a television programme was asked, 'Don't the animals count at all?' he replied, 'Why should they?' It is to these people that discretion over pain is handed over.

In 1982, seventeen cases of infringement of the Act or licence conditions were brought to the Secretary of State but fifteen of them were merely warned, while the remaining two cases were brought to the Director of Public Prosecutions. He advised in one case that proceedings should not be brought and in the other instructed the police to issue a caution!

We might conclude then, that the Home Office Inspectorate system is all but useless, aided and abetted by a government whose policy on animal suffering seems to be 'anything goes'.

There have been just three convictions for cruelty to a laboratory animal under the 1876 Act during the 107 years that it has been in force.

Since 1977, much more detailed, if still very inadequate, Home Office statistics have been published. These show a steady decline since a peak in 1971 when over 5·6 million animals were used. 1982 figures are 3 per cent lower than 1981, the lowest recorded since 1963, yet the numbers are still immense and many experiments are intolerably cruel. This is why experimenters remain so secretive. They have so much to hide. We are not allowed to visit laboratories despite the fact that much of their funding comes from the public purse.

The greatest number of experiments are carried out on mice – 2,442,702 in 1982; next came rats (932,335), birds (251,818), fish (165,833), rabbits (164,993) and guinea pigs (154,740). 13,146 dogs were used, 7,341 cats, 5,654 primates and 475 equines. In addition the laboratories used many other rodents – including hamsters and gerbils, ferrets and other carnivores, sheep, goats and cattle, reptiles and amphibians. Many people dismiss rodents as objects of fear and hate, yet laboratory rats and mice are clean, intelligent, likeable creatures – I knew one personally, a former laboratory white rat who became a perfect pet.

The testing of cosmetics, toileteries, food additives, tobacco and its substitutes, pesticides, herbicides and all kinds of environmental pollutants – which will be marketed and used in any case and which will continue to poison us and upset our environment – constituted a large proportion of experiments carried out in 1982, for profit.

Toxicity testing very often involves the LD50 (lethal dose 50 per cent) test. Here is an example: 'To determine the LD50 of a herbicide, animals were injected with various doses. Two days after injection the greater part of the lungs had collapsed in many of the animals, several of them dying before the period for killing was reached.' (Report, *Journal of Pathology*, 1979).

Despite what many scientists are saying about the crude LD50 test in which animals are force-fed a substance, be it food additives, toothpaste, detergent, substances used in packaging material, or face cream, until 50 per cent of them die, this useless procedure still goes on.

These products are all unnecessary. When, fourteen years ago, my four-year-old son drank a bottle of moisturising lotion, I rang the company who made it. They make natural products using no harmful chemical ingredients or animal products. They confirmed that nothing would happen to him. They were right.

Here are some of the things which have been said about the LD50 test:

'The LD50 test is certainly the most misunderstood, misinterpreted and misused of all tests. No valid case can be made to determine with accuracy the LD50 value in any animal species.' Chemical Industries Association, press release, 1977.

Mr P.S. Rogers, managing director of Hazleton Laboratories, Europe Ltd., stated: 'There is really little scientific justification for the test because reproducibility is not good, it can vary from day to day.'

A report of the Home Office Animal Experimentation Committee on the LD50 stated: 'The LD50 in itself affords no information as to the consequence of long-term exposure to the same substance.'

Thousands of fish and birds are used for pesticide tests – fish are immersed in these substances and the effect on their skins observed. Thirteen new pesticides have been put onto the market in the last twenty years with the 'ethical' argument that food is being saved in and for the Third World. The real answer is that the western world is making a huge profit out of these substances.

Note: India earned £4.3 million from the export of frogs' legs to the West in 1976-7. This cruel harvesting has created a gaping ecological hole and insects formerly eaten by the frogs thrived. India imported £17 million worth of pesticides in 1976-7.[1]

The Swiss company Ciba-Geigy, one of the world's leading manufacturers of pesticides have been marketing Galecron, a very dangerous substance, since 1966. Already in 1932 British workers contracted serious bladder disease caused by a substance connected with Galecron. In 1972, scientists reported that a decomposition product of Galecron was producing cancer in mice. In 1976, it became too dangerous for Ciba-Geigy and there was a halt in production with an estimated loss of 100 million Swiss francs. In 1978, it was reintroduced despite its carcinogenicity having been confirmed in the meantime. Swiss workers wear protective clothing and undergo constant checks, but in the Central and Southern American countries where it is freely sprayed about, unprotected workers are unaware of the real dangers. Ciba-Geigy did not stop at animal testing – they tried it out on a small group of unprotected Egyptian children and 'after one (spraying) flight 3 in 6 of the urine samples already showed values exceeding the maximum admissible value per day.'[2]

Springing from the notorious Agent Orange, a dioxin defoliant of the Vietnam War – with its untold number of human victims – we now have the agri-herbicide 245T. Such herbicidal chemicals had already been tested on animals in the mid-1960s in America with ghastly results – the newborn of various species arriving with such abnormalities as no eyes, no eyelids, double eyeballs, no lower jaw, cleft palates, cystic kidneys, incomplete fusion of the face and incomplete closure of spines etc.[3]

The *Daily Telegraph* (7.3.80) reported that in 1968, forty-one men were exposed to dioxin after an explosion at the Coalite and Chemical Products plant in Derbyshire. Impaired liver function and chloracne were found. A full report on their condition was made but a different version was issued by the company. A second investigation was carried out on eight of the

[1] Report on the destruction caused by the export of frogs' legs by Dr Humayun Abdulali and Dr A.G. Joshi of the Bombay Natural History Society, 14 June 1979; UN Statistics.
[2] *Soil Association Quarterly Review*, Summer 1983, from a Swiss report.
[3] *Outrage*, May/June 1980.

men by a woman pathologist. Shortly afterwards her house was broken into and these medical records stolen. Eleven companies are producing 245 T in Britain. It is used freely by farmers, gardeners and councils. The government's Advisory Committee on Pesticides composed of selected doctors and scientists say 245 T is still all right to use and 'quote *studies* to say that the allegations of risks from using the chemical have not been substantiated'. How many animals died in these studies?

Animals are suffering not only for such sinister, but also for the most trivial reasons. I heard it said at a committee hearing in the House of Commons by the then MP for Totness, 'It would be a pity if our children would have to do without what they like best, fish fingers, for example.' That is, the attitude that processed foods, packed with additives – no matter how unhealthy – are here to stay. Green peas should look greener and white cotton-wool bread whiter – all promoting ill health, yet an 'essential' part of our affluent life-styles. Must thousands of animals die for a chemical we do not either need or want in a new packaged or frozen food which little resembles the natural foodstuffs we should be eating to keep us healthy?

Here is one example of doubt in this area: 'Coumarin (a good flavouring) was found to produce liver damage in the rat and dog but not in the baboon. It is questionable whether the rat is a suitable test model.' (*Food Cosmetic Toxicology*, 1979, Vol.17.)

Even when these extraneous doctoring ingredients are tested, their effects are not necessarily translatable from animal to man.

This same doubt applies to chemical ingredients in cosmetics: 'Chinese hamsters respond quite differently to Syrian hamsters when exposed to Aluminium Chlorhydrate. The Syrian hamsters get a form of cancer but the Chinese do not.' (*International Journal of Cosmetic Science*, 1979.)

As far back as 1948, similar things were being said: 'It is notoriously dangerous to apply experimental results from animals to the treatment of human beings, because human and animal physiology show subtle but important differences,' said an editorial in *The Lancet* (3 July 1948).

Industrial companies making anything from antifreeze to lipstick and bath salts, use such agonizing tests as the LD50 and the Draize eye and skin tests – where substances are dripped into mostly rabbits' eyes or put onto patches of stripped (abraded) skin to test the effects – purely as a form of insurance, or indeed PR – 'they've been tested on animals' is meant to have a reassuring ring.

In fact the testing of non-medical cosmetics is not mandatory in this country, whereas the Health and Safety at Work Act requires the testing of industrial products (not necessarily with the use of animals), yet people are still suffering from chemically induced industrial diseases – there is, for example, a link between PVC and petrochemicals and skin disease and cancer. Many industrial products are causing dermatitis. That asbestos dust was damaging was known at the turn of the century, yet nothing was done about it for years. Profit comes before human safety and partly because of this, animal testing counts for little. As in all other testing, what happens to laboratory animals will not necessarily apply to non-laboratory humans and dangerous products continue to be produced and marketed because profits speak louder than health.

Even so, not all men working in an asbestos factory will get lung cancer – individuals vary in their reactions to potentially harmful substances and environments. If this is so, how much more so between animals and humans?

Weapons are also tested. These are not listed separately in government statistics because this is the most secret area of research, for radiation, chemical, biological, ultrasonic and photic as well as conventional explosive or ballistic weapons . . . most of this is conducted at Ministry of Defence establishments such as the Microbiological Research and Chemical Defence establishments at Porton Down in Wiltshire. It has also been reported that the animals are used in hundreds for radiation experiments at the Atomic Energy Authority's laboratories at Harwell and Aldermaston,[1] yet radiation effects are now well known.

At Porton Down weapons more sinister than the atomic bomb are tested on thousands of animals. Here is an example:

Monkeys were exposed to a nerve gas (Soman) and given various doses of the drug to look at its ability to protect the animals from the effect of nerve gas. The drug effect involved many of the animals dying. Weakness, convulsions and

[1] Richard Ryder, *Victims of Science*, NAVS, 1982.

breathlessness affected the rest. Some of the monkeys attempted to crawl across the cage floor but often collapsed. A number lived for some time in a moribund state (*Journal of Pharmacy and Pharmacology*, 1979).

Some monkeys were infected with a bacteria which resulted in severe disease after 3 days. Large amounts of mucous fluid poured from the animals' eyes and nose. They had high fevers, lost their appetites and had difficulty in breathing. They were left in this state until death came on the 5th, 6th or 7th day. Some animals were virtually dead when killed. (P. Hambleton, A. Baskerville, P.W. Harris Smith, M.E. Bailey, Microbiological Research Unit, Porton Down, 1978).

Councillor Austin Underwood of Salisbury labelled the 7,000 acre establishment at Porton 'an animal Belsen'. At its Allington Farm, thousands of animals, including monkeys, are bred for use in experiments.

Animals are used in agricultural research – the Agricultural Research Council lists forty-one research establishments in Britain. Most of the research at these establishments is directed towards more 'efficient' meat production. Scientific breeding and nutritional experiments are carried out and sometimes experimental surgery. A vet who worked in research told me he thought it 'absolutely right' that animals be experimented upon so that food production for animals could be improved; that is, that we may consume more milk and meat.

When Animal Liberationists broke into the Animal Physiology Institute at Babraham, Cambridge, in 1980, to obtain photographic evidence of experiments there, they found 'pigs with electrodes in their brains and sheep with holes in their bodies', while according to the *Daily Star*, a spokesman for the Institute said the 'farm animals are accustomed to quiet, sympathetic handling'!

Not only are animals subjected to one of man's greatest vices – warmongering – but to the effects of other damaging activities uniquely human, such as alcohol, drug and tobacco abuse.

Alcohol research began in 1926 when Curt Richter carried out the first experiments with rats.[1] Animals are subjected to

[1] *The Liberator*, May 1982.

force-feeding of alcohol and then sometimes to brain surgery in order to examine the effects on the brain. All of the alcohol work is fatuous and only demonstrates what we already know about its effects. Two scientists, Blum and Geller[1] placed animals in the dark and discovered that this increased alcohol consumption; then they blinded them and found that the increase in consumption continued. Ellis and Pick[1] showed that monkeys experiencing withdrawal symptoms had tremors, vomited, showed fright reactions and many died after violent fits. These and many more 'ingenious' experiments form a part of so-called medical research.

Meanwhile many animals, mainly rodents, are still being subjected to smoking experiments every year, despite the large public outcry against it and its uselessness.

'Despite the association between smoking and lung cancer in humans, it has not proved possible to induce lung cancers in animals by exposing them to tobacco smoke by the inhalation route.' F.J.C. Roe in G.W. Gorrod (ed.), *Testing for Toxicity*.

Some who would like to see animal experiments abolished still feel that there is a place for medical experimentation. Yet the facts show, as Alexander Pope said, that 'The proper study of mankind is man'.

Paul Hamilton Wood, MD, MB, BS, FRCP, wrote in the *British Medical Journal* (April 1951): 'Findings under highly artificial experimental conditions in animals do not necessarily apply to healthy intact man,' and Clifford Wilson MA, MD (Oxon), FRCP, wrote in *The Lancet* (19 September 1953):

> The results of animal experimentation have been too readily and uncritically applied to the problem of human disease. Well established facts about human disease – both in its clinical and histological manifestations – have been ignored by experimenters and have had to be rediscovered before fallacies were recognised and corrected.

Even more telling, René Dubos wrote: 'The experimenter does not produce nature in the laboratory. He could not if he tried, for the experiment imposes limiting conditions on nature, its aim is to force nature to give answers to questions devised by man.'[2]

[1] *The Liberator*, May 1982.
[2] *Mirage of Health*, Allen and Unwin, 1959.

Ivan Illich in *Medical Nemesis* wrote that 'the drug industry is becoming a risk to public health' and it is estimated that a third of those in hospital are suffering iatrogenic (drug induced) disease.

The thalidomide tragedy is now well known because the drug, taken for somewhat trivial purposes, had such dramatic and devastating results – a generation of deformed humans. Richardson-Merrell distributed it in the early 1960s despite the fact that animal tests had shown it to cause 'shivering, vomiting and ultimately death in rats and dogs'. Tests showed it to be toxic and to have a lethal dose. But the company went ahead with clinical trials without revealing these results to the Federal Drug Agency. Ironically, the Committee on Safety of Medicines increased its call for increased animal testing – even though the disaster was *the result of animal tests being ignored*.

This company had previously marketed an anticholesterol drug, Triparonoa, which had to be withdrawn after it was found to cause hair loss and cataracts. And now the same company, Merrell Dow, have been marketing a drug called Debendox, when animal studies suggested it caused an increased risk of deformity in babies when mothers had been taking the drug.

One Debendox mother, Mrs Valerie Alexander, wrote of her experience in the Animal Aid journal, *Outrage*.[1] Her son was born with half his right arm missing and mismatched ears in shape and position. Her MP collected statistics and found 140 other cases – one child had no properly formed joints in her body and underwent ten major operations by the age of six months, while another had to have his 'hideously malformed legs' amputated at twelve months. This mother, who had previously believed that some experiments might be a 'necessary evil' is now firmly convinced otherwise and wrote that animal torture of 'inconceivable proportions' brings only one guaranteed benefit to humanity – a financial one.

Professor Goldberg, Chairman of the Committee on Safety of Medicines, stated: 'No drug is completely safe', 'Anyone taking drugs is at risk', 'Any active drug has risks associated with it.'

A quick look through *The Data Sheet Compendium*, the drug companies' representatives' handbook reveals the number of contraindications associated with nearly all drugs. There is just one problem – it is not for sale to the public.

[1] July/August 1980.

The late Dr Edward Bach, probably the most advanced medical man of our time, denounced the cruel and immoral use of animals in medical research and the crude, blanket methods of treatment used by his profession. He found that the personality of the individual was of even more importance than the body in the treatment of disease.[1] If this is so, animal experiments become even more inexcusable.

What is more, the mentality which counts life only in objects or tools of science and statistics, motivated largely by ambition, power and greed, will show little concern for human life.

Drug companies fund research units in hospitals – most large hospitals house them. The companies try to use these for the exclusive testing of their own drugs, depending on how strongly they are resisted by consultants and administrators. They conduct clinical trials – both blind and double-blind tests, the latter in which neither the doctor nor the patient knows who is getting the drug. A geriatrician in a London hospital stated that old people, especially those with no families around to ask too many questions, are often the subjects of these trials.

In his book, *The Dark Face of Science*, John Vyvyan wrote that Dr Ruff, tried at Nuremberg, when asked whether he had any scruples when requested to experiment on camp inmates said,

> I had no scruples on legal grounds, for I know that the man who had officially authorised these experiments was Himmler. . . It was a wholly new experience for us to be offered prisoners to experiment on. Accordingly, both Dr Romberg and myself had to get used to the idea.

Dr Whittal points out in his book *People and Animals* that the torture methods used by some governments today on humans are similar to the methods which experimenters have been practising on animals for years. Both Dr Whittal and Richard Ryder note the gruesome head transplant experiments carried out on dogs and monkeys. Of transplants, former microbiologist, Catherine Roberts wrote: 'I would say the time has come to die when a dying person, young or old, can be kept alive only by means which have arisen out of scientific violation of both human and animal creatures.'[2]

[1] See *The Medical Discoveries of Edward Bach, Physician*, C.W. Daniel, 1973.
[2] See *The Scientific Conscience* (Centaur Press, 1974).

Cancer research is an enormous subject, an industry which consumes millions of pounds and eats up millions of animal lives for what have been called by Professor Smyth, former Chairman of the Research Defence Society, 'trivial returns'. We are, many years later, and millions of deaths later, no nearer to a cure. Here is one example:

> 80–100% of female C3H/He strain mice carrying a cancer virus, develop tumours within 8 to 18 months after birth when studied under normal environmental and housing conditions. Research showed that by varying housing, handling and stress the incidence of cancer at 400 days varied between 0% and 92% (*Science*, Vol.189).

It is estimated that between 80 and 90 per cent of cancers are preventable, yet still the millions are poured into cancer research to find a 'cure'.

Animals suffer in dental research despite the opinions of experts who say that animal teeth are not the same as human teeth: Bill Jordan, former RSPCA veterinary surgeon commented on experiments done with dogs: 'the pH of the dog's mouth and the bacterial flora are different from man.'[1]

When I learnt that monkeys were being used at Guys Hospital to try and develop a vaccine for tooth decay, I mentioned it to my dentist, saying that there must be a commercial interest behind such a ridiculous scheme, because the obvious answer to less tooth decay is less refined food and less sugar. He was sure that the Royal College of Dental Surgeons would be funding the research themselves and registered surprise when on the next visit I told him it was Mars Ltd who were putting up the money for the monkeys – who do not normally get tooth decay – to be fed on their products, while still denying any link between sweets and tooth decay![2]

Perhaps even more disturbing was the 207 per cent increase in experiments inducing psychological stress (other than by electric shocks and other aversive stimuli) in 1982 over 1981.

Psychological and behavioural experiments must rank among the most futile. Dr Alice Hcim, herself a behavioural psychologist, who went through the brainwashing of the system

[1] See *Victims of Science*, p.64.
[2] *Observer*, 28 December 1980.

has written: 'I believe that many of the questions posed by psychologists are trivial or highly specific – and indeed, that many of the answers are knowable in advance – in which event the suffering inflicted on animals is not justifiable from any viewpoint.'

To disguise what he is really doing, the behavioural experimenter uses jargon to help compartmentalize the reader's mind when he publishes his work. Students start this process early. Dr Heim remembered Professor Roger Russell once remarking with amusement on a student who described an animal dying as 'exhibiting lethal behaviour'.

Dallas Pratt, MD,[1] condemns behavioural experiments and writes that

> the method of studying behaviour of animals used by many investigators is, paradoxically, not to study animal behaviour. What they seem to be interested in are the distortions, the pathology of behaviour: either the fragments which remain after surgical or other mutilations have destroyed the marvellous wholeness of a functioning organism, or the reflex jerks teased out by any of the myriad of prods, punishments or pleasures which the ingenuity of a researcher can devise.

He goes on to say that perhaps the researcher is offended by the splendour of the whole animal in its wild, natural state and is somehow uncomfortable until it is 'subdued and transformed'. 'The instruments of transformation are the drug, the knife and the electrode . . . the cage, with its accessories.'

Such grisly experiments as the primate surrogate mothers (where baby monkeys are taken away from their mothers and put with wire, cloth or spikey inanimate surrogates) are now well known. These babies exhibit extremely disturbed behaviour and physical malfunctioning. Who needed such cruelty to produce such 'clever' results?

The behavioural psychologist uses many means to torment his victims – interfering with the animals' senses, with the brain, with the central nervous system, use of aversive stimuli, electrical or other, or the use of devices for 'inducing a state of psychological stress'.

[1] 'Alternatives to Pain', in *Experiments on Animals*, Argus Archives USA.

Richard Ryder described how he saw students in California cut off a cat's tail and blind it and put it on a revolving wheel from which it could not emerge. The wheel was left turning for days and nights so that it couldn't sleep. Every few hours they would take it off the wheel, wrap it in a blanket so it couldn't scratch them, while one of them stuck a needle in its spine to draw off fluid from its brain. This was supposedly to discover something about sleep deprivation.

Many psychological experiments are being carried out in Britain today. Here is an example: 'Monkeys were operated on and the frontal eye fields in the brain removed. They were then given the task of finding and retrieving a peanut from a display of visually similar objects. It was reported that the group with frontal eye fields removed by surgery made more errors than normal monkeys,[1] and 'Conscious rats were subjected to electric shocks resulting in convulsions for periods up to 10 days. These rats and another group not shocked were then given various chemicals to look at activity response. The work was carried out to look at hormone release from the brain after shock treatments.'[2]

Yet Dr Robert Drewett, Lecturer in Psychology, DSP, said in 1983: 'Very few experiments on animals in departments of psychology have anything to do with the understanding and treatment of distressing neurological conditions' and from the British Psychological Society:[3] 'Scientists should be aware of the temptation to carry out experiments because they are possible rather than because they contribute to knowledge. Every field produces such unnecessary experiments and the case for their elimination on both ethical and scientific grounds is overwhelming.'

As Brigid Brophy has said, 'Our whole relation to animals is tinted by a fantasy – and a fallacy – about our toughness. We feel obliged to demonstrate we can take it; in fact it is the animals who take it.'[4]

Psychological and behavioural experiments can tell us nothing about man – except how cruel and unfeeling he can be – and the best studies of animals have been by their keen and

[1] N.G. Collin, in *Behavioural Brain Research*, 1982, vol.4(2), 177–93.
[2] *Neuropharmacology*, 1982, vol.21(9), 881–4.
[3] 1979, Bulletin, (Vol.32; 44).
[4] *Sunday Times*, October 1965.

respectful observers like Konrad Lorenz and Allan Boone.

Meanwhile the amount of animal research being carried out is probably holding up progress rather than increasing it. Ambitious scientists fail to communicate findings and so experiments are constantly repeated and there is far from enough recourse to centralized information retrieval systems. Dr Edward Bach, his entire medical career devoted to healing the sick, immediately published his findings so that they were readily available – not for the enlightened, the egocentric secrecy of the insecure and careless.

There are many possible alternative methods available for research which include: techniques which draw on biogenetics, mathematics, virology, biochemistry, radiology and microbiology – which include tissue culture, organ culture, microorganisms, computer studies, mathematical modelling, the use of films and video recordings, the use of fertilized eggs, human investigations and epidemiological surveys.

There is a great deal of money to be made by the laboratory animal breeders and thousands of laboratory animals pass in transit through London's Heathrow airport. The Research Defence Society joined with similar societies abroad to fight possible legislation which might curb the freedom of researchers in The Research Animal Alliance. Two years ago, it was handed £1¼ million by Charles Rivers, the monkey breeding company. Those fighting animal experimentation are not fighting anything so admirable as science, but huge vested interests.

Nature's secrets can never be wrested from a torn animal imprisoned in a laboratory, nor can man ever hope to save himself any major or minor discomforts by their theft.

Until man heals himself of the psychological sickness which allows him to carry on creating victims, he can never find health nor happiness.

Source material: As stated through chapter, with special help from Angela Walder.

The Blackest of all Black Crimes: Thoughts on Vivisection from Dr Donald Whittal

This is what Gandhi called experimentation on animals and rare as he is, Dr Donald Whittal is a medical man who agreed with him. Formerly a GP, Dr Whittal was unaware of the horrors of vivisection until very late in his career. When he did discover them, he devoted a large amount of his time and energy to making others more aware, in the hope that public opinion would eventually end the torture done in our name. The following extracts are from a talk I was fortunate enough to have with him before a stroke so cruelly damaged his health.

If you gain advantage by doing something that is wrong and revolting, like vivisection, you will gain no ultimate benefit. In actual fact a good amount of disease has been caused by research on animals – the side effects of drugs, for instance. A large number of people go to hospital because they are suffering from diseases caused by doctors and that is because conventional medicine concentrates on suppressing the symptoms and not treating the person as a whole.

There is much talk about vivisection being a complex problem. In one sense it is, but in another, it isn't, because I really think that you will never get rid of it unless you say *it is a crime and therefore it should be stopped.* It is no good saying, well, we must first take a little step and when we've done that, take another little step, then another. That is not the way to get public support. The public must realise the facts of what is done to animals and then there will be public pressure and the law will change to abolish it.

Many people believe that the 1876 Act stops animals from being tortured in laboratories. It doesn't of course. All the atrocious experiments being done are perfectly legal. People don't know this – I didn't until a few years ago. I knew that there was vivisection, but I suppose I was brainwashed. It wasn't until I read John Vivyan's book, *The Dark Face of Science*, after picking it up in the library out of curiosity, that I realized. I was horrified and had to find out if it was really true. I wrote to him and went to see him and got in touch with an anti-vivisection society and found that it was all true. I felt then that

I must write and tell people who didn't know about it – I wrote to the Archbishop of Canterbury, but I was surprised, because I found that such people were not against vivisection. That is a terrible thought.

John Papworth's book, *Human Guinea Pigs* gives examples of experiments on humans in this country in quite a few hospitals. If you have an attitude of mind in which you accept experiments on animals, it will spill over onto humans. The two things run parallel. It is quite simple – would you, or would you not, torture a living creature for any purpose?

I once had an interesting conversation when I was handing out leaflets with the widow of a vivisectionist. She was a naive person, but was trying to defend vivisection on the grounds that certain discoveries had been made through it. After half an hour, I asked her, 'Would you be prepared to torture an animal if some advance was going to be made? Logically, you are in favour of that.' She replied, 'I know, but I wouldn't.' It is frightening.

Animals are used quite unnecessarily in school biology classes. I think it is unnecessary for a doctor, let alone for anyone who isn't going in for any further scientific pursuit. I never did any dissection in school. During medical training, the only dissection I did was quite useless. It taught me nothing. I dissected a dogfish. It had no bearing on anything and was a complete waste of time. There were frogs which were pierced – that is, part of the brain had been destroyed. Whether you can feel pain after being pierced, I don't know. We saw the heart beating and watched a tracing of the heartbeat. I didn't know what it was all about. A lot of people didn't know. It was quite useless and a total waste of time.

You could train to be a doctor without using animals at all. You can learn biology quite well from books and plastic models. They are much better than living animals. Dissection is just a mess which does the students psychological harm – it conditions them into treating animals as things to be used. Quite apart from what happens to the animals, it is harming the humans as well.

This attitude on the part of doctors carries through to the patients. That is why doctoring is so totally bad, because it is smothering symptoms more and more with tranquillizers, painkillers, antibiotics and so on, not getting at the causes at all.

*As long as vivisection goes on, medicine will get worse and worse and
disease will increase.*

I was brainwashed more than I realized as a medical student.
I saw diagrams in the textbooks of physiology of what they call
a decerebrate cat – a cat which had had part of its brain
destroyed, but was still alive. That was accepted by other
people; it was officially accepted by my elders and betters and I
kind of accepted it as well. Why didn't I say, 'look that is
ghastly'? In some extraordinary way, you can accept ghastly
things if they are presented to you in a certain way and if a
whole lot of other people believe it's all right.

It takes time to break through conditioning. I became a
vegetarian and this was reinforced when I had to visit a patient
who was the wife of a man who ran a slaughterhouse. Simply
being on the premises made me feel I could never eat meat
again.

'My views are different from most of my colleagues. Of
course the medical profession really is totally credulous. It
writes off anyone who doesn't agree with what it says. They
write off osteopaths, homeopaths and so on as quacks. They
laugh at them. I did myself, not so many years ago. It was pure
prejudice, I didn't know anything about homeopathy or
osteopathy, but it was quackery!

When I read John Vivyan's book and realized that what was
done to animals was all part of medicine, it completely shook
my confidence in medicine. I saw hospitals not simply as places
where people were healed and kindly actions done, but places
where horrible tortures on animals were carried out. (Most
hospitals have animal departments.) It is a terrible thought
that a hospital contains a torture chamber. I suddenly realized
and my ideas changed. I no longer took a lot of things for
granted. I enquired to see how I'd been mistaken and criticized
myself, and things appeared to be very different.

I have been a doctor since 1948. About 1971, I began to
question. I must admit that I had always had a certain distrust
of science – a kind of odd sort of mechanistic way of looking at
things. I have always been rather repelled by that. But
nonetheless, I was brainwashed.

Medicine has become so specialized – everything is put into
little departments, as if everything were separate, when in fact
nothing is separate. It is a totally wrong attitude towards a

human being. How can you be a proper doctor if you don't know what human beings are like, what they really are? If they are simply a bunch of physical organs, you are not going to do any good at medicine.

I'm against transplanting, I think it's a revolting idea. I would not personally take a transplanted heart, or any other organ – the cornea is not quite in the same category. Apart from the fact that it is wrong in a lot of ways, it does involve the torture of animals. One method which is claimed to be applicable to learning about transplants is parabiosis. Animals are sewn together so that the circulation mixes, like siamese twins. They then inject one and see what happens to the other. Learning about transplantation is the excuse for this monstrous practice as it is for head transplants. Scientists justify themselves by saying they might just hit on something useful, while admitting they don't really know what they are doing. But if you argue along those lines, there's no limit to the horrible things that you will do. Ultimately, it seems, if vivisection goes on, and increases, we will get a monstrous world.

I have noticed when giving out leaflets during demonstrations that someone will say in a very vicious way, 'But what about people?' And you feel pure hatred and resentment, almost like a physical force. Fear and hatred seem to go together. It is fear of cancer in one respect, which makes people keep on with vivisection. But they will never find a cure for cancer if they go on investigating it by tormenting animals. That is the wrong approach.

I do seem to have found that people with cancer very often seem to have had some sort of stress or discord in their lives or family or have been under tension in some way. I do think that with most illness, the cause is stress.

The tendency to think that only what you can see is real – you know a thing is solid, it exists, you can put your finger on it, is misguided. It isn't like that at all.

You can feel the atmosphere just walking about in the streets – sometimes there is something evil which comes in waves which is much more noticeable where there are concentrations of people.

Dr Whittal gave a very simplified, concise summing-up of the state of our sickness as a race, a complete diagnosis, which only such a good doctor could give. But his prognosis was grim. Perhaps that is why illness overtook him. He was hurt and depressed, but at least his book was written before his physical health deserted him, a book which will remain an outstanding tribute to his great understanding.

What You Can Do

* Support the anti-vivisection societies and distribute their literature, display their posters.
* Become as well-informed as possible on the issues involved in experimentation.
* Write a concise informed letter to your MP stating your views – he may know very little on the subject. He has to take notice of his postbag. Ask him to write to the Home Office deploring current conditions on your behalf.
* Write to your Euro MP.
* If you can, join the Research Defence Society and be informed as to what they are doing.
* Join in specific projects suggested by the anti-vivisection societies – the more who join against specific targets, the greater the concentrated effect.
* Boycott products you know to include animal products and which have been tested on animals. There are now plenty of alternative cosmetics, for example.
* Lead a healthy life and practise preventative medicine on yourself, with a fresh vegetarian diet, exercise and relaxation. The British Association of Homeopathic Pharmacists has declared that it will never use animals in research. Homeopathic and Naturopathic medicinal cures are extremely effective through good practitioners as are many other forms of alternative medicine.
* Take responsibility for your own health and well-being – avoid as far as possible taking drugs. Ask intelligent, searching questions about health care.
* Do not use commercial pesticides and weedkillers.
* Spread your views through all possible channels – local media, for example.
* Form a local animal-rights group in your own area or raise funds for the larger societies.

Organizations to Join

The British Union Against Vivisection

The BUAV was founded in June 1898 at Bristol by Miss Frances Power Cobbe after she had left the Anti-Vivisection Society when it decided to campaign in Parliament for measures other than total abolition. The aim of the Union was to 'oppose vivisection absolutely and entirely, and to demand its complete prohibition by law, without attempts at compromise of any kind'.

The BUAV began with branches in several different parts of the country, which it sought to increase and endeavoured to educate the public through its journal, *The Abolitionist*.

From its dynamic beginnings in the first part of this century, the BUAV gradually fell into a backwater and became a rather bumbling entity which achieved little and whose executives showed little of the passion or imagination of their forebears: that is, until 1979/80 when concerned about the way in which their organization was being run, and in particular the waste of public money and alleged corruption, a group of active animal rightists made the complicated facts public and successfully proceeded to take over the BUAV, managing to elect a new, radical committee and thereby employing young, dynamic staff who have managed to completely change the image of the organization and who have proved their worth by their immense activity and ability, in fighting vivisection on every possible front, and especially in maintaining excellent and continuous contact with the media and initiating new and intensive campaigns, including the inception of a section for young people, an intensive assault on dissection in schools, and relationship with Islington Council which has brought about the adoption of an Animal Rights Charter which has since been adopted by Lewisham and stands to be adopted by other councils. Its energy has helped other societies with which it is working for the abolition of vivisection, producing new impetus.

The Union as a pressure group now stands in the forefront of the fight against vivisection. Membership has increased dramatically from under a hundred new members per month under the old management, to hundreds and sometimes over a thousand per month in 1983.

New, informative fact sheets on various issues and on how to campaign are available on request.

BUAV, 16a Crane Grove, London N7.

National Anti-Vivisection Society

The NAVS was founded in 1875 by Frances Power Cobbe, a dedicated nineteenth-century animal-rights campaigner. Together with Dr and Mrs Hoggan, Archbishop Thompson of York and Lord Shaftesbury, she began what was originally known as the Victoria Street Society. History has handed down to us a philanthropic Lord Shaftesbury omitting to include, let alone emphasize, his concern for creatures. He loved all animals and was a great supporter of the movement against vivisection. He felt that to save a man from, or convince him of, the evil of cruelty, was as much a help to him as to save him from dishonesty or intemperance.

The Victoria Street Society came into being during the time when the first Royal Commission on vivisection was in progress, on 15 August 1876. Lord Carnarvon's 1876 Bill – modified in his absence to protect the vivisector against prosecution – was given Royal Assent. Miss Cobbe, intensely disappointed, stated firmly that she would remain in office as Honorary Secretary of the society only if the principle of abolition were adopted. On 22 November 1876, the following resolution was passed: 'That the society would watch the existing Act with a view to the enforcement of its restrictions and its extension to the total prohibition of painful experiments on animals.'

Miss Cobbe was probably right when she stated that they had at first thought to leave science all possible freedom, but that all hopes of compromise had now passed away. She resigned from her honorary secretaryship in June 1884. The Honorable Stephen Coleridge became Honorary Secretary in April 1897 and, in 1898, Miss Cobbe severed her connection with the society she had founded. It was by then called the National Anti-Vivisection Society, because it resolved that 'while still demanding total abolition, it would not be precluded from making efforts in Parliament for lesser measures'. Miss Cobbe did not approve and so founded the British Union for the Abolition of Vivisection.

Dr Hadwen of the BUAV and the Honorable Stephen

Coleridge thenceforth came to stand for the two factions of the anti-vivisection movement: the total abolitionists and the gradualists. It is interesting to note, however, that the position today has changed. The NAVS is an abolitionist society, as is the BUAV, but the latter campaigns more aggressively.

Aims The NAVS today asks for total abolition, stating that all experiments, regardless of purpose, are morally wrong and indefensible. Realizing that vivisection cannot end overnight, they ask that the government should stop the most wretched and cruel experiments and phase out all others, seeking viable alternatives. Money already being poured into scientific work should be syphoned off for this purpose. They demand new legislation to phase out completely all animal experiments and a ban on the issuing of new licences from the date that the legislation comes into effect.

To these ends, the society works in the political field as much as possible, and only within the confines of the law. They can understand the frustration of those who break the law but believe in working through legal and democratic means. They endeavour to use their supporters in Parliament and have sponsored many bills in the Commons and Lords. One of these was a cosmetic bill introduced by Baroness Phillips, but her work was obliterated by the industrial lobby. They spend large sums of money on educating the public through the media. Local radio is used almost weekly. They supply lectures who are officers of the society who talk at schools and universities. They have a number of films. *Curiosity Kills the Cat* won a British Academy Film and Television Arts award. Their latest films are *Quantum Pharmacology* and *Suffer the Animals*, a revealing documentary.

One department of the NAVS, the Lord Dowding Fund supplies grants to scientists who are using alternatives.

The Articles of the NAVS state that it will work in all corners of the world and to this end the International Association Against Painful Experiments on Animals was founded in 1969.

The NAVS is a thriving, well-established society and has a good deal of success in gaining media coverage. Its magazine is informative and always contains good photographic material. The society publishes numerous booklets, pamphlets and is now breaking into book publishing. It hopes to work with other societies, but states that it cannot support any society which does not have a policy of total abolition.

societies, but states that it cannot support any society which does not have a policy of total abolition.

This rigorous stand, admirable from a moral viewpoint, limits the kind of campaigning it can carry out, but does not limit the society's usefulness as several different approaches are needed. Total abolition is something which all anti-vivisectionists aspire to, but work towards with often very different strategies.

National Anti-Vivisection Society Ltd., 51 Harley Street, London W1. Tel. 01-580 4034.

Animal Aid

Animal Aid is an activist anti-vivisection organization which aims primarily at educating the public about the true facts of animal abuse.

It was founded in autumn 1978 by Jean Pink, a teacher who by chance read a copy of Peter Singer's *Animal Liberation*. Formerly unaware of how humans were abusing animals, she was shocked into action, quickly disillusioned by the existing societies which seemed to have achieved little or nothing despite having been in existence for many years. Starting locally with a handful of people and working from her own home, she achieved rapid results. Membership has grown in two years to over 7,000. Animal Aid now has a busy office and employs several staff. Jean Pink's work grew so much that she had to relinquish her teaching job to work full time as an anti-vivisection campaigner.

Having seen the drawbacks of committee and bureaucracy, she retained control without a committee to enable her to make quick decisions – something often necessary when arranging specific demonstrations and campaigns.

She aims to educate the public to the horrors of vivisection, by leafleting, demonstrating, holding rallies and informing through any possible outlet – the media, university debates and so on.

Animal Aid is one of the most effective publicity machines for anti-vivisection; it has a rapidly growing membership of 'pacifist activists' who want to act, not just pay membership fees into an ineffective bureaucracy.

Its bi-monthly magazine, *Outrage* informs with facts, carries anti-vivisection news, encourages alternative medicine and a lifestyle which avoids unnecessary exploitation of animals.

Literature – leaflets and papers – is available for individual information and for distribution.

The society has nationwide contacts who arrange local activities.

Animal Aid: 7 Castle Street, Tonbridge, Kent TN9 1BH.

The Animal Liberation Front

The ALF was formed in June 1976 at which time about thirty people were involved. It grew out of a smaller direct action group called The Band of Mercy, which came together in 1972. When the Band of Mercy started, only about half a dozen people took part, but now hundreds of people are attached to the ALF – many as activists, some as supporters.

Two of the original founder members suffered stiff prison sentences in 1973 for rescuing animals, but since that time the activist movement has gone from strength to strength simply because so many people are frustrated by the fact that animal exploitation has grown, not decreased, after a hundred or so years of campaigning.

In the long term, the ALF look to end the persecution of animals, but meanwhile it does its best to liberate as many animals as possible and has indeed managed to rescue thousands from laboratories, factory farms, fur farms and laboratory animal suppliers. In addition, the ALF has damaged property and equipment connected with animal exploitation and torture to the tune of millions of pounds as it feels that this frequently results in the prevention or diminution of persecution, either directly, or because the money which has to be spent on restoration or extra security may be redirected away from its original course.

The ALF are a non-violent group of people who believe in reverence for life and who do not consider damage to property to be in itself an act of violence. Personal threat or violence is not part of their policy and every care is taken that no harm should come to animal or human life when activities are being carried out. They do, however, reserve the right to defend themselves in the face of physical attack or to kill an animal – by an humane method – which they find in an extreme of suffering.

Contrary to the belief of many, laboratory animals will not 'simply be replaced' when rescued. Some are specially bred strains which cannot be replaced; in other cases it will be too expensive to replace them.

It is not known how many members the ALF now have. Operating in secret its activists are organized in well-run cells, which have now become international. Members are told that they must be prepared to put their personal freedom at risk in the liberation of animals. However, it welcomes all kinds of support from others who cannot make such a courageous or drastic commitment.

Supporters of the ALF can supply permanent or temporary homes for rescued animals, give money – especially on a regular basis by subscribing to the supporters group – carry out intelligence work in places where animals are exploited or tortured, perhaps even by taking a job in a laboratory or similar establishment. The ALF simply asks that other animal rights societies should support them, while it never condemns individuals who feel they cannot participate in direct action. As it has stated, 'The Animal Liberation Front is not so much an organisation, but a state of mind.'

While others, like those in Hitler's Germany, turn away and pretend these concentration camps do not exist in our midst, the ALF is prepared to go in and liberate the innocent victims with, as Hans Reusch has said, 'nothing to be gained for its members and much to be lost', while others fight for prestige and status in the Animal Rights Movement or 'talk and weep' ('Every vivisector's laboratory is a Belsen or a Dachau, and they exist and are in continual operation in thousands throughout the world').[1]

Animal Liberation Front, Box 190 Peace News, 8 Elm Avenue, Nottingham.

Research into Alternatives

The main organizations giving grants to scientists for research into alternatives to animal experimentation are:

The Fund for Research into Alternative Methods of

---

[1] Geoffrey Hodson, *Animals and Men: The Ideal Relationship*; Theosophical Society.

Experimentation (FRAME), 312A Worple Road, London SW20 8QU. Tel: 01-946 1450.

The Humane Research Trust, Brook House, 29 Bramhall Lane South, Bramhall Stockport, Cheshire SK7 2DN. Tel: 061 439 8041.

The Doctor Hadwen Trust, Hendon and Aldenham Kennels, Tylers Way, Watford Bypass, Watford, Herts.

The Lord Dowding Fund, a department of the NAVS.

Although well-intentioned, societies set up to give grants to alternative research can be deluded by scientists who, failing to obtain grants from the MRC and the ARC, often turn with unimaginative projects to these charities and call them alternatives. Pressure should rather be coming from anti-vivisection societies to push government into giving money for scientific research into alternatives. BUAV separated from the Dr Hadwen Trust because it felt that the society could not become truly progressive while working so closely with scientists and decided that all its energies should be poured into educating public opinion and pressuring government for change. FRAME is not against vivisection.

While serving an intermediate role of possibly temporary and probably stimulative value – they have made scientists think about alternative research – the Alternative Research charities will achieve little, so long as public opinion does not rise in outrage at live animal experiments and so long as massive state funding is not put into alternative research with alternative units in existing laboratories rather than the present wasteful animal research.

The Scottish Society for the Prevention of Vivisection

The Scottish Society for the Prevention of Vivisection was founded in 1902 as a branch of the National Anti-Vivisection Society as a result of one of its founders, Miss Netta Ivory, witnessing a pet dog being killed by strychnine.

In 1911, the Scots resolved to act independently and founded the Scottish Co-operative Anti-Vivisection Society which later became The Scottish Society for the Prevention of Vivisection.

Since its inception, the society has played a prominent part in the campaign for animal rights. In 1969 it set up the St Andrew Fund as a Registered Charity to take over the clearly charitable aims of the society's work – the protection from and prevention of cruelty to animals.

In recent years the society, under its director Clive Hollands, played an important part in bringing together a united campaign for animal rights beginning with Animal Welfare Year in 1976/77 in which most of the societies in Britain came together for a common purpose. Following this, the society formed the first united political campaign – Putting Animals Into Politics in the run-up to the 1979 General Election.

Unlike the other three societies, the Scottish Society does not see total abolition as realistic – although it does remain the ultimate ideal. In the words of its director, 'The Society takes a realistic view of achieving its final aim and believes that where legislation is concerned reform can only be achieved within the limits of public and parliamentary opinion at the time.'

It is up to the individual whether he or she agrees with this view of the fight against vivisection; but we have to ask whether it makes for compromise, and shouldn't campaigning societies be advancing, not simply representing, public and parliamentary opinion?

The society produces a Year Book on trends and developments in animal exploitation and the campaigns against them, together with factual pamphlets available on request.

The Scottish Society for the Prevention of Vivisection, The St. Andrew Animal Fund, 10 Queensferry St, Edinburgh EH2 4PG.

8 Conservation: A Troubled Issue

It really seems as if we wish to produce a human race in solitude, but in solitude that human race will have no chance of surviving (Mario Pavane).

Conservation is a fashionable word – it sounds like it is for the good of everyone, including animals, but it can be dangerously anthropocentric. In contrast to Animal Rights, conservation is beginning to be scientifically acceptable, largely because man sees the extinction of species as something which might possibly affect him; his enjoyment, comfort, survival, whereas the concept of animal rights involves concern for its own sake. The majority of mankind is as yet not that unselfish. Conservation can cover a multitude of ills. Its exponents are however, doing some good work and they are giving certain issues an airing which might never be allowed to come before the public were they presented under the animal-rights umbrella. But it is something which the intelligent person concerned about life on Earth must explore with a questioning approach before reaching conclusions. It runs a gamut from out-and-out materialism on one hand – humans wanting to preserve creatures for their own use, pleasure, well-being, and so on, in a world which they can now manipulate by virtue of their mental skill or artfulness – through genuine concern and appreciation of creatures by knowledgeable and sensitive humans to total condemnation by extreme animal rightists, who take the view that if a species of animal dies out, it simply will suffer no more at the hands of man and so enjoys release. Conservation is in danger of merely maintaining living museum pieces for humans' sake rather than preserving individual lives for the creatures' sakes. All life, after all, whether it be that of an endangered species of tiger or ape, or that of a domestic dog or

cat, must logically be considered equal since all living creatures
enjoy the will to live.

Bill Jordan, a veterinary surgeon of many years' experience,
former Wildlife Officer of the RSPCA, a man with progressive
and humane views, sees this as the basic difference between his
organization, the People's Trust for Endangered Species (see
pp.221–5), and other wildlife organizations. Bill Jordan is an
unusual scientist: he was one of the handful of people in the
workaday animal rights movement who mentioned the word
'spiritual' when we talked. He sees the future of animals in the
balance, depending on a spiritual as against a materialistic,
view of the world.

The World Wildlife Fund, for example, has produced a
document entitled 'World Strategy for Conservation' which
presents a philosophy which postulates that an endangered
species or any threatened species must pay for itself, pay for its
own survival, whether it is in products like meat or skins, or
tourism; that somehow or other, a species, or a reserve, must be
economically viable. If this were not the case, Third World
countries, in which most of the reserves and endangered species
live, will simply declare wildlife reserves uneconomical and will
get rid of them in order to turn them over to agriculture.

The tentacles of materialism spread to the furthest reaches of
our planet. Let us suppose we are trying to protect sea turtles
which like to browse on nice sandy beaches in, for instance,
South America. That country might find it far more profitable
to build a large hotel on the beach to encourage tourists. That
would be the end of the turtles because they would no longer go
onto the beach and even if they did, their eggs would be
smashed. And so, to persuade such a country of the necessity of
conserving the turtles, it must somehow be given some return; a
deal has to be struck. Perhaps this would mean a farm in which
case enough would be kept wild to preserve the species but a
good deal of money would be made from the farming of them.
This sounds like common sense in a materialistic world, but
materialism is just one philosophy and in fact it cannot sensibly
apply any more. It is a great pity that it should be applied to
conservation because there are certain species which cannot
produce a profit. Even the symbol of the World Wildlife Fund
itself, the panda, could not do this, and so the very symbol of the
WWF gives the lie to its basic philosophy.

The various international conventions function under

similar terms of reference. The International Whaling Commission was set up to maintain whaling, not to protect whales. The Convention on International Trade in Endangered Species, CITES, began as a convention to protect threatened species, but to protect them for the continuation of trade. Many of the EEC regulations are designed to protect trade – Europe is being bonded together by materialism, trade agreements (note, the power of the farmer in the EEC is carte blanche to create waste). Most international agreements put trade, that is, materialism, first and conservation as a very poor second. Even our national legislation falls under such directives. In that kind of a world animal rights do not enter into the thinking of politicians. Any benefit that animals derive is simply a fringe benefit.

Whales epitomize conservation because they are an international resource, because they are highly intelligent and because their numbers are going down and everyone knows and believes these three facts. There are also very important problems with some of the large land mammals. Elephants, for example, may be poached in one reserve, yet officially culled in another. There is a good deal of pressure on the people in the reserves. They are shrinking, and as the reserves shrink, so these is too little space for such big animals as elephants and rhinos. They need huge areas and therefore they are beginning to destroy their own habitats; because of pressure from increasing human population.

A report sent by Dick Pitman from Zimbabwe[1] in 1981 demonstrated this sad fact. Here, in short, is what he said:

Most local conservationists have now accepted the National Parks' case for elephant population control – Zimbabwe is now thought to hold about ten times the number of elephants as it did at the turn of the century, because of practical conservation methods and the outlawing of uncontrolled hunting. Ecologists fear that many animals will die off if population control is not carried out. (Wankie now has 15,000 animals compared with less than 1,000 in the 1920s.) The meat produced by these cullings is distributed to local tribespeople living on the borders of the parks and this helps reduce the friction between parks and locals. Further up the continent in East Africa reports indicate that hunting is to be resumed and a degree of harvesting of game animals may take place in order to feed a

[1] *The Beast*, Summer 1981, No.10.

large, hungry and fast growing populace. Kenyan conservationists have greeted this with a mixture of approval for the principle, and fears for its controlled implementation in the face of possible corruption and unbridled slaughter. The fact that the present population, seven million, is expected to double to fourteen million by the end of the century in Zimbabwe, means that it may face similar possibilities in coming decades. Its wildlife resource may come under increasing scrutiny in the future, although at present game reserves or parks are seen as enclaves in which the sanctity of wild life is respected as far as sound ecological management practice will permit.

A recent move has been the appointment of black wardens in tribal areas outside the designated wildlife estate. Many of their duties centre on the education of local people in the value of game animals as a renewable resource – education probably based on economics, not aesthetics, at least in that descending order. Until recently the bushman lived as a predator in balance with wildlife, but now the West has made a turnabout from wildlife slaughter to conservation awareness – so trying to overturn a deep-seated attitude in a population which suffers very low standards, undernourishment, and so on.

The kind of vocabulary Dick Pitman was forced to use in his report tells everything. Euphemisms like culling and harvesting, population control, while man expects to increase himself by one hundred per cent bode ill for those mighty beasts whose natural lifespans are longer than those of his wiley predator.

There are not necessarily too many humans on this planet, but their distribution and their methods are to blame for current disasters. The West and highly developed countries like Japan are to blame for their self-indulgence.

Ideally the responsibility should rest with these developed countries who should pay the underdeveloped countries not to kill off their wildlife instead of making the wildlife pay by such things as tourism or the selling of products. We should instead pay these countries not to kill the animals. We should actually give grants, for nothing, stating that if so many million hectares are set aside for elephants or other animals then they will be paid for doing it as if we were paying a kind of rent for every year that they practise conservation. We can afford to do this and there is no good reason not to do it. If we want preservation, we should be willing to pay and to support it in an *unselfish* manner. We pay for things to be protected within our own country, and such a move would merely be a logical extension, for other countries can afford protection far less than us in the West. We *should* be more enlightened, because we have been through a similar process. We are, as Bill Jordan says, 'poachers turned gamekeepers' – we have been great ravagers, especially the Americans. They have eliminated many species, devastated their lands. Europeans have been the culprits so they should pay.

The main interest in conservation is now coming from younger people who realize the appalling state of their world and want to do something about it. Small, concerned organizations like PTES are simply filling in as best they can for the time being.

Source material: Dick Pitman. *The Beast.* Bill Jordan of PTES.

What You Can Do

* Learn as many true facts about conservation as possible.
* Support those societies whose conservation philosophy you agree with.
* Make MPs and Euro MPs aware of conservation from the point of view of the animal's well-being, not necessarily humans' profit and convenience.
* Spread the idea of giving unselfishly in order to preserve animals for their *own* sake – they have as much right to be here as we do.

Organizations to Join

People's Trust for Endangered Species (PTES)

The People's Trust for Endangered Species was started in 1977 by Larry Behrman. He had had experience as an advisor to Age Concern and Oxfam and felt he could do the same for animals. He found three trustees who decided they should collect money on a mail-order system. Behrman felt the PTES would occupy a unique niche in that it collects and spends money in a different way from other organizations. There is no bureaucracy and absolutely none of its money is wasted. Only four staff are employed – two full-time and two part-time, plus one or two others on contract such as lecturers who visit schools.

The object of the trust is to educate and to fund research into the true facts of any given situation – because in many cases animals are in danger but the fact has to be proved to the world. To this end PTES has funded a great deal of research, especially into the condition of whales – which has been used by the International Whaling Commission.

PTES also funds education in countries which have particular problems and pays for anti-poaching equipment. It has also, for example, contributed £20,000 to help the otter in England and a similar amount to help the mountain gorilla in Luanda. The money helps to pay for two researchers out there who are studying and protecting the population of gorillas: there are only 200 left.

£25,000 was given for a spotter plane, radio equipment and fuel and servicing for two years to protect elephants in Uganda. The idea is to put radio contacts on to the next leader elephants spotted for the plan. The plane can then spot the leader elephant and direct the reserve guards to the elephant herds so that they are always there to protect them, and incidentally any other animals as well.

The trust is very small but has produced some excellent and productive material. Bill Jordan, its director, a vet with longstanding experience in animal welfare and wildlife, sorts out projects put up to the trust and advises the trustees on feasibility – meetings for decisions are held monthly. The structure of this small society enables it to act quickly when a species is immediately threatened: a sudden problem can be dealt with suddenly.

Sometimes projects are put up, sometimes they are originated. Part of Bill Jordan's job is to be on the lookout for projects the trust can initiate. The only publicity the trust receives is that which arises naturally from its successful work. It has no PR department, so has to rely on chance and the proof of its good works.

Some of its most impressive work was the research on pirate

whaling done by Nick Carter, a former employee. He produced
two important reports on pirate whaling which, in Bill Jordan's
words 'pretty well closed pirate whaling as far as the rest of the
world is concerned'. As a result of its findings a resolution was
passed that no IWC country would buy meat from pirate
whalers.

PTES has also funded research into the population of whales.

PTES hopes to grow as an organization in the amount of
money it has at its disposal, but will not employ extra staff –
only experts on a contract basis, just as scientists are now
employed on contract to carry out studies into the different
species.

The Trust badly needs money which is not bespoken. At
present people are mailed and asked to give money for a
particular project and those people will know exactly where
and how the money will be spent. Other wildlife societies collect
money on an unspecified basis – they work in a different way.
But PTES needs money that is not previously accounted for so
that it can protect less attractive species like crocodiles,
iguanas, bats – an appeal to protect bats is likely to get a rather
small response.

The goal of many conservationists is a managed world. The
World Wildlife Fund, for example, is saving life for *humans*, but
PTES seeks to educate man to live alongside creatures for their
own sake. To this end it aims to inform the public; lobby
authorities; fight legal battles; fund the necessary scientific
research to conserve and nurture species, and to carry out the
many other activities which may arise in connection with
conservation of species.

Bill Jordan sees his job as protecting what animals he can
until the world comes to its senses:

> We are not trying to change people, it's too big a job for a
> little society, but what we can do is protect some of these
> species so that when the world does come to its senses, there
> will be some left so that they can allow them to breathe and
> increase again.

He sees the issue in two parts: first comes the one in which
'Traffic' and other such organizations are involved, in
decreasing the huge numbers of animals being killed for fur.

Second, the method of killing. The problems can be tackled in different ways. It is possible to work through CITES, to try and reduce the numbers being killed. It can be tackled through publicity, in an attempt to dissuade affluent Western people from thinking that furs are fashionable or prestigious, and by trying to obtain legislation, demanding more humane methods of killing. 'But with tongue in cheek,' he adds, 'because it is difficult or impossible to do and to bring to the attention of the public that this is so cruel.' We can tackle these problems both worldwide through CITES and in Europe through the EEC.

We are not now, hopefully, importing the skins of endangered species into Britain as an Act of Parliament prohibits this. It also demands that any threatened species (that is, one on Appendix 2 of the Convention (CITES)) has to be licensed, so although the trade is not forbidden for all these species (the threatened species), it is monitored; we know what the numbers are; if it looks as if the species is becoming threatened, it can be moved onto Appendix 1, which prohibits all trade.[1]

The concept of conservation and the way it works is something to be carefully thought about. Bill Jordan, who works from a pleasant Surrey office feels that conservation should, if possible, work out of good, natural – that is, beautiful – surroundings. His words are a reminder to everyone to seek their emotional roots in the natural world:

> When you are spiritually awakened and you can see what Nature really has to offer, you feel for Nature. If you are living in the worst part of a big city, you may either become too angry to be talking sense at all, or you would be totally disillusioned about the whole thing. It would change you if you could get out and be in Nature again and then you can work from your heart. It is like saying to someone you can't love others unless you are loved. It is very difficult for a person who has come from a home in which there is no love to feel love for other people. And in the same way that is why I feel people do much better work if they are amidst Nature. Basically it's a very subtle thing we are trying to do. We can't just shout down at people.

[1] Obtainable from the Dept of Environment, John Goldsmiths, Bristol. CITES refers to the Convention on International Trade of Endangered Species.

People's Trust for Endangered Species, 19 Quarry Street, Guildford, Surrey GU1 3EH.

Greenpeace

When the earth is sick
The animals will begin to disappear
When that happens the Warriors of the Rainbow
Will come to save them.

Greenpeace was started in about 1970 by a small group of people in Canada and has been active in Britain since 1977. The name of one of its three ships, *Rainbow Warrior*, which has sailed to the help of seals and whales is taken from the moving Red Indian saying above.

Greenpeace is a non-violent direct-action movement which defends the environment – not talking, but action is its method. For this reason, there is no official membership as it is felt that the time and energy involved in assembling and maintaining membership files is better spent in organizing campaigns.

Current wildlife campaigns have been very successful – Greenpeace has joined with others to combat sealing and whaling: the Canadian hunt was much reduced in 1983 – no pups were killed; the Orkneys grey seal hunt stopped in 1983; Greenpeace is still pressurizing the Whaling Commission; only three countries – Japan, Russia and Norway – are holding out on the whaling ban due for 1986 (Peru withdrew its objection to the ban after pressure in July 1983).

As its campaigns have been so successful, in addition to combatting nuclear waste problems, Greenpeace is now campaigning against the slaughter of kangaroos in Australia, and the exploitation of Antarctica which they hope will eventually become a world park.

Anyone who supports Greenpeace in any way – by giving donations, showing their films, distributing their leaflets, wearing their T-shirts – is helping their campaigns. They publish an infrequent newsletter which is sent to people who donate over £5 or who request to be on their mailing list.

Greenpeace Ltd., Graham Street, London N1. Telephone: 01-251 3020.

Friends of the Earth (FOE)

Friends of the Earth began in San Fransisco in July 1969, its founder, a well-known American environmentalist, David Brower. His aim was to build an international organization which would campaign aggressively for the preservation of the environment. A friend of his living in Paris, Edwin Matthews, was given the task of representing FOE Inc. in Europe and starting up new European groups. In August 1970 FOE Ltd was formed and in May 1971 it was formally incorporated with Graham Searle as the director.

All national FOE organizations are members of Friends of the Earth International which is recognized by the United Nations as an international non-governmental organization which gives observer status at the UN and other inter-governmental agencies. FOE International helped to set up of the Environmental Liaison Centre in Nairobi which coordinates relations between environmental groups and the UN Environment Programme and also to establish the European Environment Bureau which coordinates environmentalists' relations with the EEC in Brussels.

Members of FOE International are autonomous and self-supporting, but linked by their commitment to saving the environment. Among other issues FOE fight for wildlife as they have for the whales, for the seals and for many endangered species. FOE were instrumental in getting an important ban on certain fur skins in 1972, Baleen whale products in 1973 and in pushing forward the Endangered Species (Import and Export) Act passed in 1976.

FOE depends to a large extent on donations. Members receive a newsletter three times a year. Information to be made use of may be obtained from the office during working hours.

Friends of the Earth, 377 City Road, London EC1. Telephone: 01-837 0731.

Protection and Conservation of Animals and Plant Life. PCAP International

PCAP was conceived in 1975 by Daniel Lindsay of Liverpool but was born in 1977 when he began the task of setting up a local network. He started PCAP as a local organization because he felt that the national societies concentrated their efforts in the south. With experience of running a vegetarian restaurant, and having become a shop steward in his current job, Daniel Lindsay set about using his wholefood contacts in England and abroad and was able to bring several European groups into his organization and then he began to use his direct line to the unions, having decided to specialize in getting trade unions involved in animal rights. After three years of hard work, during which a hundred unions were lobbied, he managed to get Liverpool, Glasgow and then the TUC to agree to black whale imports. That was 1980. In 1982, the European ban on whale imports was passed and the initial goal had been achieved.

PCAP then turned to environmental issues, especially the dumping of nuclear waste. It also worked on the seal issue and in March 1982, shortly before the EEC decided on an import ban into Europe, it had the support of all the big unions so that Terry Duffy of the AUEW was able to obtain a petition signed by the TUC council which represented its 12½ million members, Duffy and Lindsay heading a delegation to Downing Street to present the petition to Mrs Thatcher. As of 1 October 1983 the EEC implemented a two year voluntary ban on the importing of seal products but in September 1983, Daniel Lindsay met with Moss Evans of the TGWU who has pledged that should the ban be lifted after two years, the unions would black imports of seal products.

Another PCAP victory was won against a Liverpool fur shop selling a leopardskin coat. This was illegal under the Endangered Species Act 1976, but neither the police nor the DOE were keen to prosecute. Mr Lindsay took out a private prosecution and, after a seven month legal battle, won the case and the shop was fined £750, the largest sum ever imposed under the Act. PCAP were awarded £500 in costs. (During 1981 so many species of plants or animals were made extinct there was one for every day of the year.)

This created great media interest with the result that PCAP gained many more supporters – it now has over 6,000. PCAP has a lively programme in Liverpool, Manchester and Birmingham with demonstrations and leafleting every week. However, it will remain a specialist organization aiming to work with the unions – the British TUC, the European TUC and the International Confederation of Free Trade Unions (ICFTU).

There is no official membership, but supporters receive a quarterly newsletter and those actively involved in the Liverpool area also receive a monthly news-sheet.

Daniel Lindsay now has a good working relationship with the main trade union leaders and plans to show other organizations how they can work with the unions on their own specialized issues, bringing union muscle to bear on animal-rights issues.

PCAP International, European Secretary, 29 Broughton Drive, Grassendale, Liverpool L19 0PB.

9 Legislating for Compassion

Right before the face and across the path of Tyranny (Lord Macaulay on John Hampden, 1594–1643)

In 'civilized' society it becomes necessary to legislate for compassion. Materialism, vested interests, status and power play their part in creating pressures which can bring ordinary kindness and decency to breaking point. This is why, apart from consciousness raising, which is the only true basis for radical change in our attitude towards animals, it is necessary to use the cruder tool of politics. It is therefore important to be politically aware. This means knowing how the system works and how the individual can attempt to make it work for him or her.

Influencing MPs

If you favour a political party enough to become a member, or if you decide to favour a party because it seems the most likely to support animal-rights issues, then becoming a member and working at grass-roots level in your constituency is a good idea. To do this, go along to your local constituency party committee, attend meetings and push forward your views, which as a member you have a right to do. Proposals will be voted upon and will be on their way to being considered at the Annual Assembly. To gain a place in the party manifesto, issues must filter up through pressure from party members. Proposals passed by a large majority at annual assemblies will usually get into the manifestos.

Once an issue is included in party policy, it does not

necessarily mean that it will be acted upon when that party comes into power, and so it is important to lobby MPs at every opportunity and to keep in constant touch with MPs through informed correspondence, putting on extra pressure when an issue is current and may make progress.

There are three ways in which you can make your views known to your MP: by writing letters, seeing him at his local surgery or lobbying at the Houses of Parliament. Lord Houghton with his long political experience feels that MPs are far more affected by the letters they receive than by lobbying. This may be so, but Arthur Latham, formerly Labour MP for Paddington, believes in lobbying and valued meeting groups of constituents anxious to put over their opinions while receiving their MP's point of view at first hand. However, he deplores the rules and traditions which make this democratic right hard to exercise.

Writing to MPs

Letters to and interviews with MPs should be concise and well prepared with correct facts and well reasoned arguments. An MP is not supposed to enter into correspondence with an individual outside his constituency, so although you may write to as many MPs as you wish, you cannot expect replies from any other than your own. Every politician must take note of the size of postbag and the number of letters on any one subject. His position in a democracy depends upon the support of his constituents. Moreover, while in office, he represents them, and if he should receive vast amounts of mail on an issue which does not particularly interest him, it is his duty to become interested and it is your right to press for this.

Lobbying MPs

There is actually nothing in our constitution which allows for lobbying. Visitors to the House are called 'strangers' and can be turned out at whim. What is more, there is no pervading attitude that MPs and the staff of Parliament are public servants, rather that admission is a privilege.

Arthur Latham stated: 'In my view, it (Parliament) has learnt to cope with the mass lobby to such an extent as to make it ineffective apart from the valuable broad propaganda effect which a demonstration may achieve.'

Even if thousands of lobbyists arrive at the House, they will be herded into queues and only a few hundred may be admitted to the Central Lobby. The rest will be allowed in in batches into the Grand Committee Room in Westminster Hall.

Once they are in there, some MPs will address the lobbyists from the platform – usually the converted talking to the converted – and a limited number of questions and contributions will be put from the floor before the lobbyists are sent out through Old Palace Yard, back into Parliament Square. Then the next batch may be allowed in.

Back in the Central Lobby, a few may have got to see their MPs, but they are usually likely to be frustrated in their attempts. Lobbyists are given a green card on which they must state which MP they wish to see, the purpose of their visit and their name and address. These cards are given to a messenger who then has to find the MPs – a system which doesn't work with ease.

Only constituents with specific advance appointments can be sure of seeing their MPs, but if the lobby is very big, even this may be hard to achieve. Apart from getting through the crowds to the letter holders' queue, it may be so long as to prevent admission anywhere near the time of the appointment. In addition to all these difficulties, the Sergeant at Arms has been authorized to refuse MPs all accommodation to interview lobbyists other than in the Grand Committee Room in Westminster Hall. This, Arthur Latham said, was 'a decision I for one resent very much'.

These then are the awkward conditions which lobbyists have to face. Their only hope of achieving some success is media coverage in which case the lobby would have to be large and vociferous.

The lobby has its place – and perhaps should be given a more prominent one by an easing of the rules, but the power of the postbag must never be underestimated.

Legislation

As the Animal Rights movement is seeking new legislation to safeguard the rights of animals to life, liberty and freedom, it must not only remain alert to all proposed changes in the law, but must play an active part in bringing about any changes.

Proposed legislation must pass through three stages – a bill going through Parliament must pass through a first, second and third reading and possibly a report stage which will usually be between its second and final reading.

At the first reading, it is simply introduced and there is no debate; on the second reading, it is usually debated, but sometimes this is not so, especially for a private member's bill where time begins to run out. An attempt is made to get a bill through 'on the nod' and if one single member stands up and says, 'I object', then the whole process comes to an abrupt halt and the bill has to be debated. Because only a limited time is allowed for private members' bills, and that time almost inevitably runs out, these bills have to be put back to a day when there will be time. Certain Fridays within a parliamentary session are allocated, but even then, because private members' bills are not very important to government, they often fail as there is rarely enough time for them.

It might be very difficult to get a private member's bill through its second reading. Almost on the nod, the Speaker puts a question and the question is implicit – 'Does anyone raise the objection to the 2nd reading of this bill without a debate?' – without his asking the formal question. If there is silence in the chamber, then the second reading is taken and the bill's passage moves on to the third reading. But through usage – 'slovenliness', as Lord Houghton has called it – the Speaker doesn't bother to put the question because he must push on through the timetable and as a result does not bother to put the formal question at all; thus the formal objection is not put. A front bench spokesman might just say "ject' or the Chief Whip might have ticked the bills to which they are going to object on the Order Paper on which the day's debates are set down – the Chief Whip would probably just tick whatever is to be objected to and so the Speaker will actually know beforehand, so that he really feels he has no need to spell out the formal question.

Whether private members' bills get through or not depends on how skilful the sponsor is and whether he's done his own whipping (lobbying for support). There will be no government whipping, no party whipping on something like an animal rights bill as there is no great grass roots support in the parliamentary party and very little in the chamber (the House of Commons). The reason why private members' bills rarely get passed, especially if they are at all controversial, is because the government does not want them to get through. The government always tends to avoid controversial legislation, and most private members' bills that do get through are bills which the government has asked a private member to sponsor. A private member wins a private members' bill ballot and the government, because it always has too full a programme, might ask that private member (MP) to take on a piece of legislation in private members' time, because there is a certain amount of parliamentary time allocated to private members' bills, but it is never enough. However, if the government asks for a piece of its legislation to be put up in this time, and supports it in the chamber, then it will go through.

But that is only an extension of government legislation. For controversial or unpopular topics, the battle is hard, and rarely won. The MP sponsoring the bill must do a good deal of whipping himself, must inform members of other parties that he is dealing with a very important issue and ask for support. Then he must make sure they actually get to the House to vote, because there must be a minimum of forty members voting on such a bill, otherwise it will be lost. If it is ten o'clock in the evening and there are only fifteen members in the House, the fact that they all vote for a piece of legislation is meaningless because there will not be enough votes to get it through.

Legislation put forward by government is quite a different matter. The government whip is the man who orders the business of Parliament, who literally runs the government programme in the House, together with the Leader of the party. They organize what legislation the government aims to get through Parliament.

Campaigning to Change the Law

If you do not already know who the MP for the area is, ring the Houses of Parliament and ask. To campaign within a party, lobby any MP; if your man or woman is not interested in your cause, find one who is.

Campaign locally. Call your local council offices and find out who the councillor for your ward is. Get him or her interested and informed on animal issues which can be dealt with at local level.

Pressure the relevant ministeries on various issues. The Home Office deals with experimentation but it is not such a good idea to write to the Home Office yourself. Always get your MP to write on your behalf. When you write as an individual member of the public, a fairly low-level civil servant will respond, but when your MP asks a question or tackles the issue in Parliament, far more care will be taken with the reply and it will come to the notice of a much higher civil servant. Higher civil servants give the job of researching replies to lower-ranking officers but the facts will be double-checked by more senior persons.

If hundreds of people write in and complain on an issue it becomes a minor irritation but has no real effect. It can even be said that the closed institution of a ministry is fairly contemptuous of the public. Most ministries, and most certainly the Home Office, are almost a law unto themselves. Little changes there, regardless of what is happening in the world outside.

The Home Office has an extremely small department dealing with animal experimentation in proportion to the number of animals used every year in experiments but it is part of the Probation and Aftercare department which is in fact one of the largest. However, its smallness can be taken as an indication of their contempt for the subject – 'only animals', not human beings.

The benefit arising from the smallness of the department is that details can be lost in a great, slow-moving bureaucracy, but this does not necessarily mean that they are either more concerned about the subject they are dealing with or work any closer to its details.

There is no minister for animal research – which arguably should come under the DHSS or even the DOE, but even if a minister were appointed, it would not necessarily make any difference. He would be the most junior minister – parliamentary under secretary – and his being there would not be significant unless the right kind of laws existed to be upheld. At the moment the laws are so weak and ineffectual that it makes no difference what gets said or done and existing laws would give a minister sufficient room to manoeuvre and wriggle out of any queries put before him.

It is worth noting, especially in regard to legislation on experimentation, that it might be much easier to undermine the current state of affairs by bringing a private member's bill to amend an existing act rather than bringing in a whole new bill. Such small gains could possibly be far easier to achieve and make for quicker change.

10 Campaigning: Taking the Initiative into Our Own Hands

Thoughts and Ideas Arising from Talks with Henry Spira, US Animal Rights Leader

> If there is no struggle, there is no progress. Those who profess to favour freedom, and yet deprecate agitation, are people who want rain without thunder and lightening. They want the ocean without the roar of its many waters. Power concedes nothing without a demand. It never did and it never will. (*Frederick Douglass (Abolitionist leader)*)

Effective campaigning, especially in an area which concerns non-humans, where awareness still needs a good deal of awakening, is not easy. Histories of the anti-vivisection movement reveal that enormous amounts of energy have been expended by courageous and dedicated campaigners for the last hundred years, yet the situation is probably worse, not better. Vegetarianism, for instance, has been taught by the leading lights since antiquity, but humans still insist on violent eating habits. For the concerned, the outlook seems bleak, but Victor Hugo was certainly right when he said: 'There is something stronger than armies – an idea whose time has come.' Even in the darkest days of materialism and tyranny over creatures, there is no reason to give up. In the 1980s, we may have good reasons to believe that the day is dawning when ideas of compassion are beginning to enjoy a fuller range of expression.

There are many lessons to be learnt from the past; slavery was theoretically abolished because its time was over – though the slave mentality still persists almost unnoticed in vast numbers of humankind; how many people truly *think for themselves*, how many dare to say no when told to say yes? But nonetheless, in that great movement, certain key people were the all important catalysts for change.

The 1960s saw a breakthrough into what was called 'freedom' from the more puritanical restraints which had persisted into the gloomy 50s, and an upsurge in the Civil Rights Movement in America. One man who involved himself in that movement is now one of the foremost animal-rights campaigners in that country. A Belgian by birth, an American citizen, he is applying the experience he gained in union work in the merchant navy, in General Motors where he worked on an assembly line and in human rights work in the Southern States, to protest on behalf of non-humans. Awoken to the cause by the ideas of Peter Singer, author of *Animal Liberation*, he has brought clear thinking, initiative and cohesive planning to a movement that was at last beginning to gain momentum, becoming a force to be reckoned with, thanks to the efforts of campaigners who have, especially in the last fourteen or so years in England, brought their own kind of expertise to bear on the task of combatting government-sanctioned cruelty to animals.

Henry Spira is a strategist; a man of humility and single-minded dedication to the cause, he has been able to demonstrate the effectiveness of careful planning. It was he who successfully organized protest against the infamous sex experiments on cats at the Natural History Museum in New York which led to those experiments being stopped, and to a new policy for the museum on basic research, and was important in the formulation of new guidelines by the National Institute of Health for research on animals. He also played a part in obtaining the cessation of the Amnesty International electrical torture experiments on pigs and in achieving repeal of the Metcalf/Hatch Act which permitted laboratories to take animals from American pounds and shelters for research.

More recently, he initiated the forming of a coalition of animal-welfare organizations to campaign to abolish the Draize test in which all kinds of chemicals – household products, shampoos, hairdyes and much more – are tested by being put into the eyes of rabbits. They suffer enormously in the process, eventually go blind, and are killed, if they have not already broken their backs through struggling in the

restraining stocks.[1] The research community itself reported
that results from the Draize test are crude and unreliable, yet it
has remained unchanged for thirty-six years. Revlon was
chosen for the spotlight as it is one of the biggest companies
using the test. Revlon's vice president, Frank Johnson,
admitted that the coalition had picked a good target. The
campaign eventually linked up with Animal Aid in Britain and
nationwide protests gained enormous publicity. The result has
been a promise of money to fund research into alternatives. If
genuine efforts are forthcoming, everyone will be delighted, but
if promises are not kept, then pressure will be re-applied.

Revlon came up with $750,000 to fund a three-year research
programme at Rockefeller University into an alternative
against the Draize test.

When Avon learnt that Animal Aid was about to campaign
against them once they had achieved a result with Revlon, they
announced they were making a donation of $1/4 million to the
CTFA (Cosmetics, Toiletries and Fragrances Association) and
would pledge $1/2 million to fund any research project in
alternatives that was acceptable to them, but they want to
maintain some control over what is being done. The CTFA, the
industry trade group, set up a Test Systems Task Force on
alternatives in April 1980 and is making some attempt to help
eliminate duplication by compiling a computerized list, by
chemical composition, of materials already tested.[2] FRAME
(Fund for Research into Alternatives in Medical Experiments)
of Great Britain, presented good working proposals drawn up
by their toxicology committee. These were sent to Avon, who
asked for more detailed documents. The request was complied
with, but at the time of writing, nothing more has happened.
The CTFA set up a fund with a maximum target of $5 million:
Estee Lauder has contributed $250,000; Bristol Meyers – who
make hair colourants – gave $200,000. When Henry Spira
approached the soap and detergent trade association and the
chemical manufacturers association, they sent their toxologists
and not their PR people to talk with the coalition, which is a
hopeful indication that it has been taken seriously. He chose the

[1] 'Rabbits can break their backs on the stock . . . if it does happen, you replace the
rabbit.' (Don Abrutyn, Conference on testing guidelines, Washington, 30 October
1979.)
[2] *Lab Animal*. Conversation with Henry Spira, Draize Test Activist, Jan/February 1980.

Draize test because it gave a good opening, for reasons already mentioned. The coalition was able to make it visible through newspaper advertisements and demonstrations. Encouraged by the results, or at least potential results, Spira moved on to a campaign to abolish the LD50 (lethal dose 50 per cent) test. In this particularly obnoxious poisoning test, a group of animals is force-fed with a substance until 50 per cent of them die – be it weedkiller, hair dye or whatever. When we talked in May 1981, he outlined his current ideas:

The Draize coalition is being kept together to expand into the LD50 – if necessary, the two can be used together as companies like Avon do use the LD50 test. The idea is still to publicize the true facts. The LD50 is the most widely used test which by definition causes pain – at least half the animals in any one test will be killed and the rest will be suffering and extremely traumatized. What is more, scientists don't really know what is the question that the LD50 is an answer to. It is particularly ridiculous when considering the fact that you can kill anyone with practically anything if you give them a large enough dose. Scientists are capable of far better work than this 'super crude' method when really what is being sought is the point at which minimal damage occurs.

This test was chosen as the next target because it is not only very dramatic, it is scientifically not valid. Science can do better, and moreover, many scientists are showing concern on this issue. The idea is not to ask for an 'LD5' either, but to suggest that a *non-animal* system be used.

A campaign such as this can promote ripple effects as did the Draize protest. Abolition was asked for, but a lot of Draize testing has since been done away with – bureaucratic anachronisms, things being tested when the results were already known, for example. Some of the material is being given in a more diluted form; in some cases three instead of six rabbits are being used. The campaign was for alternatives, but in the process of spotlighting the issues, various minor concessions or partial reforms were made as the companies wanted to take the heat off themselves. Money has not been promised to fund research into alternatives. Gradually, the test could be phased out.

Fatuous behavioural experiments are also in line to be tackled. They can simply be abolished: 'The alternative, the other option, is simply to safeguard, in other words, to raise the quality of life in order not to create more victims.' Henry Spira intends to promote local campaigns where people can discover what is going on in their universities and colleges and make their feelings known.

Under the Freedom of Information Act, facts are easier to obtain in the United States than in England. Most of the experiments are funded by tax money, so it is possible to look up exactly what is being done, who is doing it, how much money they use, what happens to the animals, and so on. In England some information is kept secret. Here we have to distribute leaflets in places where we know that experiments are going on and ask people to make contact with additional information – assuming that there will be some workers who are not too comfortable about such developments. (During an Animal Aid leafleting session which I attended in Oxford, one or two people did approach us telling of horrific experiments being performed in their establishment. These people felt helpless, did not know what to do, nor who they could complain to.)

Henry Spira suggests that people register for side courses in universities to have them find out first hand exactly what is happening. It is interesting to note that an official group of animal welfarists, while visiting Babraham Research Laboratory in England last year, were not shown animals undergoing experimentation, yet Open University courses were actually putting some of them out on the television screen. Spira says:

There is a whole range of things you can do, just using your imagination. One of the benefits of a local campaign is that a huge number of actions can be developed which keep focusing on the university or research institution in various areas. Taking into account the present economic climate, we know that the enormous experimentation programme is taking away from the quality of our lives and money is going into almost criminal type experiments. Public money is going into research which is merely creating new victims.

The excuse for psychology experiments is that they will create a healthier society, but there is no way you are going to create a healthier society by the concept that might makes right and in the process helping to create more victims. Also, if we are going to consider survival of the species, I think a species is more likely to survive if it has a mindset (attitude) on concern with others rather than a mindset where it can do what the hell it likes and get away with it.

Another burning issue is the use in schools and community colleges of animals for experiments. These serve absolutely no purpose as they have been done hundreds of times before. Experiments on animals have to be taken out of the curriculum.

As a high-school teacher himself, Henry Spira thinks the best course of action is to become involved in the parent-teacher association in order to put forward the position that a parent doesn't want the school to be used to desensitize his or her children, that teaching is for understanding others, not the opposite:

> Just from the point of view of something worth learning, I imagine kids would be a lot better off learning what the human body is all about, how it functions and how they can take care of it. That way they would be learning something useful rather than the fact that you can get away with hurting those who can't fight back.
>
> The point is that activity per se doesn't do the animals any good; activity should be tied in with productivity where there is a goal and one step can be used as a stepping stone to the next thing. It is also important to realise that none of the struggles have ever been won by people just using all their energies in parliamentary gabbling.
>
> It is important to take one thing at a time – if you try and do too many things at once, everybody sees that you are hopping about all over the place and no one has to worry about you, whereas if they see that you are targeting on them and you're not going away till the battle is won, then that's a message you'll get responses to.

Spira also feels that only one company at a time need be tackled because precedents can be set and other similar companies will, hopefully, fall into line:

> They didn't integrate every single lunch counter in the USA – they integrated just some of them and then the rest fell in

line. You don't have to target on all the companies – if you do
it with Revlon, and maybe half a dozen of them, then all the
others will fall in line one way or another, or else you'll force
them into line. But once you have set the pattern, it becomes
simpler; you're winning a lot more than one particular fight.
I think it's clear that if you're in a campaign, you're in there
to *win*, not to *fight*, and you should not move away from there
till that one is finished. Just the idea that your procedure has
been serious and those are your intentions, is very important.

He feels it is useful to compare animal and human rights
campaigns when deciding how to set about protesting for
animals. It's a good idea to spend a little time in the library to
find out how the Anti-Slavery movement functioned, how the
Women's Movement has operated and so on:

I think we are in the same fight, but we have to remember
that the victims can't be mobilized in defence of their own
rights. One of the basic laws is that if you follow the rules that
the power structure sets for you, you will fail. The power
structure does not make rules in such a way as to encourage
outsiders to get into the system; people say Parliament is the
way to go, or the vote is the way to go, but the vote is not
going to make any difference – they're fooling themselves;
they're just getting into the same system. Part of what the
system does is to programme people into *inconsistency*, so they
care about cats and dogs and not about the other animals
used in labs. It also distorts belief in where the levers of
power are, and the levers of power are not in the vote. The
power system plays games – it can also unmake and
circumvent its own rules to suit its own convenience and
interests. If you are not a part of it, then it's really irrelevant
what you do. If you are going to set up the candidates in the
first place, and you don't have the apparatus or the
machinery that the powerful political parties have, you are
really just playing their game. It's never been done before,
and there's no reason why it should happen now because of
the simple fact that the system sets out hundreds of rules and
regulations precisely to frustrate people who want to change
the system, and not only to frustrate them, but give them
'occupational therapy'. This is the way to keep yourself busy

and struggling, where it's all going to be ineffective, but you have the illusion that you're doing something – educating people, getting people to vote and all this sort of thing.

I think educating has to be done in the course of action campaigns and it has to be done at the bottom line so that you can mobilize the enormous energies of the people out in the street, where you can raise enormous media pressure, and create economic pressure, bringing them into an orchestrated whole. I think that pushing people's energies into the election game is not just wasteful, but it is really frustrating and it is betraying the whole struggle for animals. If you were part of the power structure, then the animals wouldn't be where they are, so obviously the fight for animal rights is not a part of the power system, as I have said before, it isn't inviting people to come in. It is keeping everybody out and themselves in. . . People are told that one vote can make all the difference, this way they have the illusion that they have something to say, but in reality they have very little voice, if any. Things are often made worse this way. Then people complain that things don't happen, when in fact they have been made part of a huge confidence trick.

This is the way Spira sees leaving your conscience at the ballot box.

Comparing animal rights to civil rights and looking back, it is plain to see that it is not yet a battle won. By asking why, we could perhaps learn from omissions and mistakes, of which he thinks there are many:

I think part of the trouble was that the blacks allowed themselves to be co-opted by the power system, they started to rely on poverty programmes, to rely on the government to do things, instead of relying on themselves, on their own people. I think they neglected to make alliances with other groups. But part of their failure was nothing to do with them. It is the fact that there is less need for skilled labourers – most of them are unskilled, and what is more, the economy is shrinking instead of expanding, and the blacks are going to be the first ones to get pinched out. All the blacks in the USA could strike and it wouldn't make any difference. They don't have a lot of levers. They don't have any big alliances with

other movements – they never hooked themselves in with the
anti-nuclear movement, the anti-war movement. They just
never had that mindset, *that this was all part of the fight for the
quality of life* [my italics].

Should we be linking up with other movements in the UK at the
present time? The anti-nuclear movement is not interested in
animal rights; it is human-orientated, while the ecology
movement so far seems to be half-hearted in its concern for
animals.

Henry Spira feels that the animal rights movement must first
well and truly establish itself as viable before attempting to
forge such links:

> It really doesn't make sense to link up with other movements
> if you don't have any clouts to link up with. You have to get
> your own act together before you can ally yourself with
> others. To hook up with the environmental movement would
> be quite natural. We are saying, for instance, we need a
> better toxicology, and in order to test all the pollutants in the
> atmosphere, they too, need a better toxicology. There was a
> big anti-nuclear march on Washington early in 1981 which
> included a banner for animal rights activities. After the
> march they had a non-violent food stand. In that sense, it's
> certainly a good way to go. We should have our presence at
> these anti-war, anti-nuclear activities. We should certainly
> make the point that *what we want is a non-violent society* [my
> italics].

But governments want just the opposite. They are making huge
amounts of money from arms manufacture and export. The
vested interest is so great, there is no economic incentive for any
government to withdraw from the arms race. Spira makes a
point worth noting about the animal rights movement in this
context:

> It is possible that many of our demands can be met without a
> challenge to the entire power system – concessions can be
> made without it being undermined. Alternatives could
> certainly be developed, animals could be phased out of labs,
> behavioural experiments could certainly be done away with

and we could surely do without slicing up animals.

(This of course discounts the many animals used in nuclear and biological warfare testing. For example we are housing in England the biological warfare research in Porton Down that Nixon removed from America when it became an issue too hot to handle after the Pentagon Papers scandal.)

None of those things really gets at the basis of the power system, so in one sense, we really have to maintain our independence. At the same time, sections of the animal rights movement would see our struggle as part of the whole struggle for justice and rights. In a practical sense, we must retain a certain amount of independence because we can legitimately win a lot of our demands within the system. This is one of the reasons why it is so outrageous that no victories have been won, specifically because they should have been from the point of view of practical politics, whereas fighting against a war economy, like the fight for a just society, in general, almost always undermines the entire system. There just isn't a system without exploitation but the phasing out of animal suffering can be won if there is a powerful enough movement. It would also move the human justice campaign forward in the process. Whether we do or do not become part of the other movements, I think our movement will affect the one for human rights, and I can certainly see there will be overlap where there will be support for various different issues from the animal rights movement relating to human rights struggles – and all of the struggles for a non-violent society.

In a system which is cutting out benefits for humans – as in the present recession – there certainly should not be money spent on torturing animals. At the very least, we can do away with that sort of nonsense, and use the money to meet the needs of the people who are suffering from the cuts. We have to be realistic and see where we can create bridges, cutting out, for instance, all of the tax money that is not only being wasted, but is being used without people ever knowing where or how it is being used, in secret, to serve no other purpose than to enrich animal experiments, to create more victims. We have to be involved in practical politics, not just in the sense of maintaining our principles, but being very practical, very realistic, very political, deciding where to hook in with what is happening today in order to win some victories.

I feel that animals are the ones who are being exploited and tormented the most and whose misery and suffering is most rapidly expanding. We owe to them an obligation to win the quickest and fastest victories. Part of this is to study what is happening within the system, within this society, to judge where it is most vulnerable, where we can make most impact, where we can win. One area is the use of tax money for behavioural experiments. I would get the hell out and use these funds for the needs of people.

(To the California State University system in 1980, the US government gave \$79 million, most of which was spent on animal experiments.)

Should or can we work with the trades unions? Spira had some union support in his protest against the New York Natural History museum. Many people backed the protest on the basis that tax money should not be used to hurt others, but rather to raise the quality of life. He has made inroads into the National Institutes of Health in the United States. There is now a proposal that there should be a forum inside the science and technology department of the government that would include scientists and regulators, trade unionists, people in the animal-rights movement, and consumers; a forum which would focus particularly on developing a new toxicology. It would be protecting public health without harming animals. He feels there has not been as much cooperation with unions as there could be. One potentially good area is that of the trade in live food animals – we should be working with maritime workers and longshoreman (dockers) on this issue.

To attack the consumer end of the animal rights issue would be to diversify too much:

I don't think we can afford to get into extraneous issues and so divert the struggle to other areas where people are already working. Many people are, for instance, questioning the whole structure of medicine today, whether it is just creating more sick people, and so on. We can't afford to get into such issues because that would simply divert attention elsewhere.

There has been too much diversion in the last hundred years which has really been a betrayal of the animals, because the more you isolate yourself, the more you work against the cause. We already have enough difficulties in reaching people's minds and to push more and more issues at them will only isolate us more and more. It isn't fair to the animals. We have to be absolutely clear about this and avoid all extraneous issues.

The new campaign against the LD50 test will be given as much publicity as the anti-Revlon campaign. The aim once again is to push experimenters into alternatives. A specific company is chosen as a target – because it is big, because it does a lot of testing, because it is a household name and its products are identifiable. This makes it vulnerable. Proof of testing was easily come by in the States because the tests have to be put on government files, and are signed by the companies concerned. (In England we only have the Home Office returns on animal experiments and cannot easily gain information on various companies.) Proctor and Gamble has now been chosen for an international campaign because it can be asked to fund research overseas, because that is where it is making a great deal of its profit.

The company will be asked to contribute say, 1 per cent of its revenue to research into alternatives. What it spends on a particular household product is a vulnerable target. If alternatives for the LD50 were developed for household products then that could well produce a ripple effect so that alternatives could be used for pharmaceuticals and so on. Many people will agree that developing a new soap powder is not really going to raise the quality of anybody's life, and so this kind of target is much more viable than a pharmaceutical product. It is important to define one thing at a time, this gives leverage. It has to be a household name – there is no leverage when you protest against a generic chemical.

Despite, and because of, Spira's very strong feelings on the subject of animals is pain, his calm, calculated, rational approach works to good effect. Here is a summary of the basic points he emphasizes:

* Animal-rights people still tend to be regarded as anti-

intellectual, anti-science sentimentalists and this image has to be combatted by a professional approach.

* The movement must make use of experts – sympathetic, neutral and adversary, in order to establish credibility.

* There are professionals within the ranks of the movement – scientists, lawyers, writers, journalists and so on, who will be useful in drawing up fact sheets, preparing papers for presentation (both scientific and legal), in publicizing the cause, spreading awareness, bridging the gap between those involved with animal experimentation and all the vested interests appertaining to it, and the public.

* The neutrals can give useful advice – Spira sought the advice of media people, asking 'if you were us, what would you do?'

* Adversaries too, cannot be ignored. Sensible dialogue with a senator who had consistently blocked the repeal of the Metcalf/Hatch Act, despite this man's tenacity to his position regarding that issue, gave the protesting voice a very fair chance to be heard in democratic debate. The senator was later thanked in the victory statement – something which the press found worth reporting.

* Not only are the services of experts important, but it is also vital that the rank and file of the movement makes itself well-informed, armed with verifiable facts which will greatly lessen vulnerability to attack.

* They also need a good communications network. Spira's coalition against the Draize test finally amounted to 409 organizations all cooperating on one single issue. The kind of energy that can be generated by communication and agreement of this sort is enormous. Organizations can lend their individual skills, abilities, or whatever they choose, to the task in hand. The Millenium Guild in New York sponsored full-page advertisements in major daily newspapers, aided by the fact that (a) the coalition was making a scientific approach, and (b) that collaborative approaches had previously been made to Revlon, before a public campaign against them was launched. (For eighteen months prior to the protest the company was given scientific suggestions drawn up by two doctors. Only after it refused to respond did the coalition go into action.)

* Only one immediate issue is chosen, the emphasis being on issues and not on intentions. Name calling doesn't help the cause and neither do disseminated vagaries.

* An understanding of the scientific world helps – it is possible to find the weak spots in the system and drive in wedges in the most vulnerable places. Some scientists are uncomfortable about certain processes and would be glad to see some changes as regards tests which serve no truly useful purpose. Because of this, the adversaries can be split, and certain tenacious individuals may well become isolated by their colleagues as happened in the Natural History Museum cat experiments protest.

* The approach that scientists can do better than waste their time, energy and abilities on ridiculous experiments can help, emphasizing the potential of more imaginative, more refined research: 'that non-intrusive science is more imaginative, more elegant and likely to produce more relevant data'.

* Very important is the dedication and energy of the protesters. Concerted, organized pressure must be maintained until there is a victory – odd demonstrations, odd exposés, are easily dismissed and forgotten, leaving only frustration in their wake. The idea is to win battles, step by step, getting bigger each time, working within time limits, to keep up the pressure.

Protesters need to involve themselves in constructive use of the media in whatever way they can – sending letters and information to papers, radio, and so on. Our attitude needs to be one of 'outrage combined with political realism'.

It is the awareness, the wishes, the energy and dedication of animal-rights workers which really counts. Says Spira, 'No Congressional Bill (Parliamentary Bill), no legal gimmickry, by itself will save the animals.' We should not work just for these, but work with a total concept – which will involve breaking the barriers of conservatism, prejudice, unawareness, across the entire structure of our society: 'A victory in the Draize campaign, made possible through the evolution of science, will have an enormous real impact – a possible beginning of the end of live animal safety testing.'

The Draize test has been taken very seriously where it was meant to be noticed. The industry arranged top level meetings, they did attempt to seduce Spira into the power structure, something which can so easily be achieved if you are naive enough not to notice what is happening to you. (Attempts at such seductions have been made in England – of Animal Aid – and of course rebuffed.) It is a basic diversionary tactic – first-class plane trips, expensive hotels, consultant status and without knowing it, you're sitting on their side of the fence and nothing is really happening. Singlemindedness in pursuit of a goal helps avoidance of this kind of seduction. Seats on apparently high-powered committees instigated by the established system don't usually mean too much in terms of what we are trying to do for animals. Henry Spira did make a breakthrough early in 1981 when an important US scientific magazine *Lab Animal* ran an interview with him, helping to prove the point that his approach is working.

How it goes from now on depends on all of us:

The lab animals who suffer intense pain from birth to death, who never have a good day, cannot defend themselves, but we can, and together, we will. We are beginning to make things happen, but we must escalate. There are no brakes nor speed limits in the fight for justice.

11 Animals in Other Countries

Although cruelty and neglect are world-wide problems its manifestations vary according to the cultures and traditions of various countries. But if we in England perpetrate the most horrific, sophisticated and insidious crimes against animals, we do have a complex network of organizations and bodies doing their best to help and improve the lot of animals. Probably the United States of America and Australia are the only other countries in which a book like this could be written.

British individuals have set up organizations in their own country to help animals suffering from cruelty or neglect in other countries, and these societies link with existing organizations abroad to improve functioning and help progress and funds. There are not many of these, but they play an important part in international animal welfare and their existence is essential for the linking up of awareness of the plight of animals. Now that so many people can travel to many different countries on holiday, they can play their part in spreading compassion and taking action to fight cruelty and neglect wherever they see it in foreign countries.

Australian Animal Welfare Groups

Animal Liberation

257 Broadway, Sydney, 2007 NSW. Tel: 660 4242.

Issue: Battery hens, intensive farming, export of live sheep, cruelty on the farm. Conservation of wildlife.

Co-ordinator: Genny Young.

Australian Association for Humane Research

Box 356 PO, B roadway, Sydney. NSW 2007. Tel: 520 4584.

Anti-vivisectionists. Small group but highly effective particularly in schools where they campaign against experiments on animals in classes.

Chairman: Elizabeth Ahlston.

Beauty Without Cruelty

Box 5, PO Rosanna Vic. 3084.

Publicize and oppose cruelties inflicted on animals by the cosmetic and fur industries.

Fund for Animals

2/14 Sydney Road, Manly, NSW, 2095 (PO Box 371).

Wildlife issues, whales, Antartica. Large group with a branch in Victoria.

Contact: Michael Kennedy.

International Fund for Animal Welfare (Australia)

Private Bag 1, Bondi Junction, 2022, Sydney, Australia.

Major campaigns: saving the Australian kangaroo, killing and eating of dog, anti-vivisection, whales, dolphins and wildlife. Largest animal welfare group in Australia.

Contact: Sue Arnold and Graham Bicknell.

Project Jonah

399 Pitt Street, Sydney, NSW 2000.

Whales, dolphins.

Contact: Pam Eiser.

The Anglo-Italian Society for the Protection of Animals

AISPA originated in 1874, and has now over 3,000 members in England. It aims to prevent cruelty to animals and to encourage kindness to them particularly amongst the young. Italy not only carries the ancient Roman legacy of cruelty, but also suffers from the orthodox Catholic doctrine that animals have no souls and therefore cannot suffer, and are on this earth to be used by man. Education, teaching by example and the support of those who want changes in the law in their own country are their methods, as they were over a century ago. AISPA provides ambulances and other vehicles for rescuing injured animals; veterinary equipment and medicines and pentobarbitone for animals to be put down when necessary. The stray dog problem is enormous and attempts have been made to spread the idea of spaying and neutering. Financial help is given for kennels for stray dogs and cats and humane slaughter is promoted – thousands of captive bolt pistols and cartridges are provided. All slaughterhouses use a humane killer for cattle, but Italians will not use it on sheep as they sell and eat the brain. AISPA campaigns against the export of live animals and has been active in its disapproval of the live horse trade into Italy. It has also helped to create the Italian Bird League which is becoming an influential conservation force in Europe. 20,000 young Italians now belong to the Italian Society for the Protection of Birds. Local protection societies lecture at schools and have established good relations with the authorities.

AISPA has played a big part in rescue operations – especially after the floods and earthquakes in Italy but its main success most recently has been to alleviate the slaughter of the migrating birds in Italy.

AISPA (Anglo-Italian Society for the Protection of Animals) 136 Baker Street, London W1M 1FH.

The Greek Animal Welfare Fund (GAWF)

Work for Greek animals was begun by Mrs Eleanor Close in 1959. Her small society became autonomous after her return to

England, changing its name to the Hellenic Animal Welfare Society (HAWS). GAWF in England exists to support their work and that of the animal shelter in Salonica; Mr Michael Garby, who runs an animal shelter at Harvati outside Athens; Lady Melina Kemp and others who feed stray cats in Athens.

HAWS, under the direction of Mrs Patricia Stathatos, rescues starving, sick and abandoned animals which are rehomed where possible. It has a clinic in Athens where animals are treated, spayed and neutered. It visits experimental laboratories and looks after neglected animals, giving them blankets or beds to lie on as they are otherwise left on bare concrete, completely without care.

GAWF sends representatives to Greece annually, offering help and information. The Fund hopes to instigate a Humane Education campaign in Greece, to be run by Greek nationals, with GAWF supplying funds, ideas, and experience. Though it only has 900 subscribers, it contributes to the alleviation of animal suffering in Greece. Leaflets from GAWF give addresses to contact so that distressed or injured animals may be reported to welfare workers.

Greek Animal Welfare Fund, 11 Lower Barn Road, Purley, Surrey.

The Society for the Protection of Animals in North Africa

SPANA was started in 1923 by Mrs Kate Hosali. By 1929, she had set up twenty free treatment centres in Algeria and Tunisia. After the war, the work was extended to Marrakech and Morocco. SPANA has fifteen hospitals and refuges and fifty dispensaries throughout Morocco, Algeria and Tunisia. In 1970 SPANA opened the largest hospital and refuge in N. Africa in Marrakech. It has extensive accommodation for horses, mules, donkeys, camels, dogs and cats. Rest, refuge and treatment is now given to over 200,000 animals every year.

Since 1966 SPANA has been running a very successful and humane bit campaign to replace at no cost the traditional N. African bits – which can and often do cause the animals a good deal of agony – with comfortable bits. It has also attempted to improve the fourrières, or dog pounds – in the words of Nina

Hosali (Kate's daughter), these are 'the canine counterparts of Belsen'. The fourrières exist because of the fear of rabies – all dogs are supposed to be muzzled and leashed in the streets, but this law is mostly ignored. Wandering dogs are caught by Dog Captors by means of a noose and hauled into hand carts in which there are small cages. Charges and fines are made to owners seeking to retrieve their dogs and so pets are often captured deliberately. Dogs are kept for varying lengths of time, but if unclaimed, they are destroyed. In most towns the Municipality was obliged to capture loose dogs but was not given money to feed them, and so they starved in tiny unhygienic cages. Often after complaints improvements were made, but later lapsed. SPANA has been allowed to provide food for the dogs and drugs for humane killing to vets who will use them.

SPANA now has over 6½ thousand members and subscribers. Miss Nina Hosali retired as organizing secretary in 1963, but joined the council and became honorary secretary. In 1976 she received an MBE in recognition of her services to animal welfare. Her fascinating story can be read in her book, *The SPANA Story: Kate Who Was Called The Toubibe*, an inspiring tale of courage and compassion for humans and animals. All proceeds are going towards helping the continuing work in North Africa.

SPANA, 15 Buckingham Gate, London SW1E 6LB.

Brooke Hospital for Animals, Cairo

Brooke Hospital began as an Old War Horse stables in 1932. In 1934, Dorothy Brooke opened her free hospital for the working animals of the poor, continuing until she died in Cairo in 1955. Kathleen Taylor-Smith then carried on the work raising funds for eighteen years. Mrs Brooke's son, Philip Searight, became Chairman in 1966 and her daughter, Pamela Blenman-Bull, honorary treasurer in 1973. Branches in Alexandria and Luxur were set up after Mrs Taylor-Smith took office in 1955.

All animals are brought in *voluntarily* by their owners; in most cases these animals are the sole source of livelihood of their owners and their families. Patients belonging to poor owners receive free treatment and food while in hospital. The few who can afford to pay small changes are asked to do so. *Every patient receives the same care and treatment. No animal is discharged from hospital until it is fit for work.*

The hospital deals with other welfare problems, such as the selling of horses to the Middle East – once their value declines they may be sold to the poor and ignorant of villages where they are literally worked to death. At the hospital's Alexandria clinic there are also kennels for stray dogs.

The hospital also sponsors investigations and has recently campaigned against animal abuse in countries as far afield as Australia.

Brooke Hospital for Animals (Old War Horse Memorial Hospital), British Colombia House, 1 Regent St, London SW1 Y4PA.

Japan Animal Welfare Society (JAWS)

JAWS was founded in Tokyo in 1954 to help alleviate the desperate plight of animals in Japan. After World War II, Lady Gascoigne, wife of the head of the UK Liaison Mission, founded the Japan Society for the Prevention of Cruelty to Animals (JSPCA) in Tokyo for which she purchased land, and built and endowed a fully equipped clinic in 1950. By 1954 (after Lady Gascoigne had left Japan), the property and equipment so generously donated for animal welfare work was effectively lost. The position of the non-Japanese members of the JSPCA Board having been made untenable, they got together and founded the Japan Animal Welfare Society (JAWS) to deal with the vital animal welfare work that the JSPCA would no longer do and for which the Society had originally been founded.

JAWS in London began in 1956, when Mrs E. Close returned to England, with the help of Lady Gascoigne and the RSPCA. Again, Lady Gascoigne generously donated funds and help. This society is supported entirely by voluntary contributions and JAWS, London, raises funds in England to maintain animal welfare workers in Japan and to support various welfare activities in that country to supplement funds raised by JAWS,

Tokyo. It also supplies drugs for euthanasia.

Japan is one of the countries whose animals are most in need of care and support. Suffering in an animal is condoned and often not allowed to be terminated by a merciful death, even in experimental laboratories. In private homes, pets are in an intolerable position: dogs are kept as watchdogs and status symbols and are often poorly fed. The incidence of sickness is high and veterinary attention rare. Dogs are not allowed to run free in the streets, in parks or even in private gardens and the necessity of exercise is little understood. Abandoned dogs are caught by wire nooses and taken to pounds. Tight nooses left on the animals sometimes kill them as the wounds suppurate. Most dog pounds outside Tokyo are very unpleasant, and methods of killing are prolonged and painful – electrocution, skull smashing, strychnine poisoning, inefficient compression chambers. There is no tradition of painless euthanasia. It is estimated that two million unwanted dogs are killed in Japan each year. Official reported figures verge on ¾ million. The same is true for cats, but there are no official figures.

Some 40,000 dogs and cats are sent from pounds to medical and ironically, to veterinary training institutions each year where they are used for uncontrolled experiments or practice surgery along with many other kinds of animals. Most of them suffer extreme pain and distress for long and often repeated periods, without pre- or post-operative attention, or even water or food. Both JAWS and NAVS have ample evidence of extreme cruelty in Japanese laboratories.

Exported dogs and cats may meet a terrible fate in Japan. Strays will often die an agonising death from eating poisoned bait left in the streets. In remote areas traps are set for strays with notices saying trapped animals should not be fed. And so they often die of thirst, starvation or exposure.

As a result of continual pressure from JAWS and other AW bodies, an Animal Protection Law was passed in 1974, but there is as yet no inspectorate to police it, so there are few, if any, prosecutions. The police disclaim knowledge of and responsibility for that law, referring enquirers to Hokenshos (municipal health centres). The Hokensho people often profess ignorance, saying these matters are for the police. But a gradual awareness is growing among the people and JAWS field workers are more in demand.

JAWS has some thirty workers in Japan and nine centres. It has trained two Japanese vets in England who are now working in their own country, and hopes to train more in the future.

JAWS is trying to educate pet owners and visits establishments where animals are used, to maintain attendants, provide food and medical comfort where possible, to change the attitude of indifferent researchers and untrained animal keepers. It is maintaining an animal rescue centre in Kobe-Osaka and trying to establish others elsewhere. It is trying to reach children and young people through educational programmes in schools and universities and organises essay contests for children and students. It visits zoos and pet shops and runs a branch of the Kindness Club of Canada.

JAWS has supporters in Australia, S. Africa, USA, Canada, Switzerland, Germany, Austria and Singapore and would like to hear from anyone in any country who would be interested in supporting this charity.

Japan Animal Welfare Society Ltd, 88-90 Weston Street, London SE1.

Society for Animal Welfare in Israel (SAWI)

SAWI was formed in October 1957 by Miss Silverman, a veterinary surgeon who is still its Secretary. She appealed to people in the UK to help fund the establishment and maintenance of SPCAs, animal clinics and hospital facilities in Israel and also to help educate the children in animal welfare. By 1966, there were six SPCAs in Israel, and people in Haifa started a Cat Lovers' Society specializing in birth control for cats and the humane destruction of newborn kittens. The Federation of Israel Animal Welfare Societies was established to liaise between the government and the SPCAs. One of its main aims was education, and with the help of the Ministry of Education it instigated an annual 'National Animal Week'.

Israel's animal problems are unique because of its cultural mixture. On the one hand there are people from Europe who know how animals should be treated and on the other, there is a mass of Middle Eastern people who are poor and uneducated and therefore ignorant of animals' needs. The inclusion of Arab areas within Israeli boundaries placed a greater burden on already overworked animal workers. War conditions, when they occur, naturally affect the animal population. Hoardes of stray dogs wander over the border and rabies scares mean wholesale strychnine poisoning of these poor creatures. Animal protection laws do exist and are supposed to be enforced, but the Arab population does not appreciate or care about cats, for instance, and work horses and donkeys are often sadly neglected. Mr Elie D. Rolbag, MRCVS, president of the Israel Arab Horse Society affiliated to the International League for the Protection of Horses works to ease the lot of sick, injured and starving equines and was instrumental in the passing of an Act to protect horses in riding schools and riding establishments. He is encouraged by the general improvement evident in the care and treatment of equines in Israel.

The Cat Lovers' Society is having some success in controlling the feral cat populations with the Pill. But Israel's soaring inflation is causing enormous problems. Increasing numbers of animals are being abandoned as food costs increase and there is not enough money for the upkeep of existing shelters. SAWI sends Israeli workers money, drugs and advice when required (Kibbutz animals are not included as they are the responsibility of the individual communities and their vets).

SAWI has only a few hundred members. Based in London, it has a branch in Johanesburg. Miss Lieselott Richtmann of 34 Bethel St., Ormond 3204, Victoria, works independently in Australia, sending money to Animal Welfare in Israel, and is in regular contact with SAWI which welcomes both Jewish and non-Jewish members and supporters.

SAWI, 4 North Mews, London WC1N 2JP.

Dingo – Anglo-Venetian Group for the Protection of Stray Animals

This group began as a result of a visit to Venice in 1965 by Mrs Helen Sanders who found the city swarming with thousands of starving, sick cats. Help came towards a programme of neutering, spaying, treating and putting down newly born. Now the population has reached manageable proportions and since 1969 the Anglo-Venetian Group has been a registered charity. It also established a dog refuge on an island which was subsequently taken over by the Italian Dog League. Dingo's veterinary bills amount to over £2,000 a year; the work is supported by a small number of English, Canadian and Swiss people.

Anglo Venetian Group for the Protection of Stray Animals, The Chairman, Condurro Cottage, St Clement, Truro, Cornwall TR11 S2.

World Society for the Protection of Animals (WSPA)

WSPA is the amalgamation of what was the International Society for the Protection of Animals based in London and the World Federation for the Protection of Animals based in Zurich, Switzerland where its quarterly magazine *Animals International* is produced, and where technical reports and campaign plans are co-ordinated.

ISPA was an offshoot of the RSPCA, founded in 1959 to co-ordinate humane societies in different parts of the world. At a meeting of the RSPCA, the American Humane Association, the Massachusetts SPCA and the Animal Rescue League (Boston, USA), its main objects were determined: to promote effective means of prevention of cruelty and suffering of animals, to maintain liaison with local organizations with similar objectives, to provide facilities for affiliation of all approved animal welfare societies and to organize conferences.

WSPA's main areas of concern are farm livestock (breeding, rearing, upkeep, handling, transport and slaughter), wild animals (preservation and rescue), laboratory animals and pets. It aims to promote legislation in favour of animals and humane education. WSPA undertakes investigations in the field and provides scientific advice where it is needed.

WSPA in London lacks the large funding which could make it a more effective international force, but working in conjunction with other societies it can help to alleviate areas of particular suffering in many parts of the world.

WSPA, 106 Jermyn Street, London SW1Y 6EE.

12   Prominent Animal Societies

The International Fund for Animal Welfare (IFAW)

The International Fund for Animal Welfare, one of the most dynamic organizations of its kind, began and exists because of the initiative of its founder and executive director, Brian Davies. A Welshman in his forties, he emigrated to Canada, joining the Canadian army as a young man. There he did a good deal of voluntary work for animals and when he came out of the army was offered the equivalent job of RSPCA inspector with one of the Canadian Humane Societies. This was over a decade ago.

Public grumblings began at that time about the seal hunt, so much so, that the Canadian government offered for two of the leading humane organizations to send two experienced inspectors onto the ice, to witness the hunt, and obviously, also to whitewash it. Unlike those in Britain, Canadian and American humane societies receive some state aid and this fact tends to govern their direction. Therefore the two societies had to bear in mind that the report they submitted to the government would be likely to affect their status – after the event they stood to receive more money, or none at all.

Brian Davies, who knew nothing of the hunt and who had never been on the ice in his life, went along with an open mind and was subsequently appalled at what he saw. He wrote a very critical report which his boss refused to submit. However, he refused to make any alterations and on a point of principle resigned from his post, despite having a family to keep. He then began a small organization of his own, called SOS – Save Our Seals. Together with a group of friends he managed to arouse public indignation and to raise enough money to employ himself full-time in the fight against the seal hunt.

It was at this point that IFAW came into being in New Brunswick. He immediately learned to fly a helicopter knowing that that was the only way in which he could tell the world just what was going on, by getting the media out onto the ice, something the Canadian government had never been anxious to do, for obvious reasons.

He was successful in obtaining tremendous world-wide coverage of the hunt, which angered the Canadian government. In order to make it impossible for the media to witness the hunt in the future, they brought out a law which stated that it was a criminal offence under the Seal Protection Act to fly a fixed-wing aircraft within two miles of the seal herd or below 2,000ft, and that it was a criminal offence to land a helicopter within half a mile of a seal herd. Brian Davies decided to test the law and took the BBC *Horizon* team out onto the ice. He was arrested at gun point, put in jail for three days and the helicopter was impounded. Then a riotous mob, composed mainly of sealers, stirred up trouble, so much so that a hundred specially trained riot police had to be flown in. Davies' life could have been in danger.

The helicopter was released on a bond of $50,000 and to make life difficult the government added that Mr Davies would have to report to a Canadian embassy wherever he was in the world, once a week, despite the fact that he would sometimes be 3,000ft up in the Andes saving other wild creatures. However, it was a deliberate attempt to make his work difficult. He was eventually sent for trial and sentenced to two weeks in jail, but was allowed four days off for good behaviour.

The Canadian government continued to harass the organization which proved the anxiety it felt, and still feels, over this campaign which has aroused so much public protest. Furthermore, it decided that any charity which attempted to alter existing laws or to bring about new ones would forfeit its charitable status and its goods and chattels. As IFAW was the only charity campaigning in this way, the reason was obvious. And so IFAW moved to Cape Cod, USA.

IFAW is a small commando-type organization. It is dedicated to ending the seal hunt, but also moves in on other areas of exploitation. It differs from other groups and societies in that it is not bound by committee procedures and it is therefore capable of a fire-brigade approach. It does not criticize other organizations which work in a different way, but with the approval of its two tough trustees, it can move in on an emergency situation anywhere in the world. Its biggest success appears to have been in bringing certain critical issues before the public on such a large scale.

IFAW moved in on the Vicuna cull in Peru which was being carried out very carelessly and hence cruelly and for commercial reasons under a bogus cover of 'conservation'. It went to help the cheetah in Namibia which had grown out of control under altered conditions. IFAW planned to trap them humanely and move them off to other areas because the cheetah is the rarest spotted cat in Africa. There were difficulties but they did manage to release twenty into a national park in the Kalahari.

For four years IFAW looked after polar bears in Churchill in the Arctic Circle. Churchill was built overnight to accommodate oil people. A town was built where polar bears had always lived for part of the year. These creatures are really quite docile, but might easily take the head off a screaming child, for example, with a swing of the paw, not knowing their own strength. Therefore the inhabitants were nervous of having the bears rooting around their dustbins. They didn't want to shoot them, but asked for advice and help. IFAW flew in a chartered Dakota with two vets and special containers, tranquillized the bears and flew them 500 miles north. This holding operation worked very well, and now any bears which turn up are accepted by the townspeople, tranquillized, and held in an enclosure, fed for two months and then released when they will migrate north again.

IFAW has had failures – its huge campaign to ban the leghold trap in Central America failed – the other side spent $100,000 more on its campaign.

A large and important scientific workshop on alternatives to culling was sponsored by IFAW, the results of which have been published by them in book form.

It has mounted, with the help and co-operation of other organizations, an enormously well organized campaign against the Canadian seal hunt. The battle is not over, but IFAW has demonstrated how powerful the animal-rights movement can be when it moves in an expert and coordinated way to make public opinion into a cohesive force to be reckoned with.

Tubwell House, New Road, Crowborough, E. Sussex.

Royal Society for the Prevention of Cruelty to Animals (RSPCA)

On 16 June 1824 the first known society for the prevention of cruelty to animals was formed. At the first meeting in St Martin's Lane in London, the chairman was Fowell Buxton, MP, brother-in-law of Elizabeth Fry, the Quaker prison reformer. Also present were seven other MPs including Richard Martin – who had introduced a Bill passed in 1822 to prevent the cruel and improper treatment of cattle – and William Wilberforce, together with the convener of the meeting, Reverend Arthur Broome, an humane reformer.

Two committees were set up – one to influence public opinion, the other to inspect the markets and streets, slaughterhouses and conduct of coachmen. Richard Martin stated that the society's main emphasis should not be on prosecution, but that it should aim to 'alter the moral feelings of the country'.

In the first half of 1824, two men who had been employed to look out for cruelty brought in sixty-three offenders who appeared in Court, but magistrates were still hesitant to prosecute under the new Act.

In 1835, Joseph Pease, MP, a Quaker industrialist and member of the society's committee, introduced a Bill to increase Martin's Act to cover bulls and domestic animals. In 1939 came two more Acts – the Hackney Carriage Metropolitan Act which restrained drivers in their treatment of horses and one which empowered the Metropolitan Police to enter premises where there were suspicions of cockfighting.

The society's influence had spread and in 1835, Royal support was sought; the Duchess of Kent and Queen Victoria became patrons. In 1840, Queen Victoria made it the Royal Society.

Legislation had to be enforced and from the late 1830s inspectors were organized to do this work. However, after a raid on a cockfighting gang one inspector, already ill from tuberculosis, was beaten up and died in hospital. Subsequent to this unfortunate event, the inspectors were put in uniform and given truncheons.

The RSPCA inspired the establishment of similar societies abroad – France, Germany, Scotland (still autonomous), Holland, Belgium and the USA.

An interesting historical point which more than answers accusations that those who care about animals do not care about humans is that the NSPCC started as a result of the RSPCA. The American SPCA took on a case of a battered child and was subsequently inundated with similar cases which led to the founding of a New York Society for the Prevention of Cruelty to Children and within a year, the NSPCC was formed in London. It was proposed by Lord Shaftesbury, largely through the influence of John Colam, then Secretary to the RSPCA.

In 1845, the society began an educational campaign in schools and later in the century a junior movement – the Band of Mercy – was founded by Mrs Catherine Smithies, an anti-slavery worker.

By 1874, the society had firmly established itself with its headquarters in Jermyn Street, where it remained for nearly a hundred years. By 1884, it was employing eighty inspectors up and down the country.

In 1911, the Protection of Animals Act was passed – the most progressive law so far, due in a large part to the society's activities.

From those early years, the RSPCA has grown into an enormous institution with 213 autonomous branches, 249 inspectors and an annual turnover of around seven million pounds.

Still highly regarded throughout the world, its solidarity and expertise is an essential part of the ongoing campaign for animal rights, but it has suffered greatly in recent years from infighting and an inability to accept and implement imaginative, radical ideas. Older societies with their roots in the nineteenth century and strong traditions built up over long years tend to find change much harder than younger organizations and they can tend, instead of being ahead of public opinion, drawing it along, merely to keep up with it.

A long battle was fought before the RSPCA came out against fox hunting, an issue finally resolved after the formation of a reform group in 1970, put together by fifteen enlightened members who saw foxhunting as incompatible with the ideals of an animal protection society.

The RSPCA has been seen by some who have studied it as 'solidly middle-class', 'hostile to anything unconventional and drawing the line at vegetarianism' with its 'stuffy respectability'.

It has been a pity that the RSPCA has attacked direct-action groups and so has appeared to condone large-scale commercial cruelties, whereas it has always been very good at prosecuting in cases of individual cruelty.

It has failed to prosecute commercial concerns, despite evidence of cruelty from its own inspectors. On one occasion some of the society's own vets said they would give evidence *against* the society if it took proceedings against a large pharmaceutical company.

Attempts have been made – and in one case succeeded – to expel the most progressive people from the society.

Vested interests obviously want to ensure that the RSPCA – potentially one of the most powerful of all pressure groups in Europe – remains restrained by a conservative, bureaucratic majority. This means that unless the RSPCA governing council and staff are prepared to be more radical, the society could become a power to block reform in favour of animals, rather than being a vehicle for change.

The RSPCA's status, prestige, staff of experts, educational role, inspectorate with its vital day-to-day work, voluntary workers in the branches who raise funds and deal with homeless animals are all vital and positive aspects of this great organization. It now remains to be seen whether the RSPCA can allow itself to become rewardingly infected with the zealous mood of the growing animal-rights movement and place itself at its head as the powerful force it should be.

The RSPCA, The Causeway, Horsham, Sussex.

Crusade Against All Cruelty To Animals

Crusade Against All Cruelty To Animals is a non-profit-making association limited by guarantee and a registered charity founded in 1955. It works vigorously to prevent cruelty to animals, to advance education in the humane treatment of and regard for the animal kingdom and to promote in man humane and ethical standards of behaviour towards the animal kingdom.

Because humane-education must start at an early age, Crusade has made many contacts with schools and has organized school parties to visit its lecture theatre for talks and filmshows.

Crusade founders were pioneering in their work for animals before 1955, and in 1956 were the first society to publicize the horrors of the sealing and trapping industries. In 1960 it began the fight against factory farming. Its campaign against the cruelty involved in *pâté de foie gras* production is now twenty years old and in 1983 the issue was at last brought before the European Parliament as a result of its efforts.

Such an important feature as its lecture theatre at headquarters is something which should have been instigated by bigger societies long ago as such work is vital, especially to combat propaganda aimed at children by animal exploiters.

Crusade Against All Cruelty to Animals, Humane Education Centre, Avenue Lodge, Bounds Green Road, London N22 4EN.

Animal Vigilantes

Animal Vigilantes is an Educational Charitable Trust which was set up to work exclusively among young people in 1965, when its founders recognized the special need not filled by other organizations. Dedicated to fight all cruelty to animals, it teaches reverence for all life. Having attracted support from other societies, it now has representatives in over forty different countries.

Working individually or in groups, members raise funds, distribute literature, collect signatures for petitions, seek new members, hold discussions and meetings in order to spread the facts of cruelty to animals perpetrated by man. A bi-monthly magazine is published for members.

Friends of Animal Vigilantes is an adult group formed to support the trust.

Animal Vigilantes, James Mason House, 24 Salisbury Street, Farding Bridge, Hants SP6 1AF.

Co-ordinating Animal Welfare (CAW)

CAW is a loose association of animal rights activists without official membership or a committee, but founded in 1978 by Fay Funnel, Angela Walder and Kim Stallwood, all well-known figures in the movement. It has sought to bring together the disparate parts of the movement, feeling that too many separate organizations all working on their own were not always effective and often did not communicate with each other. CAW set out with the following aims:

*   To analyse the dilemmas facing the established animal welfare societies and encourage people to become members in order to be active in improving the effectiveness of their policies.
*   To point out that animal abuse is now perpetrated by big business and multinational corporations on a scale which cannot be controlled by holding jumble sales or street pickets.
*   To encourage a more direct approach by infiltration of companies who profit from the abuse of animals by encouraging people to become shareholders and by using the legitimate and political might of trade unions.
*   To act as a watchdog in the affairs of existing animal welfare societies.

CAW was successfully used as a vehicle for coordinating the struggle to revolutionize the BUAV and instigated the successful campaign to shut down Club Row animal street market.

CAW is open to all those who want to contribute to the battle for animal rights. Meetings are held approximately every three months.

CAW, PO Box 61, Camberley, Surrey GU15 4EN.

Universities Federation for Animal Welfare (UFAW)

UFAW was founded as the University of London Animal Welfare Society in 1926, as a scientific animal welfare society. Its aim was to 'promote humane behaviour towards wild and domestic animals in Britain and abroad so as to reduce the sum total of pain inflicted on animals by man'.

UFAW has carried out research into the welfare of battery-caged hens and animals undergoing transport. It is financing research into tissue culture to attempt to discover whether laboratory animals can be replaced for the routine testing of certain drugs. It also researches methods of estimating population size and humane ways of controlling (where control appears necessary) wild animals such as seals, badgers and moles.

The Federation has an educational programme and teaches methods for the care and management of animals. It has published many leaflets, booklets and technical publications which are useful for reference and in establishing scientific fact and has held many symposia on various animal-welfare issues.

During the summer months UFAW's Field Study Centre on Holy Island, Firth of Clyde, is available for members, university departments and schools for the study of biology and of a wide range of wild species.

UFAW also cooperates with animal-welfare societies and interested individuals overseas with whom it exchanges information.

This organization considers itself to be different from most other animal-welfare societies in that it cooperates with the academic world – and indeed, arose from within it. This is where UFAW and animal rightists will part company, for it is not a campaigning society as such and is *not* aiming to abolish animal experimentation, but simply to 'make life more comfortable' for laboratory animals. Its stated policy has been not to engage 'on either side in public controversies relating to the legitimacy of making scientific experiments on animals' (Russell and Burch, *The Principles of Humane Experimental Technique*, 1959).

It survives on voluntary contributions and its ordinary

voting membership consists of university graduates and those with professional qualifications.

UFAW, 8 Hamilton Close, South Mimms, Potters Bar, Herts. EN6 3QD.

The Blue Cross

A small society called 'Our Dumb Friends' League' for 'the encouragement of kindness to animals' was formed by a small group in London in 1897. They had taken the name from a speech by Queen Victoria in which she had referred to the need to care for 'the dumb creatures of the earth'.

In 1906 the first animal hospital was opened to provide treatment for animals of needy owners at Hugh Street, Victoria, London. This hospital has always remained open, throughout the night during the two World Wars. It was in 1912 that the Blue Cross symbol originated; and then became famous in the First World War.

The society has an impressive history of rescue work and campaigning for dogs and horses. In 1948, The Horse Protection Scheme to rescue ex-army horses from unnecessary suffering abroad was set up. This saved 1,000 horses from cruelty, neglect and premature slaughter during the ensuing ten years as the society involved itself generally in the campaign to save horses from slaughter. From 1951–64 it also became involved in a further campaign to stop the export of horses from Eire to Europe.

In 1953 the society went to the rescue of animals involved in the Canvey Island Flood disaster. It then undertook a modernization programme of its hospitals and homes until 1976.

The Blue Cross Horse Protection Scheme still operates today as it did when its Balkan War Horse work began in 1913. Horses, ponies and donkeys are rescued from slaughter and then remain the society's property. Some are loaned out, under agreement, to good homes which are regularly inspected, but some remain at the rest home. It also takes in horses from owners who can no longer take care of their animals but wish to secure a safe future for them. The society's horse ambulances attend shows and sporting events in England and Southern Ireland.

The Blue Cross endeavours to rehome animals which arrive via the branches as well as dealing with accident and emergency cases, including the rescue of trapped animals and strays. The branches board pensioners' pets in cases of genuine need and of other owners in emergencies. Advice and help on diverse animal problems as well as veterinary treatment is provided and speakers are available for illustrated lectures to schools and societies.

The Blue Cross, The Secretary, Animals Hospital, Hugh Street, Victoria, London SW1V 1QQ.

Animal Aid Emergency Unit

Animal Aid Emergency Unit was formed in January 1978 by Cliff Goodman to provide a twenty-four-hour rescue service for animals in the Northampton area. It was formed to fill a need – RSPCA inspectors are uneven in quality and efficiency and there are no other nationwide emergency services for animals. Volunteers work for this organization in their spare time in varying shifts to fit in with their regular employment. Emergency calls are received by telephone at a private home. Volunteers use their own vehicles and equipment and Animal Aid Emergency contributes when possible to petrol expenses involved in rescue work. Where veterinary costs are not recovered from owners, it pays for these. Permanently injured wild animals are given sanctuary and suitable homes are sought for abandoned animals and those whose owners cannot be traced.

However, the housing of sick and injured animals pending recovery or rehoming has always been a great problem for the unit. No animal-welfare society in the Northampton area has any kennelling or hospital facilities. It was decided that all the local animal-welfare societies and interested individuals should come together to form a trust fund for the sole purpose of setting up a sanctuary and hospital to provide after care for the sick, trapped and homeless animals in the country. It was estimated that £50,000 was needed to start the venture. No money is to be spent until sufficient funds are available to purchase the necessary land and buildings. In the meantime the trust will perform an educative task by encouraging people to solve the problem of unwanted pets – neutering and spaying of cats and dogs and taking on an animal if they are sure they have the time, knowledge and financial resources to look after one properly.

Money has come from donations, membership subscriptions and general fund raising activities. The unit manages to gain a good deal of local publicity.

This organization gives every animal it handles a better chance. Its volunteers are all dedicated, sincere people; its founder-organizer is a well-known animal-rights activist. Animals are rescued, not put down. Every area could do with this kind of service. If you think you could start one in another area, ask Cliff Goodman for advice.

Animal Aid Emergency Unit needs volunteers, donations and new members.

Address: 36 Swale Drive, Northampton NN5 7NL. Tel: (0604) 53730.

The League of Venturers

Patronised by Prince Charles, this is a voluntary organisation of teenagers who go to the help of people and animals in physical danger or distress on land or sea. Donations welcomed.

Venturers Search and Rescue, 'Courage House', Wellands Road, Lyndhurst, Hampshire SO4 7AB. Tel: Lyndhurst 2787.

13 Religious Organizations for Animal Rights and Welfare

Gradually the Church is awakening to its responsibilities towards animals. There are groups within the Church who are doing something to propound the true teachings of love and compassion for all things.

This anonymous prayer, printed by The Fellowship of Life, in one of its newsletters, seems very appropriate for such a movement.

Lord, keep us from arrogance, which thinks it knows all the truth,
Lord, keep us from apathy, which is content with mere half truth,
Lord, keep us from cowardice, which is afraid of new truth.

The Christian Consultative Council

The Christian Consultative Council, convened by the Dean of Westminster, is a group of representatives of religious animal-welfare societies who meet together every three months to pool ideas and decide how best to approach current animal issues.

The Anglican Society for the Welfare of Animals

The Anglican Society for the Welfare of Animals, whose president is the Very Reverend E.F. Carpenter, Dean of Westminster, was inaugurated in 1970 for clergy with laymen, following the Report of the Church Assembly, 'Man In His Living Environment'.

The society's objects are to promote 'prayer, study and action on behalf of animals'.

This is to include teaching to congregations, through sermons, discussions, prayer and animal blessings services, their duty to be 'merciful to the animals in their power'; an effort to seek the inclusion in the Church liturgy of 'prayers of repentance for our treatment of living creatures, and for our indirect encouragement of cruel exploitation', and also to include in the liturgy 'prayers for those who have special responsibility for animals, and to press for the recognition of these aims on all festivals connected with the theme of creation'; an attempt to 'keep members of the Church accurately informed on the exploitation of animals wherever they are subject to man's use or pleasure'; cooperating with other organizations, religious or secular, which have compatible aims; the organizing of 'a Christian protest where it may be deemed necessary'; recognizing 'God's love for the whole of his Creation', and then to 'appreciate, love and respect all living things'.

The Anglican Society for the Welfare of Animals, Hon. Sec., 10 Chester Avenue, Hawkesbury, Tunbridge Wells, Kent.

Quaker Concern for Animal Welfare

Towards the end of the nineteenth century some Quakers became increasingly concerned at the growth in experiments on animals. They formed a group and established the Friends' Anti-Vivisection Association on 22 May 1891. This impressive resolution read:

> That this meeting, recognising the supreme importance of justice and compassion over conditions of physical benefit, emphatically rejects the view that cruel experiments on animals can be justified by the anicipation of useful results to the human race, even were it proved, which does not appear to be the case, that such results are obtainable thereby.

The association's first president was Joseph Stores Fry and among its members was Joshua Rowntree, MP.

The objects of the society were to draw attention of fellow Quakers to the cruelty involved in vivisection and to quicken the conscience of fellow Quakers as to the need of witnessing against it.

Since that time the society has broadened its interest to include all forms of ill-treatment and cruel exploitation of animals in accordance with the Quaker Advice: 'Show a loving consideration for all God's creatures' (*Advices and Queries*, 1931).

The society has undergone certain changes – until 1978 it was known as the Friends' Animal Welfare and Anti-Vivisection Society.

The society feels concern that the Quaker voice is not heard enough in protest against man's cruel treatment of animals and tries to encourage Quakers to free their own lives as much as possible from dependence on cruelty and exploitation of animals. It is affiliated to the National Anti-Vivisection Society and works closely with the Farm and Food Society, and is represented on the Christian Consultative Council for Animal Welfare, the Farm Animal Welfare Co-Ordination Executive, the Humane Education Council and the Conference of Animal Welfare Societies. It has published leaflets and papers, provides speakers and communicates with government ministries and other authorities when possible and appropriate, makes grants to other organizations with similar aims and publishes a newsletter, usually three times a year.

This society could do much, working as it does within the Christian Community, to spread awareness and compassion in a genuine spirit of co-operation with other animal-welfare societies. Non-Friends are also welcomed as members.

Quaker Concern for Animal Welfare, Webbs Cottage, Saling, Braintree, Essex CM7 5DZ.

The Catholic Study Circle For Animal Welfare

The Catholic Study Circle For Animal Welfare arose from the idea of a handful of Catholic ladies who in the mid-1930s decided to form a prayer group especially for animals – who previously had been largely ignored.

The late Father Agius then supported them and they further

gained the support of Cardinal Vaughan who recommended
that the group keep to prayer and not interfere with the work of
any other welfare societies.

The Study Circle's official aim is to explore the positive
teaching of the Church on compassion for animals. It certainly
never gives any publicity to the negative teachings on this
subject.

Unofficially it is evident that it is doing its best to fight the
hatred of animals which has existed for so long within the
Catholic Church. It endeavours to spread the idea that religion
should not only be concerned with human beings, but also with
all of creation, in the realization that those who are going to
propound humane principles must have their theories soundly
based in factual information, which must be learned and
understood. To this end, it publishes an excellent journal *The
Ark* three times a year which explores theological and
philosophical issues to do with animals as well as giving
information on current exploitation and welfare of animals.

Their emeritus chairman is Father Basil Wrighton, a
scholarly priest, now in his eighties, who thoroughly and
absolutely supports the idea of compassion and reverence for all
life.

The Catholic Study Circle needs to grow and gain support
and influence. Both Catholics and non-Catholics are welcomed
as members and subscribers to the magazine. Its work is not to
spread Catholicism, but to spread the awareness that animals
have a right to life and liberty as fellow creatures on this earth.

The Catholic Study Circle for Animal Welfare, 39 Onslow
Gardens, London E18.

The Fellowship of Life

Founded in 1973, the Fellowship of Life is a religious/spiritual,
vegetarian/vegan group with its immediate aim of establishing
vegetarianism as a Christian ideal and virtue. It is non-political
and non-pressure, but aims 'To promote a Christian way of life
which is beneficial to ALL Creation, human, animal and
environmental' and 'To unite believers of all religions, or none,
in a way of life which neither hurts nor destroys needlessly any

part of creation, human, animal or environmental.'

The Fellowship of Life, Eynhallow, Croy, Inverness IV1 2PG.

The Order of the Cross

The Order of the Cross is an informal fellowship which was founded in 1904 by the Reverend J. Todd Ferrier, a Methodist minister who answered an inner call to give up his ministry and devote his life to doing something to help the creatures who are victims of man's ill-treatment. His work was far more radical and far-reaching than his denominational pastorate would ever have been. When he began his mission Mr Ferrier had no intention of setting up a new sect or institution but went ahead with the purpose of 'linking together Souls who upheld the necessity of abstaining from flesh-eating, and who might help one another and thus become better equipped to help the world.'

Hundreds of men and women from all walks of life followed him and groups were formed up and down the country. He was a true seer, full of absolute love and compassion for all life.

The Order of the Cross proclaims three steps towards Oneness with the Divine: Purity of Living, Purity of the Mind, Purity of the Soul, and thus its ideal are to

> endeavour by example and teaching to win all men to the love of Truth, Purity and Right-Doing.
>
> To proclaim the Brotherhood of Man, the essential one-ness of all religious aspirations and the unity of all living creatures in the Divine.
>
> To teach the moral necessity for humaneness towards all men and all creatures.
>
> To protest against, and to work for the abolition of, all national and social customs which violate the teachings of Christ, especially such as involve bloodshed, the oppression of the weak and defenceless, the perpetuation of the brutal mind, and the infliction of cruelty upon animals, viz., war, vivisection, the slaughter of animals for food, fashion and sport and kindred evils.
>
> To advocate the universal adoption of a bloodless diet,

and the return to simple and natural foods.

To proclaim a message of peace and happiness, health and purity, spirituality and Divine Love.

Mr Ferrier, who died in 1943, in his eighty-eighth year, wrote many wonderful books, including *On Behalf of Creatures*, a truly humane plea for mercy and compassion.

Information and books may be obtained from the Fellowship's headquarters:

The Secretary, The Order of the Cross, 10 De Vere Gardens, Kensington, London W8 5AE.

The Brotherhood of the Essenes: The Light of the Animal Kingdom

The Essenes are a mystical closed Order which gives out some teachings and welcomes outside supporters. It holds a midsummer night meditation for The Animal Kingdom each year at Glastonbury. This is the one religious order which recognizes the true glory of the animals.

The Secretary, Brother Stanley Brown, BCM Glaston, London WC1.

The Theosophical Society

The Theosophical Society was founded in 1875 to promote the recognition of the brotherhood of man and the unity of life, whatever its diversity in form. The Theosophical Order of Service stated in its leaflet *Animals and Men*:

> Is it not time to define our whole attitude to the animal creation? Should we not recognise that there is an interdependence between animals and humans, and that this is a part of a plan for the evolution and helping of both. This would foster true reverence for life and lead ultimately to the realisation of the One Universal Divine Life in all forms.

It is this Truth perhaps that the world needs to perceive and realise before its own peace and happiness can be attained. As long as cruelty to animals exists, cruelty to man will also continue.

The Theosophical Order of Service endeavours to further this understanding of the place of the animals in the scheme of things, and of man's responsibility as a conscious agent in the evolutionary process.

The Theosophical Society, 50 Gloucester Place, London W1.

The Vedanta Movement

Swami Avyaktananda, chairman of the Vedanta Movement in Britain came here in 1934. Previously in India, he had preached religion and philosophy and had joined Mahatma Gandhi's Non-cooperation Movement for Indian Freedom and had been twice imprisoned.

Vedanta means the fulfilment of knowledge – Veda meaning knowledge, and Anta, the end. The Vedas are the sacred books of India. Vedanta is the teaching of unity for all, it does not proselytize and emphasizes tranquillity and liberation through inner freedom.

Among the many things he lectures and writes about, Swami Avyaktananda teaches the Oneness of all Life which includes the liberation of animals:

Vedanta asks every man and woman in the world to accept the principle of eliminating every form of needless and avoidable cruelty and killing, while seeking food, fashion, sport and medicaments. . . Life remains immoral or only falsely moral, if there is cruelty and killing for the satisfaction of our daily needs.

One of the objects of the Vedanta Movement is 'To promote a spiritual mode of living from which every form of unnecessary and avoidable cruelty and killing is eliminated.'

Swami Avyaktananda lives what he teaches in his daily life. He is a vegan, feeds the mice who come to him, and has stopped digging his garden because he was distressed about disturbing

the worms. A scholar and a true lover of humanity and all
creatures, he has organized conferences on The Liberation of
Animals and has written several small books, including one of
that title.

The Vedanta Movement, Batheaston Villa, Batheaston, Bath.

Conclusion

The premise on which this book is based is that all suffering, knowingly inflicted on any creature, is wrong. Any accusations of 'sentimentality', 'anthropomorphism' or 'emotionalism' put to the animal rights lobby are simply the tormented cries of the defensive, who, taking pride in their 'intellectualism' and 'objectivity', are forgetting the danger of pride, the frightening danger of intellect divorced from feeling and conscience, indicating a state of non-integration, and that there *is no* objectivity: every human being, unable to perceive pure truth, argues from his or her own standpoint.

Sentimentality in the cloying Victorian tradition can no longer have a place in a forceful movement for rights and liberation which aims to grant dignity and respect, not bestow patronizing favours.

It is a privilege to be able to speak in any way on behalf of these voiceless ones whose true beauty and dignity – from the smallest insect to the largest whale – are largely ignored. It is a privilege to serve them in any way, because the enormous debt which mankind is building up minute by minute to the animal nation is becoming so overwhelming that by natural justice, the sad effects must come back upon the human race who 'know not what they do'.

There are many millions of nameless unmentioned ones – from the swatted fly, the poisoned slug, the diabetic dog tugged on his 'master's' lead to the arctic fox caught in the agony clasp of the leg-hold trap for a piece of coat, the screaming research-tool monkey, the torn dolphin, the murdered elephant, the exploded whale, whose blood paints the waters of our tears; the pain of them all imprisons us in interminable suffering.

One day the human race, if it survives, may relinquish its

eating of corpses and, free of guilt, be able to look with clearer sight into the eyes of the animals. Meanwhile, there is blood on our hands which only compassion can wash away.

As I write, a young man is being made ill by confinement in prison because he attempted to rescue some dogs from a laboratory. Must we not ask who is the real criminal? Is it not the society which protects its right to inflict suffering by punishing those who dare to act upon their feelings of compassion? The law will not move until the people push it into action. Parliament will not speak until the people give it a voice.

One autumn afternoon of watery sunshine and yellowing leaves Swami Avyaktananda was talking to a small group of us in a room in South London. A calm, gentle, elderly man, his voice steadied as he pointed his finger at the world:

While one human being is left suffering, I cannot go on, I cannot go in peace.

While one creature is left suffering, I cannot go on, I cannot go in peace.

Index of Animals

Index of Organizations